Lecture Notes on

Environmental and Resource Economics

A Theoretical Introduction

World Scientific Lecture Notes in Economics and Policy

ISSN: 2630-4872

The World Scientific Lecture Notes in Economics and Policy series is aimed to produce lecture note texts for a wide range of economics disciplines, both theoretical and applied at the undergraduate and graduate levels. Contributors to the series are highly ranked and experienced professors of economics who see in publication of their lectures a mission to disseminate the teaching of economics in an affordable manner to students and other readers interested in enriching their knowledge of economic topics. The series was formerly titled World Scientific Lecture Notes in Economics.

Published:

Vol. 27: *Lecture Notes on Environmental and Resource Economics: A Theoretical Introduction*
by Aart de Zeeuw

Vol. 26: *Agricultural Economics and Policy*
by David Zilberman, Ruiqing Miao and Jian Rong

For the complete list of volumes in this series, please visit
www.worldscientific.com/series/wslnep

World Scientific Lecture Notes in Economics and Policy – Vol. 27

Lecture Notes on Environmental and Resource Economics

A Theoretical Introduction

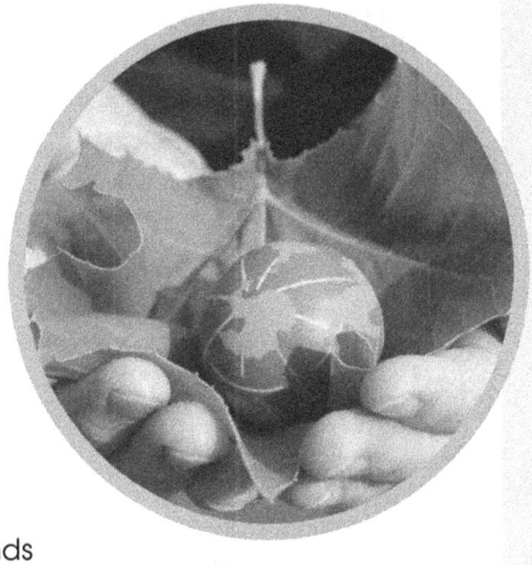

Aart de Zeeuw
Tilburg University, The Netherlands
Beijer Institute of Ecological Economics, Sweden

World Scientific

NEW JERSEY • LONDON • SINGAPORE • BEIJING • SHANGHAI • TAIPEI • CHENNAI

Published by

World Scientific Publishing Co. Pte. Ltd.
5 Toh Tuck Link, Singapore 596224
USA office: 27 Warren Street, Suite 401-402, Hackensack, NJ 07601
UK office: 57 Shelton Street, Covent Garden, London WC2H 9HE

Library of Congress Control Number: 2025010528

British Library Cataloguing-in-Publication Data
A catalogue record for this book is available from the British Library.

World Scientific Lecture Notes in Economics and Policy — Vol. 27
LECTURE NOTES ON ENVIRONMENTAL AND RESOURCE ECONOMICS
A Theoretical Introduction

ISBN 978-981-98-0801-4 (hardcover)
ISBN 978-981-98-0939-4 (paperback)
ISBN 978-981-98-0802-1 (ebook for institutions)
ISBN 978-981-98-0803-8 (ebook for individuals)

For any available supplementary material, please visit
https://www.worldscientific.com/worldscibooks/10.1142/14177#t=suppl

Desk Editors: Kannan Krishnan/Yulin Jiang

Typeset by Stallion Press
Email: enquiries@stallionpress.com

Preface

These lecture notes developed over the years by teaching an introductory course in environmental and resource economics at the advanced undergraduate level of the economics program at Tilburg University in the Netherlands.

This set of lecture notes contains basic theory in environmental and resource economics. It covers not only traditional topics, such as pollution targets and instruments, renewable and non-renewable resources, growth, trade, and valuation, but also newer topics, such as international aspects, stock pollution, and tipping points. These lecture notes focus on the main concepts, models, and results in the core areas of environmental and resource economics, as a basis for the presentation of extensions, applications, and real-world policy discussions in the courses.

This book is compact and can serve as a basic text for a course in environmental and resource economics at the advanced undergraduate level. It can also be useful as a reference text at the graduate level or for research. The mathematics in the main text is elementary, with more advanced mathematical analyses in the appendices. This book provides a precise account of the essentials in environmental and resource economics.

Acknowledgment

I am grateful to Herman Cesar, Herman Vollebergh, Daan van Soest, Cees Withagen, Sjak Smulders, and Shelby Gerking for taking turns teaching this course and for discussing the contents of the course. I am especially grateful to Shelby Gerking and Sjak Smulders for their suggestions on lecture notes 4–10, which improved the notes. Lecture note 10 is strongly based on the ideas of Sjak Smulders but the contents remain my responsibility. Finally, I am very grateful to Felix Munoz-Garcia for his comments on each lecture note, which improved these lecture notes.

About the Author

Em. Prof. Dr. Aart de Zeeuw studied mathematics at the University of Groningen, Netherlands, and received his PhD in economics at Tilburg University, Netherlands. He has been professor of quantitative economics (1989–1993) and professor of environmental economics (1993–2017) at Tilburg University, and he is now emeritus professor. From 2006 to 2009, he was co-director of the Beijer Institute of Ecological Economics at the Royal Swedish Academy of Sciences in Stockholm.

Aart de Zeeuw served as president of the *European Association of Environmental and Resource Economists* (1998–2000) and as co-editor of the *Journal of Environmental Economics and Management* (2004–2008).

At Tilburg University, Aart de Zeeuw held several other positions such as dean of the faculty of economics (1992–1994), director of graduate studies (1998–2001), scientific director of CentER (2005–2007), and founding director of the Tilburg Sustainability Center (2009–2013). He has been member of the Netherlands Advisory Council for Research on Nature and Environment and advisor to the Netherlands Environmental Assessment Agency. In 2017, he was awarded the Tjalling C. Koopmans medal from Tilburg University.

Aart de Zeeuw published in a wide range of scientific economic journals. His current research interests focus on the economics of tipping points in dynamical ecological systems and on international aspects of pollution control. In 2018, he was awarded the EAERE Lifetime Achievement Award in Environmental Economics. He became an EAERE Fellow in 2019.

Contents

Introduction to the Lecture Notes*

Environmental and resource economics is a field in economics that takes the relation with the natural environment into account. Resource economics is an old branch that exists for over a century but environmental economics in the sense of considering pollution and its consequences is relatively new. The focus in resource economics is on the optimal extraction and the price of natural resources. For a long time, the general idea was that the earth was sufficiently rich in resources, so societies did not have to worry about availability. In the early seventies of the previous century, however, the societal concern about the availability of natural resources became stronger. Economists predicted that the mechanism of scarcity, higher prices, lower use, and the search for alternatives would mitigate the problem. Indeed, availability of natural resources has not become a very pressing problem yet, although the concern is rising again. The other societal concern about the increasing level of pollution, however, has become a huge problem. Examples are climate change, due to the high level of greenhouse gas emissions, or health issues, due to the high level of air pollution. The earth is very big and has a large assimilative potential, but history has reached the geological epoch called the Anthropocene, with a significant human impact on the ecosystems. Change is always there, and change as such is not a problem

*These lecture notes developed over the years by teaching a basic course in environmental and resource economics at the advanced undergraduate level of the economics program at Tilburg University in the Netherlands. I am grateful to Herman Cesar, Herman Vollebergh, Daan van Soest, Cees Withagen, Sjak Smulders, and Shelby Gerking for taking turns in teaching this course.

unless it is detrimental to life support and to welfare. Economies and economics must start to take the relation with the natural environment into account.

Classical economics was studying economies which were mainly agricultural, and it was therefore focused on nature, such as the availability and the quality of land. Over time, economics drifted away from the natural environment. Due to the technological development, economies became less dependent on nature. Furthermore, economic activities like agriculture, fisheries, and tourism could leave the areas where natural conditions started to become less favorable and move around the world. However, the situation has changed now. Limits to the stability of ecosystems, such as the climate, are in sight. Pollution of the natural environment affects the availability of resources and directly affects certain aspects of welfare, such as health. Economics cannot restrict attention anymore to welfare generated by the production and consumption of goods and services, without considering the relation with the natural environment. The new challenge for development is to consider the broader concept of welfare, including the contribution of the natural environment. It becomes important to consider the connection between pollution and natural capital, i.e. between the output and the input of production and consumption. Environmental and resource economics focuses on answers to this challenge. At this point, it is still a separate field in economics, but it will probably become mainstream economics soon because the challenges will be a central issue in the Anthropocene with the large human impact on the natural environment.

Some people argue that economics is the cause of environmental problems and therefore cannot be the solution. It is true that for a long time, economics focused on growth and on welfare ignoring the increased importance of the natural environment. However, this has changed now, and the development of environmental and resource economics is a way to provide solutions. The concepts and techniques of economics are powerful, and it is easy to extend these to the analysis of welfare that takes a broader perspective. Economics is very well suited to consider scarcity and the different trade-offs and risks that are involved. In this way, the field environmental and resource economics can stand on the shoulders of giants in economics and handle environmental and resource problems at the same time.

These lecture notes provide an introduction to environmental and resource economics for students in economics at an advanced undergraduate level. This means that students have a basic knowledge of economics but are new to aspects regarding environment and resources. The idea is to present the essentials of this new field of economics in a clear and transparent way and to leave examples, extensions, and applications to the lecturer of the course. The reference lists only contain the seminal papers leading to the essentials and do not cover the wide range of research in these areas. The lecturer of the course can choose which areas or policy issues to discuss in more detail and which references to use for that purpose. These lecture notes are also useful for students who want to do a course in environmental and resource economics in their master's program but who did not have such a course in their bachelor's program. These lecture notes can help to quickly catch up with the essentials. The end of this introduction provides a list of selected textbooks in this field. The textbooks are different and aim at different levels and interests. Some only focus on resource economics or on environmental economics. Some are more theory oriented, and others are more policy oriented. Some require mathematical skills, and others avoid mathematics as an analytical tool. Some are very broad and extensive, and others are more selective. These lecture notes contain both resource and environmental economics. They are mainly theory oriented and leave the policy discussion to the lecturer of the course. They do not avoid mathematics but use it at a simple level in the main text and at a more advanced level in appendices. These lecture notes provide the concepts, techniques, and results that are essential for the field of environmental and resource economics in this stage of its development. The topics are mainly the usual topics of a course in this field, but valuation is only a small topic in these lecture notes and some topics are rather new and usually not part of the textbooks.

The first topic in Lecture 1 is on the level of pollution. A zero level is not compatible with the need for producing goods and services. The target is to strike a balance from an optimal welfare perspective. Lecture 1 formalizes the trade-off between the benefits of production and the costs of pollution. Cost–benefit analyses need to attach values to the environmental goods and services. Lecture 1 also provides a short introduction into the concepts and techniques of valuation. Since the natural environment is a public good, the policymaker must intervene and develop a policy to reach the pollution target. Lecture 2 presents the economic policy instruments. The Pigouvian tax is one, but environmental economics also developed tradable emission permits. Both instruments are cost-effective and do not require information on the firms. Lecture 2 also shows that in case of uncertainty, a condition exists that splits the preference for tradable permits or for taxes.

Lecture 3 extends trade theory with the aspect of pollution. It is always beneficial to open up for trade if environmental policy is in place. Otherwise, the welfare loss due to the increase of local pollution in an exporting country may outweigh the gains of trade. Lax environmental policy can be a strategic argument to attract firms, but Lecture 3 presents empirical analyses showing that this hardly works because less endowment with the factor capital counteracts this policy. Lecture 4 switches to global and cross-border pollution and international aspects of environmental policy. It is best for the countries together to cooperate, possibly with side payments, but cooperation is voluntary, and each country may have an incentive to deviate. Game theory provides a framework for analyzing cooperative and non-cooperative behavior. The acid rain game on the emission and the deposition of sulfur dioxide and nitrogen oxides in Europe provides a nice example. Lecture 5 considers the option of partial international cooperation as the equilibrium between the incentive to deviate and the incentive to cooperate. The incentive to free ride is usually stronger, so the stable coalition is small. However, the stable coalition becomes larger if the threat that countries leave the coalition becomes stronger. Lecture 5 also shows that in case of a tipping point in the ecological system (see Lecture 8), cooperation may not be needed to avoid tipping. The models in these first 5 lectures are static, but the next 5 lectures contain dynamical models.

Lecture 6 considers renewable resources such as fish. Renewable resources grow but can be depleted by overharvesting. The growth is restricted by the carrying capacity of the ecological system. The bio-economic analysis compares open access with optimal management. Models for renewable resources are dynamical and the analysis requires dynamical optimization. Lecture 6 presents the mechanisms, but the precise mathematical analysis is moved to the appendix. Lecture 7 considers non-renewable resources such as oil. Non-renewable resources do not grow but must be extracted in an optimal way. The core of the analysis is the Hotelling rule which is a condition of no-arbitrage stating that the price of the resource must grow at the rate of interest. Lecture 7 presents the optimal extraction path of the resource, under perfect competition and monopoly, and analyzes the effect of changes in parameters like the initial stock and the interest rate. Lecture 8 considers a relatively new topic, the economics of tipping points in ecological systems. Resources stem from ecological systems but at a certain level of pollution, the systems can suddenly tip into a state with a big loss of resources. Optimal management must take the possibility of tipping into account. If a model for the ecological system exists, non-linearities become part of the analysis. If tipping is probabilistic and endogenous, behavior should be more precautionary.

Lecture 9 returns to the issue of pollution in Lectures 1 and 2 but considers the dynamical accumulation of pollution now into a stock that is damaging such as the stock of greenhouse gases that causes climate change. Marginal net benefits are now equal to the present value of all future marginal net damages. Lecture 9 returns to Lecture 4 as well by comparing non-cooperative and cooperative behavior in the case of global stock pollution and international environmental policy. Lecture 10 shows when economic growth and the reduction of resource use and pollution can go together. It uses the Solow–Swan growth model and performs the analysis in terms of growth rates (inspired by lecture notes of Sjak Smulders). Lecture 10 also connects the Ramsey growth model with non-renewable resources and stock pollution and shows, partly in the appendix, that the core results from Lectures 7 (the Hotelling rule) and 8 (stock pollution) return.

These lecture notes can serve as a basic text for an introductory course environmental and resource economics at an advanced undergraduate level. They can also serve as a reference for students in a later stage of their studies. These lecture notes provide the main concepts, techniques, and results in the core areas of environmental and resource economics. Hopefully, these lecture notes will be useful for both lecturers and students and will help in establishing environmental and resource economics as part of the economics programs at the universities.

Acknowledgment

I am grateful to the other teachers of this course for discussing the contents of the course, especially to Shelby Gerking and Sjak Smulders for their suggestions on lecture notes 4–10, which improved these lecture notes. Lecture note 10 is strongly based on the ideas of Sjak Smulders but the contents remain my responsibility. Finally, I am grateful to Felix Munoz-Garcia for his comments on each lecture note, which improved these lecture notes.

Further Readings

Baumol, W.J. and Oates, W.E. 1975. *The Theory of Environmental Policy.* New York: Cambridge University Press.

Berck, P. and Helfand, G. 2011. *The Economics of the Environment.* Boston: Pearson Education.

Common, M. 1988. *Environmental & Resource Economics: An Introduction.* Harlow, England: Addison Wesley Longman Limited.

Conrad, J.M. and Clark, C.W. 1987. *Natural Resource Economics: Notes and Problems.* Cambridge: Cambridge University Press.

Dasgupta, P. 1982. *The Control of Resources.* Cambridge, MA: Harvard University Press.

Field, B.C. and Field, M.K. 2013. *Environmental Economics: An Introduction*, 6th edition. New York: McGraw-Hill.

Goodstein, E.S. 2008. *Economics and the Environment.* Hoboken, NJ: John Wiley & Sons.

Haab, T.C. and McConnell, K.E. 2002. *Valuing Environmental and Natural Resources.* Cheltenham, UK: Edward Elgar Publishing.

Hanley, N., Shogren, J.F., and White, B. 1997. *Environmental Economics in Theory and Practice.* Hampshire, UK: Palgrave Macmillan.

Hartwick, J.M. and Olewiler, N.D. 1986. *The Economics of Natural Resource Use.* New York: Harper & Row.

Kolstad, C.D. 2000. *Environmental Economics.* New York: Oxford University Press.

Pearce, D.W. and Turner, R.K. 1990. *Economics of Natural Resources and the Environment.* Hertfordshire, UK: Harvester Wheatsheaf.

Perman, R., Ma, Y., Common, M., Maddison, D., and McGilvray, J. 2011. *Natural Resource and Environmental Economics*, 4th edition. Harlow, England: Pearson Education Limited.

Phaneuf, D.J. and Requate, T. 2017. *A Course in Environmental Economics: Theory, Policy, and Practice.* Cambridge: Cambridge University Press.

Tietenberg, T. and Lewis, L. 2009. *Environmental & Natural Resource Economics*, 8th edition. Boston: Pearson Education.

Lecture 1

Pollution and Valuation

1.1 Introduction

An economy functions within a larger natural system. Classical economics was studying economies that were mainly agricultural and was therefore concerned about nature, such as the availability and the quality of land. However, neoclassical economics abstracted from the natural environment and focused on production, consumption, and related welfare. It was assumed that the availability of resources and the capacity of nature to assimilate pollution was sufficient and thus could be ignored. In recent times, the level of environmental pollution has reached the point where the mindset of economics has to switch back and integrate the natural environment again in economic analysis. Besides production, consumption, and related welfare, it is important to add resources, pollution, and the welfare associated with the natural environment.

It is unfortunate that many people perceive a controversy between economics and ecology. Both words originate from the Greek language and contain the word eco or oikos in Greek, which means house. Nomos in Greek means rules and logos description. Ecology indeed describes the relationship between living organisms and their physical environment. Economics, however, still mainly ignores the physical environment when it sets the rules for the economy. Especially in the current times, when population and affluence are growing, it is necessary that economics takes the relationship with the natural environment into account.

Almost all economic activities use natural resources and pollute the natural environment. It is therefore not possible to target for zero pollution, and pollution implies a cost that has to be taken into account. A good example is a lake which provides life support, amenities, and resources like fish and water. Pollution from nearby agricultural activities threatens these ecosystem services so that agriculture not only has benefits but also costs. The trade-off between the benefits of the economic activities and the costs of the resulting pollution leads to a pollution target. Pollution is a by-product of production and consumption. It is not generated on purpose. In economic terms, pollution is an external effect which means that the welfare of other people is unintentionally affected by the activity and that these other people are not compensated. Examples are playing loud music that affects neighbors, and greenhouse gas emissions that affect the climate of future generations. Noise is an example of flow pollution that immediately vanishes, and the accumulation of greenhouse gas emissions is an example of stock pollution (Lecture 9).

It is important to consider the level at which the pollution externality occurs. For example, if the problem only concerns a few people, like two neighbors in the case of noise, it is sufficient to institutionalize a bargaining procedure (Coase, 1960). If the problem concerns a larger number of people but within a jurisdiction, the policymaker has instruments like taxes and tradable permits to regulate the environmental problem. This is the topic of Lecture 2. If the problem is global, like climate change or pollution that crosses national borders, the optimal regulation requires voluntary cooperation between the countries. This is the topic of Lectures 4 and 5. This lecture describes the Coase theorem after formalizing the pollution target from the trade-off between the net benefits of production and consumption and the costs of the resulting pollution.

Valuing the costs of pollution is a difficult problem but it is needed to be able to compare these costs with the benefits. Economics usually values goods and services by their price on the market, but for the non-marketed environmental goods and services, other methods are required. The theory and practice of valuation is an extensive field in environmental economics, but these lecture notes only provide a short introduction.

This lecture has two goals. The first is to characterize the optimal production and resulting pollution target from the trade-off between the benefits and the damages. The second is to provide a short introduction to the valuation of environmental goods and services.

Section 1.2 presents the graphical analysis and the underlying calculus for the trade-off between the benefits and the damages. Section 1.3 introduces concepts and techniques for valuing environmental goods and services. Section 1.4 concludes.

1.2 Pollution

Pollution is a by-product of production and consumption. The examples range from noise or light that bother people to the emissions of greenhouse gases (like CO_2) that accumulate in the atmosphere and lead to climate change with possible high costs for future generations. Other examples are the emissions of particles that cause health problems, the emissions of sulfur dioxide and nitrogen oxides that cause acidification of soils (Lecture 4), the emissions of phosphorus that cause eutrophication of lakes (Lecture 8), the emissions of CFC that cause holes in the ozone layer with risks for skin cancer (Lecture 4), the release of plastics, etcetera.

Most pollution problems have a time dimension. The emissions accumulate into a stock of pollution, and the pollution stock causes damage. Nature can assimilate part of the emissions so that only the emissions above the assimilative capacity of nature increase the stock of pollution. It is a dynamical model, and the trade-off between the benefits and the damages is thus a dynamical optimization problem. This is the topic of Lecture 9. Flow pollutants, like noise and light, do not have a time dimension. Flow pollutants appear, and may bother people, but can be switched off without future damage. This section abstracts from this distinction and focuses on the concept of optimal pollution from the trade-off between the benefits and the damages.

1.2.1 *Optimal production and pollution*

The basic idea is an extension of standard microeconomics where the optimal production results from the maximization of the benefits minus the costs of production. The emissions are a by-product of the production. The damages to the natural environment due to the emissions of pollutants require extension of this analysis with the maximization of the net benefits of production NB corrected for the damages of the resulting pollution D. The optimal level of production and pollution, or the pollution target, follows from the maximization

$$\max_{y} [NB(y) - D(y)], \tag{1.1}$$

where y denotes the production. If the net benefit function NB is a concave function of y and the damage function D a convex function of y (see Appendix A), the optimal level of production is given by the first-order condition

$$NB'(y) - D'(y) = 0 \Rightarrow NB'(y) = D'(y), \tag{1.2}$$

which means that the marginal net benefits of production are equal to the marginal damages of pollution. If the net benefit function NB and the damage function D are quadratic functions, the marginal net benefits and damages are linear functions. For example, if $NB(y) = y - 0.5y^2$ and $D(y) = 0.5y^2$, the marginal net benefits MNB are given by $1 - y$ and the marginal damages MD by y. The optimal level of production is given by MNB = MD, $1 - y = y$, resulting in $y^* = 0.5$. Figure 1.1 depicts the marginal net benefits MNB and the marginal damages MD, resulting in the optimal level of production y^*. Note that y_0 (in the example, $y_0 = 1$) is the level of production where the marginal net benefits MNB are zero, so this is the optimal level of production when ignoring the damage of pollution. Taking the damage into account thus means that it is optimal to lower the production from y_0 to y^*. The pollution target becomes the resulting level of pollution. The area under the MD line between 0 and y^* represents the total damages $D(y^*)$ because this area is equal to the integral $\int_0^{y^*} D'(y)dy$. In the example, $\int_0^{y^*} ydy = [0.5y^2]_0^{y^*} = 0.5y^{*^2}$. The area under the MNB line represents the total net benefits $NB(y^*)$. This observation allows a graphical analysis in Figure 1.1 for showing that y^* is indeed the optimal level of production. Increasing the production to y_h implies that the net benefits increase by cey_hy^* but the damages increase by cdy_hy^* so that the total welfare decreases by cde. Decreasing the production to y_l

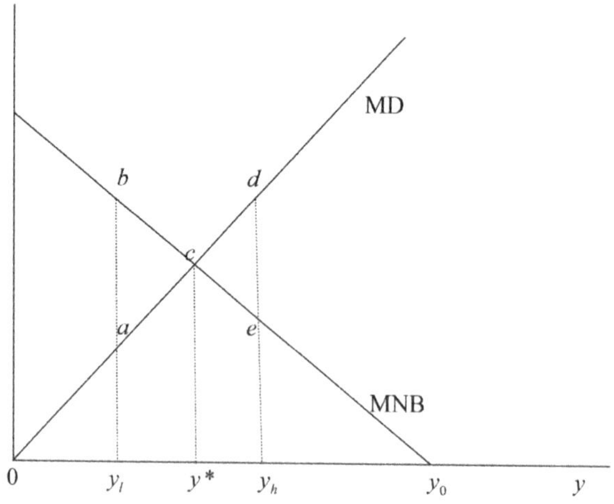

Figure 1.1. Optimal production and pollution.

implies that the net benefits decrease by bcy^*y_l but the damages decrease by acy^*y_l so that the total welfare decreases by acb. It follows that y^* is the optimal level of production.

This pollution target results from a smooth damage function D. However, many damage functions have a threshold in the sense that crossing this threshold leads to an unacceptable level of damage or to a large increase in damage. For example, exceeding a certain level of toxic waste may be unacceptable for health reasons. In such a case, the cost–benefit analysis implies that not exceeding the threshold is the pollution target (see also Lecture 8 on tipping points).

1.2.2 *Coase theorem*

Figure 1.1 also shows how a pollution externality can be solved at a low decision level that only concerns a few people. A good example is a situation with two neighbors in which one wants to play loud music and the other one is bothered by this. In this case, the MNB line in Figure 1.1 represents the marginal net benefits of the one who wants to play loud music and the MD line the marginal damage of the noise externality to the other one. The Coase theorem states that regardless of whether neighbor 1 has the right to play loud music or neighbor 2 has the right to silence, they can strike a bargain (Coase, 1960). They will agree on y^* where y indicates how long the music is played or at which volume or at which times. The reason is that for higher or lower values of y, one neighbor can compensate the other neighbor for moving to y^*. For y_h, neighbor 2 can compensate neighbor 1 for the loss of benefits cey_hy^* because the decrease in damage cdy_hy^* is larger. The neighbors can bargain on dividing the surplus cde. For y_l, neighbor 1 can compensate neighbor 2 for the increase in damage acy^*y_l because the gain in benefits bcy^*y_l is larger. The neighbors can bargain on dividing the surplus acb. The Coase theorem works if the transaction costs of the bargaining process are sufficiently low so that the net gain on which the parties bargain does not vanish. This may become problematic in the case of many parties so that it only works at a low decision level with a few parties. The core of the Coase theorem is that the optimum is reached regardless of who has the property rights, but the consequences for welfare are large. The Coase theorem assumes that the property rights are assigned, and the judicial system is functioning properly. In the example above, it is not always so clear whether someone has the right to silence or the right to play music. If neighbor 1 has the property rights, and thus can claim y_0, neighbor 2 has to pay at least cy_0y^* to neighbor 1 to reach y^*. If neighbor 2 has the property rights, and thus can claim 0, neighbor 1 has to pay at least $c0y^*$ to neighbor 2 to reach y^*. This means that either the polluter pays the victim of the pollution externality or the other way around. The so-called polluter-pays principle may not apply if the property rights are not clearly assigned to the victim. In the early seventies, for example, the Netherlands paid money to France to prevent the release of waste from the salt mines in the Elzas on the river Rhine.

1.2.3 *External costs*

This section builds on standard microeconomics where the optimal production results from the maximization of the benefits minus the costs of production and adds the damage to the natural environment as external costs. The optimal level of production that takes the external costs into account follows from the maximization

$$\max_y \,[B(y) - C(y) - EC(y)], \tag{1.3}$$

where y denotes the production, B the benefits, C the costs, and EC the external costs.

If the benefit function B is a concave function of y and the cost functions C and EC are convex functions of y, the optimal level of production is given by the first-order condition

$$B'(y) - C'(y) - EC'(y) = 0 \Rightarrow B'(y) = C'(y) + EC'(y), \tag{1.4}$$

which means that the marginal benefits of production are equal to the marginal costs of production plus the marginal external costs. If the benefit function B and the cost functions C and EC are quadratic functions, the marginal benefits and costs are linear functions. Define the marginal social costs (MSC) as the sum of the marginal costs (MC) and the marginal external costs (MEC). This also is a linear function. For example, if $B(y) = y - 0.5y^2$, $C(y) = 0.25y^2$, and $EC(y) = 0.25y^2$, the marginal benefits (MB) are given by $1 - y$, the MC by $0.5y$, the MEC by $0.5y$, and the MSC by y. The optimal level of production is given by MB = MC + MEC = MSC, $1-y = y$, resulting in $y^* = 0.5$. Note that this example gives the same result but also differs from the example in Section 1.2.1. The marginal net benefits are given by MNB = MB − MC, i.e. $1 - 1.5y$, and the marginal damages

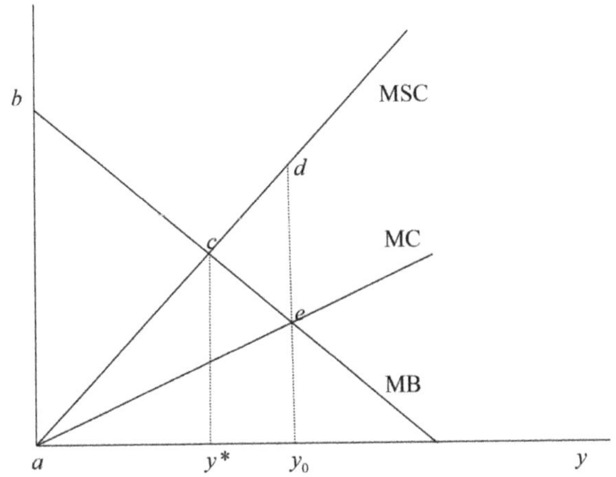

Figure 1.2. External costs.

(MD) are the MEC, i.e. $0.5y$, so that the optimal level of production results from $1 - 1.5y = 0.5y$, and this again yields $y^* = 0.5$. Figure 1.2 depicts the marginal benefits (MB), the MC, and the MSC, resulting in the optimal level of production y^*. Note that y_0 (in this example, $y_0 = 0.67$) is the level of production where the MB are equal to the MC so that this is the optimal level of production when ignoring the external costs. Taking the external costs into account means that it is optimal to lower the production from y_0 to y^*. The pollution target becomes the resulting level of pollution. It is basically the same story as in Section 1.2.1, but Figure 1.2 has different benefits and costs of production. The MEC are depicted in Figure 1.2 as a wedge between the MSC and the MC. For example, the MEC in y_0 are represented by the segment *ed*, which in the example above is equal to $0.5\,y_0 = 0.33$.

Figure 1.2 also shows the welfare gain when lowering the production from y_0 to y^*. The area under the MC line represents the total costs of production, and the area under the MB line the total benefits. The area between the MSC line and the MC line represents the total external costs because this is the difference between the total social costs and the total costs of production. For y_0, total welfare is equal to $bey_0a - ey_0a - dea$, which is equal to $acb - cde$. For y^*, total welfare is equal to $bcy^*a - cy^*a$, which is equal to acb. It follows that the welfare gain when lowering the production from y_0 to y^* is cde.

1.2.4 *Spatial analysis*

For emissions of greenhouse gases (like CO_2) that accumulate in the atmosphere and lead to climate change, it does not matter where the emissions originate. These emissions spread out uniformly and the damage due to climate change occurs everywhere. However, for emissions like sulfur dioxide and nitrogen oxides, it matters where these substances are emitted and where they are deposited. The damage in the form of acidification of soils occurs at the so-called receptors of the pollutants, but the targets must be set at the pollution sources. Another example is air pollution which causes health problems in the cities but originates from factories elsewhere. This means that a model is needed that connects the depositions d_i in receptor i with the emissions e_j originating from source j. If f_{ij} denotes the fraction of the emissions e_j from source j that is deposited in receptor i, it follows that for m sources and n receptors

$$d_i = \sum_{j=1}^{m} f_{ij}e_j, \; i = 1, 2, \ldots, n. \tag{1.5}$$

The cost–benefit analysis for a situation with sources and receptors in the different countries in Europe is presented in Lecture 4. Since it is also an example of cross-border externalities, the policy analysis in Lecture 4 becomes a game. This section only gives a numerical example to show the effect of spatial analysis. Suppose that there are two sources and two receptors. The benefits of production can be seen as functions of emissions e_j given by $B(e_j) = e_j - 0.5e_j^2, j = 1, 2$. The damage functions can be seen as functions of the depositions d_i given by $D(d_i) = 0.5d_i^2, i = 1, 2$. If the sources and the receptors coincide so that $d_1 = e_1$ and $d_2 = e_2$, it follows that the marginal benefits at each of the two locations are $1 - e_j, j = 1, 2$, and the marginal damages are $e_j, j = 1, 2$ so that the optimal levels of emission are $e_j{}^* = 0.5, j = 1, 2$. However, if all the emissions from the two sources are deposited in receptor 1, so that zero emissions end up in receptor 2, equation (1.5) yield

$$d_1 = e_1 + e_2, \; d_2 = 0, \tag{1.6}$$

and the total benefits minus the total damages become

$$B(e_1)+B(e_2)-D(d_1)-D(d_2) = e_1-0.5e_1^2+e_2-0.5e_2^2-0.5(e_1+e_2)^2. \tag{1.7}$$

The first-order conditions for maximizing (1.7) are

$$1 - e_1 - (e_1 + e_2) = 0,$$
$$1 - e_2 - (e_1 + e_2) = 0,$$

so that the optimal levels of emission are $e_j{}^* = 0.33,\ j = 1, 2$. The reason that the optimal levels of emission decrease is that receptor 1 becomes a hot spot that receives all the depositions. Since the marginal damages are increasing, total damage is larger when all the emissions are deposited at receptor 1 than when the emissions spread out over receptors 1 and 2.

1.2.5 *Summary*

Pollution targets follow from balancing the net benefits of production and the damages of the resulting pollution. The previous sections add the damage of pollution or the external costs for the people who suffer from the pollution to the cost–benefit analysis of production. In this way, the optimal level of production results that takes account of the damage of pollution or the external costs. This also defines the pollution target that balances all the benefits and costs. The graphical analysis shows the welfare gain of moving from the level of production ignoring the damage of pollution to this optimal level of production. Lecture 2 discusses the instruments for reaching the optimal level of production and the associated pollution target.

Pollution has a time dimension in the sense that pollution often accumulates into a stock of pollution and has a space dimension in the sense that pollution often does not spread out uniformly. Lecture 9 analyzes stock pollution and Lecture 4 discusses the acid rain game as an example of the spatial analysis. The previous section provides a simple example to show that the spatial analysis can have hot spots that affect the optimal level of emissions.

Pollution problems have to be handled at different decision levels. In the case that a pollution problem is a simple problem between neighbors, such as noise, the Coase theorem states that the problem can be solved with a bargaining process between the parties, regardless of who has the property rights, if the transaction costs of bargaining are not too large. At a higher decision level, but still within one jurisdiction, the policymaker can use the policy instruments that are discussed in Lecture 2. For global pollution problems, at the international decision level, the policy problem becomes a game. This is discussed in Lecture 4.

1.3 Valuation

Valuation of environmental goods and services is an important and extensive topic in the field of environmental and resource economics. These goods and services are usually not traded on markets and thus do not have a market price, but a value is needed to include these goods and services in cost–benefit analyses and to determine external costs of pollution. Some resources that the natural environment provides are traded on markets and have a market price, but extraction of these resources reduces other values at the same time. For example, cutting trees provides wood but part of the forest is lost for recreation, for preventing soil erosion, and for the sequestration of carbon. Other examples are catching fish that affects ecological systems, such as the coral reefs, and collecting ivory that results in killing many elephants. This section gives a short introduction into valuation by considering different types of values, some theories, and the main techniques that are used to infer these different types of values.

1.3.1 *Values*

Environmental goods and services have *use* and *non-use* values. Use values are attached to resources that are used for production and consumption, but enjoying beautiful nature is also a use value. Non-use values are mainly existence values. People value the existence of species and natural assets even if they do not make use of them. They may value the option for future use or for use by others or future generations, or they may have a spiritual motive. People may want to keep the Grand Canyon, for example, because they want to visit it sometime or they want others or their children to be able to visit it, or they want to respect the plant and animal species that live there. Use values can be inferred from observed behavior: on markets, of course, where these use values are revealed, but also from the efforts and costs people are willing to make to visit nature. A good example is the housing market where people reveal how much they are willing to pay to live in a house with a beautiful view. Non-use values can only be determined by asking people or by confronting them with situations in which they reveal their preferences.

1.3.2 *Theory*

The theory on the valuation of environmental goods and services distinguishes two ways to determine the value. The *compensating surplus* is the amount of money someone is willing to pay for an improvement in the environmental quality or is willing to accept for a deterioration of the environmental quality. The *equivalent surplus* is the amount of money someone is willing to accept for not having an improvement in the environmental

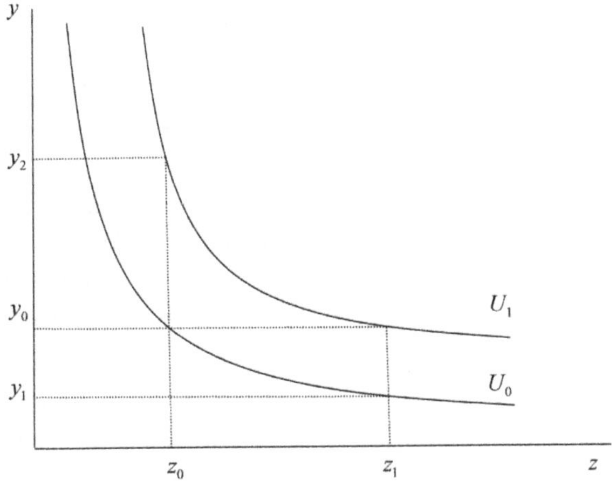

Figure 1.3. Compensating surplus and equivalent surplus.

quality or is willing to pay for avoiding a deterioration of the environmental quality. Suppose that utility is given by $U(y, z)$, where y denotes income and z denotes environmental quality. Figure 1.3 depicts two indifference curves, U_0 and U_1, with $U_1 > U_0$. For income y_0 and environmental quality z_0, utility is equal to U_0. In the case of an improvement in the environmental quality from z_0 to z_1, the compensating surplus is equal to $y_0 - y_1$ because $U(y_1, z_1) = U(y_0, z_0) = U_0$ so that $y_0 - y_1$ is the maximum amount of money someone is willing to pay for this improvement in the environmental quality. For income y_0 and environmental quality z_1, utility is equal to U_1. In the opposite case now of a deterioration of the environmental quality from z_1 to z_0, the compensating surplus is equal to $y_2 - y_0$ because $U(y_2, z_0) = U(y_0, z_1) = U_1$ so that $y_2 - y_0$ is the minimum amount of money someone is willing to accept as compensation for this deterioration of the environmental quality. The equivalent surplus has its reference at the higher utility level U_1 and is the willingness-to-accept (WTA) for not having an improvement in the environmental quality from z_0 to z_1, which is equal to $y_2 - y_0$. On the other hand, the equivalent surplus measures the willingness-to-pay (WTP) for avoiding a deterioration of the environmental quality from z_1 to z_0, which is equal to $y_0 - y_1$.

The compensating surplus restores the utility level in the case a change occurs, and the equivalent surplus restores the utility level in the case a change does not occur. Both measures are either a WTP or a WTA. The WTP is the maximum amount of money someone is willing to pay for an

Table 1.1. Compensating surplus and equivalent surplus.

	Improvement	Deterioration
Compensating surplus	WTP for change to occur	WTA for change to occur
Equivalent surplus	WTA for change not to occur	WTP for change not to occur

improvement in the environmental quality or for avoiding deterioration of the environmental quality, and the WTA is the minimum amount of money someone is willing to accept as compensation for a deterioration of the environmental quality or for giving up an improvement in the environmental quality. Table 1.1 summarizes the relationships between these concepts.

Valuation may yield different results depending on whether it is about an improvement or a deterioration of the environment and whether people must value a change to occur or a proposed change not to occur. The conceptual framework shows that valuation either extracts a WTP or a WTA from people. Figure 1.3 can also be used to derive a relationship between WTP and WTA. Suppose that the initial income increases from y_0 to y_2. In that case, $y_2 - y_0$ is the WTP for an improvement in the environmental quality from z_0 to z_1 because $U(y_0, z_1) = U(y_2, z_0) = U_1$. Furthermore, $y_2 - y_0$ is also the WTA for a deterioration of the environmental quality from z_1 to z_0, in case the initial income is y_0. The WTA is thus equal to the WTP that results at a higher level of income. It follows that the WTA is larger than the WTP if the WTP increases with income (the income effect).

Empirical studies often show a significant divergence between WTP and WTA. Although the analysis above gives an argument for this result, standard theory predicts that for small income effects, WTP and WTA should not differ much. The literature provides two main reasons for the empirical evidence. One reason is that environmental goods and services have limited possibilities for substitution and that the difference between WTP and WTA increases with a decrease in the degree of substitution (Hanemann, 1991). Another reason follows from the so-called prospect theory (Kahneman and Tversky, 1979). The point of reference matters and in absolute terms, people give a larger value to a loss than they give to a gain of the same size (loss aversion). This means that the WTA for deterioration of environmental quality will be larger than the WTP for an equal-size improvement in environmental quality. This is called the *endowment effect.* People attach more value to retaining an object that they own than to acquiring that same object when they do not own it. A nice example is a field experiment on providing financial incentives to teachers for doing a better job (Fryer *et al.*, 2022). It proved to be much more successful to give the teachers an upfront bonus that has to be returned (a loss) in case their students do not sufficiently improve than to pay them afterward (a gain) in the case of sufficient improvement. The point of reference matters and a possible loss provides a stronger incentive than a possible gain. Empirical studies confirm that points of reference and property rights also matter in valuation.

1.3.3 *Methods*

There are several methods of valuation. The revealed-preference methods derive values from observed behavior and thus can only estimate use values. The stated preference methods are based on surveys and can estimate both use and non-use values but rely on answers to hypothetical questions. The literature contains many valuation studies using different methods, but this section only provides a short description of the main method in each category.

The main method in revealed preference is *hedonic pricing* (Rosen, 1974). The idea is to model the price of a good that is sold on the market as a function of the different aspects that can explain the value of this good, among which is an environmental aspect. A good example is the price of a house which can be explained by characteristics like the number of rooms, the location, and the neighborhood but also by characteristics like noise, view, and air quality. Regression analysis on the data reveals to what extent the environmental characteristic explains the price of the house and in this way provides a value for that characteristic. For example, if houses of the same quality in the same area differ in price because they either have a view on beautiful nature or a view on a dirty industrial site, the difference in price indicates the value of the view. Using this method, the external effect of noise close to an airport can also be estimated.

The main method in stated preference is *contingent valuation* (Ciriacy-Wantrup, 1947). It is based on surveys in which a representative sample of the population is asked directly about their WTP or their WTA. This method can extract both use and non-use values but requires a very careful description of what the people are supposed to value. The main difficulty, however, is that the questions are hypothetical and that people do not really have to pay (or to accept) what they answer. They may not realize their opportunity costs, or they may have strategic reasons for mentioning higher or lower numbers. The design of the survey can explicitly warn the people that their income will be lower after paying what they answer or that the results of the survey will be reported to the authorities with possible consequences, but the survey remains hypothetical. Another difficulty is that answers to open-ended questions may differ widely and may not be very reliable because people do not have a clear view on what to answer. It is possible to anchor the questions by giving the people a set of numbers to choose from (payment cards), or by asking them to say yes or no to a proposed number (like a referendum). Anchoring will give more focus to the valuation, but, on the other hand, fixing the numbers beforehand gives a possible anchoring bias. Performing a pilot study first to get an idea about the range of values can overcome this difficulty. Finally, a contingent valuation study collects the characteristics of the respondents for explaining the variation in the answers in the econometric analysis. The literature on contingent valuation contains a wide variety of studies and discusses all sorts of difficulties, but it is beyond the scope of these lecture notes to give a complete overview. A prestigious panel with two Nobel laureates in economics, convened by the National Oceanic and Atmospheric Administration, wrote a report on contingent valuation in 1993 which concluded that despite all the shortcomings of this valuation method, it is in many cases the only game in town.

1.3.4 *Summary*

Valuation of non-marketed environmental goods and services is needed for complete cost–benefit analyses and for attaching values to the externalities of pollution and extracting resources. The theory distinguishes compensating surplus and equivalent surplus. Both concepts measure a WTP or a WTA. The compensating surplus measures the WTP for an improvement in the environmental quality or the WTA for a deterioration of the environmental quality. The equivalent surplus measures the WTA for not having an improvement or the WTP for not having a deterioration. Due to an income effect, the WTA is usually somewhat larger than the WTP, but empirical studies show that when valuing environmental goods and services, the difference can be quite large. The reason may be the limited substitution possibilities but especially the evidence of the endowment effect from prospect theory is convincing. People value a loss in absolute terms higher than a gain of the same size.

Valuation methods are either based on revealed preference or stated preference. Revealed-preference methods infer values from observed behavior and thus only measure use values. Stated-preference methods infer values from surveys and can measure both use and non-use or existence values. Hedonic pricing is a revealed-preference method inferring values from regression analysis on the different characteristics, among which is an environmental one, that can explain the price of a marketed good like a house. Contingent valuation is a stated-preference method inferring values from asking people. This method is vulnerable to several biases such as a hypothetical bias or an anchoring bias, and requires operating carefully, but there is often no alternative valuation method. Most textbooks in environmental economics have separate chapters on valuation, but these lecture notes only provide a short introduction here in this section. For interested people, a good textbook on the topic of valuation is Haab and McConnell (2002).

1.4 Conclusion

This lecture has two parts. Section 1.2 extends the standard economics with the damage and the external effects of pollution. This section provides simple algebraic and graphical analyses for determining the optimal level of production, including the environmental damages and external costs. The graphical analysis with environmental damage also proves the Coase theorem which states that regardless of who has the property rights, bargaining can solve the problem if it only involves a few parties. Lecture 2 considers environmental policy at the decision level of a country, and Lecture 4 at the international decision level.

Section 1.3 provides a short introduction to the concepts and techniques of environmental valuation. This section explains the concepts of compensating and equivalent surplus and how these concepts relate to the WTP and the WTA. It is important to be clear on what one wants to measure and to take account of behavioral aspects like the endowment effect. This section also introduces hedonic pricing and contingent valuation as the main examples of a revealed-preference and a stated-preference valuation method, respectively. Hedonic pricing uses observed behavior. Contingent valuation uses answers to hypothetical questions but can value use and non-use values and is often the only game in town.

References

Ciriacy-Wantrup, S.V. 1947. Capital returns from soil-conservation practices. *Journal of Farm Economics* 29, 4: 1181–1196.

Coase, R.H. 1960. The problem of social cost. *The Journal of Law & Economics* 3: 1–44.

Fryer, R.G. Jr., Levitt, S.D., List, J., and Sadoff, S. 2022. Enhancing the efficacy of teacher incentives through framing: A field experiment. *American Economic Journal: Economic Policy* 14, 4: 269–299.

Haab, T.C. and McConnell, K.E. 2002. *Valuing Environmental and Natural Resources*. Cheltenham, UK: Edward Elgar Publishing.

Hanemann, W.M. 1991. Willingness to pay and willingness to accept: How much can they differ? *The American Economic Review* 81, 3: 635–647.

Kahneman, D. and Tversky, A. 1979. Prospect theory: An analysis of decision under risk. *Econometrica* 47, 2: 263–292.

Rosen, S. 1974. Hedonic prices and implicit markets: Product differentiation in pure competition. *Journal of Political Economy* 82, 1: 34–55.

Lecture 2

Policy Instruments

2.1 Introduction

Lecture 1 focuses on the trade-off between the benefits of the economic activities and the costs of the resulting pollution which yields the optimal level of production or the pollution target. If the problem only concerns a few people, it is sufficient to institutionalize a bargaining procedure, but if the problem concerns a larger number of people within one jurisdiction, the policymaker has to find ways to regulate the environmental problem. If the problem is global, it requires voluntary cooperation between the countries, which is the topic of Lectures 4 and 5.

Initially, policymakers mainly relied on *command-and-control* instruments which means that the policymaker prescribes what is allowed regarding the damage to the environment. Either firms get licenses for the allowable level of emissions or firms are obliged to use the best available technologies to produce the goods and services. However, these instruments are not economical. Licenses work in the sense of controlling the total emissions but because firms differ in their costs of reducing emissions, this policy does not guarantee that the target is reached at the lowest costs. Furthermore, requiring the best available technology now does not give an incentive to improve the technology. Gradually, policy shifted to using *economic instruments* that provide incentives and cost-effectiveness. The main economic instruments are taxes and tradable permits. Taxes on emissions change the relative prices which leads to a substitution away from polluting economic activities. Tradable permits mean that the policymaker creates a market for the licenses so that the licenses get a price, and the use of licenses becomes cost-effective.

The use of economic instruments has several advantages. Emissions get a price by levying a tax or by creating a market for emission permits so that the pollution target is reached at the lowest costs. Moreover, the price always provides an incentive to further reduce emissions, which is a form of dynamic efficiency. Another advantage is that economic instruments do not require precise information on the firms. If the policymaker would want to allocate the emission permits to the firms in a cost-efficient way, it would have to know the marginal costs of emission reduction at each firm. However, the price on emissions that result from the use of an economic instrument takes care of this automatically. An important difference between taxes and tradable permits is that tradable permits also set the standard or the pollution target as the total of the emission permits while with taxes, the resulting total level of emissions is initially not clear. Taxes can be adjusted, of course, until the pollution target is reached but policy changes are costly. A final issue is equity or fairness. Environmental policy implies additional costs to firms that formerly did not have to bother about these costs, and economic adjustments take time. The instrument of tradable permits allows for an interesting way to steer this adjustment. By "grandfathering" the emission permits, which means that the permits are allocated for free and in proportion to the current emission levels, the initial costs to the firms are low, but the market will start to reallocate the permits to the firms that can produce at lower costs. By gradually lowering the total amount of emission permits, the adjustment proceeds until the pollution target is reached at the lowest costs. A nice example is the EU Emissions Trading System (EU ETS) which regulates the emissions of greenhouse gases in the energy sector and manufacturing industry in the European Union.

Lecture 1 determines the optimal level of production or the pollution target assuming that the marginal benefits and the marginal costs are known but of course, this information is uncertain. The theory on environmental policy includes the interesting result that in case of uncertainty, the relative steepness of the marginal benefit and marginal cost curves determines whether it is better to use taxes or tradable permits as the instrument of environmental policy (Weitzman, 1974). This result follows from comparing the welfare losses in the different situations.

This lecture has two goals. The first is to introduce and compare taxes and tradable permits as the economic instruments of environmental policy. The second is to show that for a certain type of uncertainty, taxes are preferred over tradable permits, or vice versa.

Section 2.2 presents the graphical analysis of using taxes or tradable permits as economic instruments of environmental policy. Section 2.3 presents the result that either taxes or tradable permits are preferred for a certain type of uncertainty. Section 2.4 concludes.

2.2 Economic Instruments

Figures 1.1 and 1.2 in Lecture 1 present the trade-off between the benefits of the production and the damage of the resulting pollution as a function of the production y. Figure 1.1 depicts the marginal net benefits of production and the marginal damages of pollution. Figure 1.2 depicts the marginal benefits and marginal costs of production and the marginal external costs which are equal to the marginal damages of pollution. This graphical analysis presupposes a fixed relation between the production y and the emissions e, and thus the same figures also apply as a function of the emissions e. As a function of e, the marginal net benefits of emissions mean the marginal net benefits of the production that leads to that level of emissions. When moving to taxes on emissions and trade in emission permits, it is convenient to use the figures in terms of the emissions e. It is important to note, however, that the relation between the production y and the emissions e is not one-to-one. Reduction of emissions can be realized by reducing production but also by substitution to other inputs or by using other technologies. The precise effect on the level of production and the marginal benefits and costs depends on these options. All the options to reduce emissions are denoted by abatement. It follows that the marginal net benefits (MNB) can also be seen as the mirror of the marginal abatement costs (MAC) of reducing emissions. Figure 2.1 is a copy of Figure 1.1 but in terms of emissions e. The area ce_0e^* represents the costs of reducing emissions from e_0 to e^*. Furthermore, the area $c0e^*$ under the marginal damages (MD) represents the damage at the level of emissions e^*. The total costs are ce_00. Minimizing the total costs leads again to e^* as the optimal level of emissions because the total costs or the sum of the areas under MAC to the right and under MD to the left are higher for any other level of emissions.

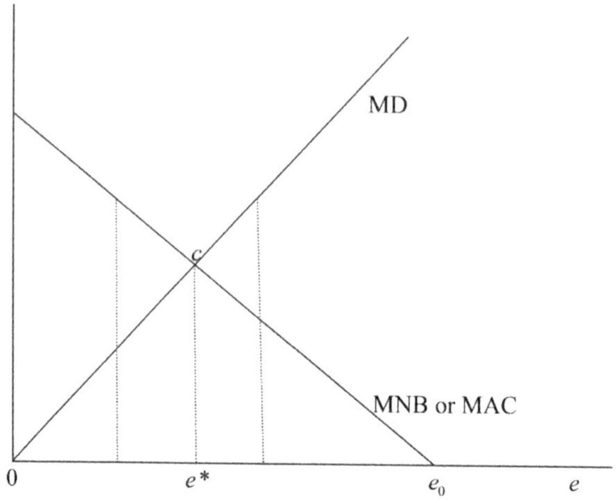

Figure 2.1. Optimal emissions.

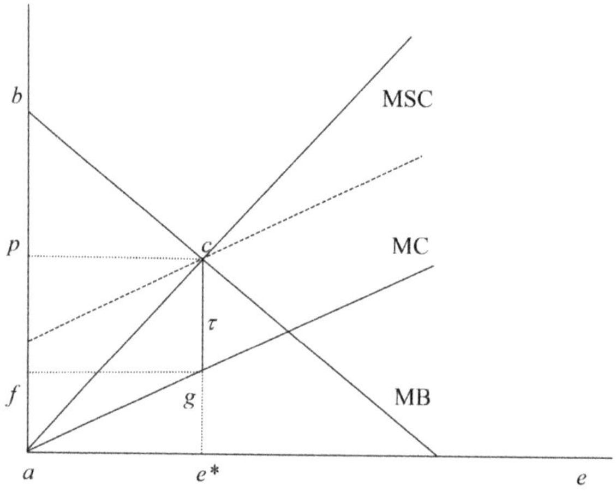

Figure 2.2. Pigouvian tax.

2.2.1 *Pigouvian tax*

A Pigouvian tax is a tax that provides the incentive to internalize external costs (Pigou, 1932). This tax is a price that affects behavior in the sense that behavior takes the external costs into account. Figure 2.2 is a copy of Figure 1.2 but in terms of emissions e (the relation between the emissions e and the production y is discussed above).

The optimal level of emissions for some tax on emissions τ follows from the maximization

$$\max_{e} [B(e) - C(e) - \tau e], \tag{2.1}$$

where B denotes the benefits and C the costs.

The optimal level of emissions for this tax τ is given by the first-order condition

$$B'(e) - C'(e) - \tau = 0 \Rightarrow B'(e) = C'(e) + \tau, \tag{2.2}$$

which means that the marginal benefits (MB) are equal to the marginal costs (MC) plus the tax τ. By comparing equation (2.2) with equation (1.4) in Lecture 1 (in terms of emissions e), it is clear that levying a tax τ that is equal to the marginal external costs (MEC) for the optimal level of emissions e^* induces this optimal level of emissions. Figure 2.2 shows that adding this tax τ and shifting the marginal cost (MC) upward to the dashed line MC + τ leads to the optimal level of emissions e^*. Note that the marginal external costs (MEC) are the difference between the marginal costs (MC) and the marginal social costs (MSC). For example, by copying the example in Lecture 1 in terms of emissions e, it follows that if $B(e) = e - 0.5e^2$, $C(e) = 0.25e^2$, and $EC(e) = 0.25e^2$, the marginal benefits MB are given by $1 - e$, the marginal costs (MC) by $0.5e$, the marginal external costs (MEC) by $0.5e$, and the marginal social costs (MSC) by e. The optimal level of emissions is given by MB = MSC or $1 - e = e$, resulting in $e^* = 0.5$. The marginal external costs (MEC) in the optimal level of emissions e^* are 0.25. It follows that for a tax $\tau = 0.25$, equation 2.2 implies that the optimal level of emissions e^* is also given by MB = MC + τ or $1 - e = 0.5e + 0.25$, resulting in $e^* = 0.5$ again. Figure 2.2 depicts the different welfare components. The gross price is p and the consumer surplus is bcp. The net price is $p - \tau$ and the producer surplus is agf. The tax revenues are $fgcp$ and these can be used for public goods and services or can be returned to the private sector, lump-sum, or in the form of lower taxes elsewhere. The different welfare components add up to $agcb$. The external costs are agc. It follows that total welfare is equal to $agcb - agc = acb$, as in Lecture 1. This analysis returns in Lecture 3.

2.2.2 *Cost-effectiveness*

Section 2.2.1 provides the overall picture but in practice, the policymaker faces many firms that have different costs of reducing emissions, i.e. different marginal abatement costs (MAC). If the policymaker aims to reduce emissions from e_0 to e^*, it is fair to demand proportional shares from each firm, but this is not the way to reduce emissions at the lowest cost. If the policymaker knows all the marginal abatement costs (MAC), it is in principle possible to allocate the obligations to reduce emissions in a cost-efficient way, but this informational requirement is enormous. When using a tax on emissions, this information is not needed.

Figure 2.3 depicts the marginal abatement costs (MAC) for two firms, i.e. firm 1 and firm 2. The lines MAC1 and MAC2 run from left to right whereas the MAC in Figure 2.1 runs from right to left because Figure 2.3 has abatement a instead of emissions e on the axis. It is optimal for each firm to choose the level of emissions and production so that the tax τ is equal to its marginal abatement cost, MAC1 or MAC2. It follows that levying a tax is cost-effective. The difficulty is that the policymaker does not know beforehand how much each firm will abate for a certain level of the tax τ and thus does not know which level of the tax will induce the total level of abatement $e_0 - e^*$. In Figure 2.3, firm 1 will abate a_1 and firm 2 will abate a_2. If $a_1 + a_2 > e_0 - e^*$, the tax τ must be decreased and if $a_1 + a_2 < e_0 - e^*$, the tax τ must be increased, until $a_1 + a_2 = e_0 - e^*$. This level of the tax realizes the required reduction of emissions and is cost-effective. Suppose that the target is to reduce emissions from $e_0 = 90$ to $e^* = 50$ so that the required reduction of emissions is 40. Suppose also that MAC1 is $5a$ and MAC2 is $3a$. If the level of the tax is τ, it holds that the abatement levels

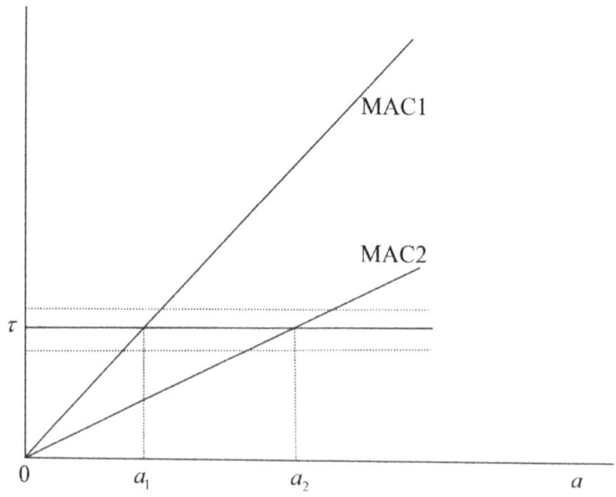

Figure 2.3. Cost-effectiveness.

a_1 and a_2 satisfy $5a_1 = \tau$ and $3a_2 = \tau$ so that $5a_1 = 3a_2$. Furthermore, the total level of abatement is 40, or $a_1 + a_2 = 40$. Simple algebra yields $a_1 = 15$, $a_2 = 25$, and $\tau = 75$. If the policymaker levies the tax $\tau = 75$, the firms react with abatement levels $a_1 = 15$ and $a_2 = 25$ so that this tax induces the total abatement target 40. The overall marginal abatement cost (MAC) in this case is $15a/8$. For the tax $\tau = 75$, total abatement is equal to 40.

Note that this reasoning leads to a circle. Varying the tax τ until the pollution target e^* is reached provides information on the overall marginal abatement costs (MAC), but as Figure 2.1 shows, this overall marginal abatement cost (MAC) was required to set the pollution target in the first place. It may be needed to reconsider the pollution target and to vary the tax τ again to reach this pollution target.

2.2.3 *Tradable permits*

Tradable permits are the instrument of environmental policy that combines two important criteria (Dales, 1968). By construction, this instrument implements the pollution target, but it also realizes cost-effectiveness. The total allowable level of emissions e^* is split into a set of emission permits, and these emission permits are allocated to the firms. By creating a market for the permits, cost-effectiveness results. The price of the permits will be equal to the marginal abatement costs.

Figure 2.4 is a copy of Figure 2.1 but shows the Pigouvian tax τ from Section 2.2.2 as the marginal damages (MD), that are equal to the marginal external costs (MEC), in the optimal level of emissions e^*. This tax τ is also equal to the overall marginal abatement costs (MAC). Figure 2.3 shows that the tax τ is equal to the marginal abatement costs of each of the individual firms. The price $\tilde{p}$ of the emission permits on the market for permits plays the same role as the tax τ and is also equal to the marginal abatement costs. The policymaker can allocate the emission permits to the firms in two ways. The policymaker can either organize an auction for emission permits or hand out the emission permits to the firms for free, usually in proportion to the current levels of emissions. The last option is called grandfathering. Initially, the total amount of emission permits is higher than the pollution target. Policymakers prefer this option, because the firms have initially low costs, so that society has less difficulty accepting the policy. Step by step, the total amount of emission permits is reduced until the pollution target is reached so that the economy has time to adjust. The resulting price on the market for the emission permits guarantees cost-effectiveness. The option

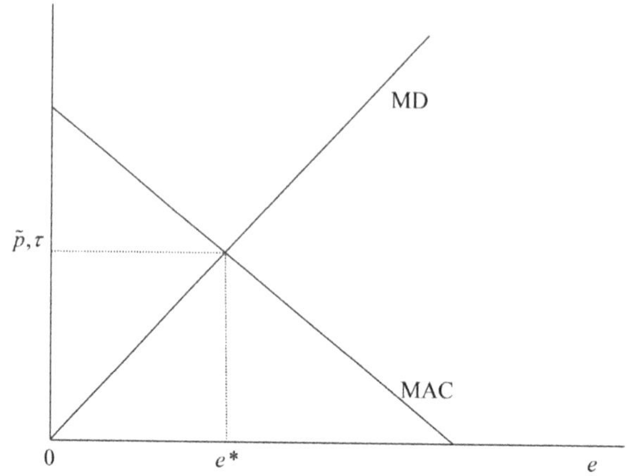

Figure 2.4. Economic instruments.

of an auction, with the total allowable set of emission permits, also yields this price of emission permits that is equal to the marginal abatement costs.

The instrument of tradable permits (*cap-and-trade*) has these two important properties but also a significant administrative burden. The market must function properly, and initially, it proved to be difficult to establish a market in emission permits, but currently, several permit markets work well. Moreover, the system of tradable permits requires the monitoring of the firms to ensure that they do not emit more than the level for which they have permits. Nevertheless, the instrument of tradable permits has been quite successful in the reduction of emissions. For example, the market in permits for emissions of sulfur dioxide under the framework of the Acid Rain Program of the 1990 Clean Air Act in the USA reduced the emissions by 50% from 1980 levels by 2007. Under the 2011 Cross-State Air Pollution Rule (CSAPR), the national sulfur dioxide market was replaced by four separate markets in sulfur dioxide and nitrogen oxides, with similar rates of success (see Lecture 4 for an analysis of the acid rain game in Europe). Perhaps the most interesting market in emission permits is the EU Emissions Trading System (EU ETS) for greenhouse gas emissions, with the aim to control climate change. It covers around 10,000 installations in the energy sector and manufacturing industry, as well as part of the aircraft operators, which adds up to about 40% of the EU's emissions. Under the European Climate Law, the first target is to reduce the emissions by at least 55% from 1990 levels by 2030.

2.2.4 *Summary*

The previous sections show the power of economic instruments for environmental policy with the aim of realizing a pollution target. The main economic instruments are taxes and tradable permits. In theory, the Pigouvian tax is equal to the marginal external costs (MEC) or the marginal damages (MD) in the optimal level of emissions. In practice, the policymaker does not know how the different firms will react to a tax, but, for any tax, the firms will equate the tax to their marginal abatement costs so that the tax is cost-effective. By varying the tax, the policymaker can adjust the emissions and realize the pollution target.

The use of tradable permits kills two birds with one stone. The total set of tradable permits yields the pollution target from the outset. Moreover, the trade in emission permits yields a price on the permits market that is equal to the marginal abatement costs of all the firms so that tradable permits are also cost-effective. The policymaker can auction the emission permits or give them to the firms for free. The last option, together with a larger set of permits initially, starts the trading process but does not immediately burden the firms. Gradually, the policymaker tightens the cap on permits, the economy adjusts, and the pollution target is realized.

2.3 Prices vs. Quantities

The pollution target can be split into a set of emission permits which can be traded on a market. The resulting price $\tilde{p}$ of permits is equal to the marginal abatement costs of the individual firms and equal to the overall marginal abatement costs (MAC). The alternative policy is to levy a tax τ on emissions which plays the same role as the price $\tilde{p}$ of permits and is also equal to the overall marginal abatement cost (MAC) in Figure 2.4. Both policies are cost-effective. When the pollution target e^* is determined, the instrument of tradable permits realizes the pollution target by construction, but the instrument of a tax requires some trial and error before the pollution target is realized. In the end, it does not matter which instrument is used but this section shows that this does matter when uncertainty is considered. There is uncertainty on the marginal damages (MD) and on the marginal abatement costs (MAC) in Figure 2.4, and thus on the pollution target e^*. This section shows, by considering the welfare losses, that in case of a specific uncertainty about the position of these lines, the relative steepness implies to prefer taxes (price instrument) over tradable permits (quantity instrument) or the other way around (Weitzman, 1974).

2.3.1 *Effects of uncertainty*

Suppose that the uncertainty about the marginal abatement costs (MAC) means that the true line representing these costs in Figure 2.4 shifts in, when the costs are overestimated, or shifts out, when these costs are underestimated. Figure 2.5 shows that if the instrument of a tax τ is used, the resulting level of emissions is uncertain and becomes either $e^{*\prime}$ when the line representing the marginal abatement costs (MAC) shifts in, or $e^{*\prime\prime}$ when this line shifts out. For example, if the line is given by $1 - e$, and either shifts to $1 - e - \varepsilon$ or to $1 - e + \varepsilon$, the tax $\tau = 0.5$ realizes either the level of emissions $e^{*\prime} = 0.5 - \varepsilon$ or $e^{*\prime\prime} = 0.5 + \varepsilon$, instead of the pollution target $e^* = 0.5$. However, if the instrument of tradable permits is used, the level of emissions stays at the pollution target e^* but the price of permits becomes uncertain and is either equal to $\tilde{p}'$, when this line shifts in, or $\tilde{p}''$, when this line shifts out. In the example, $\tilde{p}' = 0.5 - \varepsilon$ and $\tilde{p}'' = 0.5 + \varepsilon$, instead of $\tilde{p} = \tau = 0.5$.

2.3.2 *The choice of instrument*

First, note that if only marginal damages (MD) are uncertain, but the policymaker correctly estimated the marginal abatement costs (MAC), there is

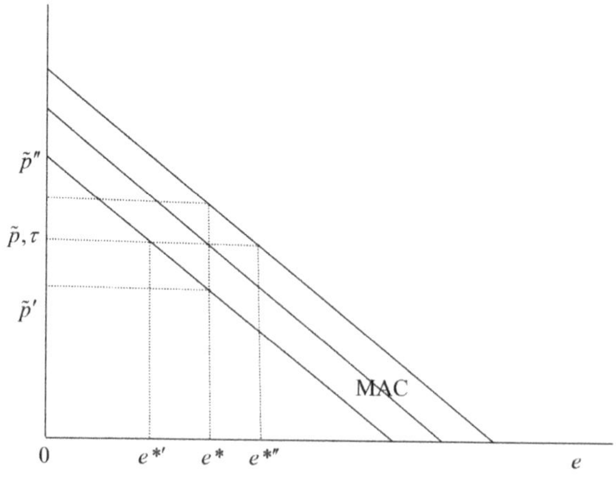

Figure 2.5. Uncertainty about MAC.

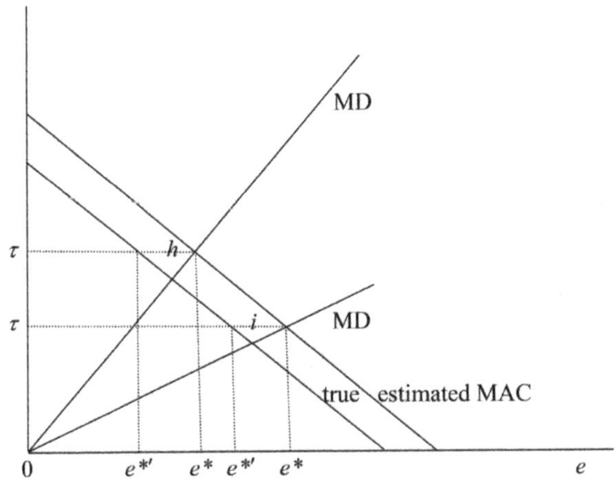

Figure 2.6. Choice of instrument I.

no difference between the two instruments taxes and tradable permits. Both instruments will realize the same level of emissions, which is the expected optimal level of emissions. This level of emissions is not the optimal level if the true marginal damages (MD) are not the estimated marginal damages (MD). This leads, of course, to a loss of welfare, but this loss is the same for both instruments.

However, if the marginal abatement costs (MAC) are uncertain, the choice of instrument can make a difference. Figure 2.6 depicts this situation for two different lines representing marginal damages (MD). The marginal abatement costs (MAC) are overestimated here so that the true line representing these costs shifts in. The intersection of the marginal damages (MD) and the estimated marginal abatement costs (MAC) yields the pollution target e^*, but the pollution target should be the level of emissions at the intersection point with the true marginal abatement costs (MAC). For the steeper line representing the marginal damages (MD), the intersection point is denoted by h and for the less steep line, this intersection point is denoted by i. If the instrument of tradable permits is used, the costs of the mistake in estimating the marginal abatement costs (MAC) is depicted by the triangle to the right of h and i, respectively. The mistake of estimating the pollution target at e^* saves abatement costs but increases damage costs, and the net increase in costs is represented by this triangle. If the instrument of a tax on emissions τ is used, the resulting level of emissions is $e^{*\prime}$ at the intersection point of the tax with the true marginal abatement costs (MAC). This level of emissions is too low because the tax τ is set too high. The mistake of estimating the pollution target at e^*, leading to a tax τ that is too high, saves damage costs but increases abatement costs, and the net increase in costs is represented by the triangle to the left of h and i, respectively. The result follows now by comparing the triangles to the right and to the left of h and i, respectively. In case of the steeper marginal damages (MD), the triangle to the left of h is larger than the triangle to the right of h. This means that the increase in costs of overestimating the marginal abatement costs (MAC) is larger when taxes are used than when tradable permits are used. In case of the less steep marginal damages (MD), the triangle to the left of i is smaller than the triangle to the right of i. This means that the increase in costs of overestimating the marginal abatement costs (MAC) is now smaller when taxes are used than when tradable permits are used. Note that the changes in the costs are the same when the slope of the MD line is the same in absolute terms as the slope of the MAC lines. The conclusion of this analysis is that tradable permits are preferred over taxes if the marginal damages (MD) are steeper than the marginal abatement costs (MAC) and that taxes are preferred over tradable permits in the opposite case. For example, suppose that in Figure 2.6 the line representing the estimated marginal abatement costs (MAC) is given by $1-e$, the true line by $1-e-\varepsilon$, the steeper line representing the marginal damages (MD) by $1.5e$, and the less steep line by $0.5e$. For the steeper MD line, the pollution target is $e^* = 0.4$, the tax becomes $\tau = 0.6$, and the resulting level of emissions $e^{*\prime} = 0.4-\varepsilon$. The intersection point h is $(0.4(1-\varepsilon), 0.6(1-\varepsilon))$. The size of the triangle to the left of h is $0.45\varepsilon^2$, and this is larger than the size of the triangle to the right of h which is $0.2\varepsilon^2$ so that the welfare loss of using taxes as policy instrument instead of tradable permits is larger. For the less steep MD line, the pollution target is $e^* = 0.67$, the tax becomes $\tau = 0.33$, and the resulting level of emissions $e^{*\prime} = 0.67-\varepsilon$. The intersection point i is $(0.67(1-\varepsilon), 0.33(1-\varepsilon))$. The size of the triangle to the left of i is $0.08\varepsilon^2$, and this is smaller than the size of the triangle to the right of i which is $0.33\varepsilon^2$ so that the welfare loss of using tradable permits as policy instrument instead of taxes is larger. It is better to use tradable permits than taxes for a steeper MD line, and the other way around for a less steep MD line.

Figure 2.7 depicts the case where the marginal abatement costs (MAC) are underestimated so that the true line representing these costs shifts out. As in Figure 2.6, e^* is the pollution target, but the pollution target should be the level of emissions at the intersection points h and i for the two

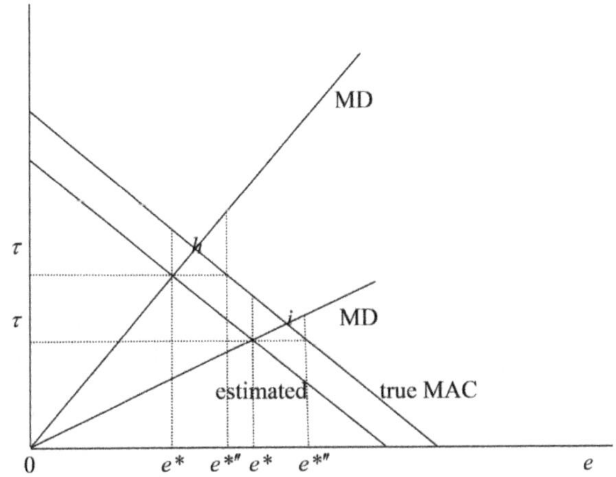

Figure 2.7. Choice of instrument II.

MD lines, respectively. If the instrument of tradable permits is used, the costs of the mistake in estimating the marginal abatement costs (MAC) is now depicted by the triangle to the left of h and i, respectively. The mistake of estimating the pollution target at e^* saves damage costs but increases abatement costs, with a net increase in costs. If the instrument of a tax on emissions τ is used, the resulting level of emissions is now $e^{*\prime\prime}$ at the intersection point of the tax with the true marginal abatement costs (MAC). This level of emissions is too high because the tax τ is set too low. The mistake of estimating the pollution target at e^*, leading to a tax τ that is too low, saves abatement costs but increases damage costs, and the net increase in costs is now represented by the triangle to the right of h and i, respectively. The result follows by comparing the triangles to the left and to the right of h and i, respectively. Since the triangle to the left of h is smaller than the triangle to the right of h, the increase in costs of underestimating the marginal abatement costs (MAC) is larger when taxes are used than when tradable permits are used. Since the triangle to the left of i is larger than the triangle to the right of i, the increase in costs of underestimating the marginal abatement costs (MAC) is smaller when taxes are used than when tradable permits are used. The conclusion of the analysis is the same as in the case that the marginal abatement costs (MAC) are overestimated, which is depicted in Figure 2.6. Tradable permits are preferred over taxes if the marginal damages (MD) are steeper than the marginal abatement costs (MAC), and taxes are preferred over tradable permits in the opposite case. For example, suppose that in Figure 2.7 the line representing the estimated marginal abatement costs (MAC) is given by $1 - e$, the true line by $1 - e + \varepsilon$, the steeper line representing the marginal damages (MD) by $1.5e$, and the less steep line by $0.5e$. For the steeper MD line, the pollution target is $e^* = 0.4$, the tax becomes $\tau = 0.6$, and the resulting level of emissions $e^{*\prime\prime} = 0.4 + \varepsilon$. The intersection point h is $(0.4(1 + \varepsilon), 0.6(1 + \varepsilon))$. The size of the triangle to the left of h is $0.2\varepsilon^2$, and this is smaller than the size of the triangle to the right of h which is $0.45\varepsilon^2$ so that the welfare loss of using taxes as policy instrument instead of tradable permits is larger. For the less steep MD line, the pollution target is $e^* = 0.67$, the tax becomes $\tau = 0.33$, and the resulting level of emissions $e^{*\prime\prime} = 0.67 + \varepsilon$. The intersection point i is $(0.67(1 + \varepsilon), 0.33(1 + \varepsilon))$. The size of the triangle to the left of i is $0.33\varepsilon^2$, and this is larger than the size of the triangle to the right of i which is $0.08\varepsilon^2$ so that the welfare loss of using tradable permits as policy instrument instead of taxes is larger. It is better to use tradable permits than taxes for a steeper MD line, and the other way around for a less steep MD line. If the marginal abatement costs (MAC) are uncertain but the policymaker has an idea of how fast the marginal costs are increasing as compared to the marginal damages (MD), there is a clear choice for taxes or tradable permits.

2.3.3 *Summary*

The previous sections consider the use of economic instruments for the specific type of uncertainty that the true lines representing the marginal damages (MD) and the marginal abatement costs (MAC) may shift in or shift out from the estimated lines. If only the MD line is uncertain, the choice of instrument does not matter in the sense that it does not affect the welfare loss resulting from the difference between the true line and the estimated line because both taxes and tradable permits lead to the same level of emissions, with the same welfare loss. However, if the MAC line is uncertain, taxes and tradable permits lead to different levels of emissions, with different welfare losses. The reason is that tradable permits fix the level of emissions at the expected optimal level, whereas taxes lead to a different level of emissions by equating the true marginal abatement costs (MAC) to the tax. Regardless of whether the abatement costs are overestimated or underestimated, there is a clear result in choosing taxes (price instrument) or tradable permits (quantity instrument). If the MD line is steeper than the MAC lines, it is better to use tradable permits and if the MD line is less steep than the MAC lines, it is better to use taxes.

2.4 Conclusion

Lecture 1 provides the conceptual framework for a pollution target or an emission target by considering the trade-off between the net benefits of production and the damages of pollution. This lecture considers the policy for realizing a pollution target by using the economic instruments taxes or tradable permits. A tax on emissions is a price instrument that lowers the emissions. A (Pigouvian) tax, that is equal to the marginal damages or the marginal external costs in the optimal level of emissions, realizes this level of emissions. In practice, a tax on emissions is equal to the marginal abatement costs of each firm. By varying such a tax, the pollution target can be achieved, without the need for information on the marginal abatement costs of the firms. This process yields information about the overall marginal abatement costs, which is the mirror of the marginal net benefits in terms of emissions. This information feeds back into determining the pollution target, and it may require adjustments to equate marginal damages and overall marginal abatement costs. Tradable permits are a quantity instrument because this fixes the pollution target. By splitting the pollution target into a set of emission permits and by creating a market for these emission permits, the permits get a price, and this price is also equal to the marginal abatement costs of each firm. Both instruments are cost-effective and realize the pollution target.

The choice between the instruments taxes and tradable permits also depends on arguments outside the framework in Lectures 1 and 2. However, when there is uncertainty about the position of the line representing the marginal abatement costs, there is a good reason within this framework to choose either taxes or tradable permits. More precisely, when the true line lies below or above the estimated line, because the marginal abatement costs are overestimated or underestimated, the choice of instrument depends on the position of these lines with respect to the line representing the marginal damages. When the marginal damages are steeper or increase faster than the marginal abatement costs, it is better to use tradable permits than taxes because the welfare loss due to the mistake in estimating the marginal abatement costs is lower. When the marginal damages are less steep or increase slower than the marginal abatement costs, however, it is better to use taxes than tradable permits because now the welfare loss of using taxes is lower. Tradable permits fix the expected pollution target that differs from the pollution target corresponding to the true marginal abatement costs, and this yields a welfare loss. Taxes lead to different levels of emissions because the tax will be equal to the true marginal abatement costs, and this also yields a welfare loss. These welfare losses differ which explains the choice for either taxes or tradable permits.

References

Dales, J.H. 1968. *Pollution, Property and Prices.* Toronto: University of Toronto Press.

Pigou, A.C. 1932. *The Economics of Welfare*, 4th edition. London: Macmillan and Co.

Weitzman, M.L. 1974. Prices vs. quantities. *The Review of Economic Studies* 41, 4: 477–491.

Lecture 3

Trade and the Environment

3.1 Introduction

Economists generally advocate free trade between countries to improve their welfare. This is based on the concept of comparative advantage which means that countries can produce certain goods or services at lower opportunity costs than other countries (Ricardo, 1817). Countries can achieve gains of trade by exporting the goods and services in which they have a comparative advantage and by importing other goods and services. This concept resulted in the basic theorem for international trade, formulated by Heckscher and Ohlin in 1933, which says that trade is determined by differences in factor endowments. A country will export those goods and services that are relatively intensive in the factors of production which are abundant in that country and import those goods and services that are relatively intensive in its scarce factors of production. For example, if a country has an abundant supply of capital, it will focus on goods and services for which the production is capital-intensive. Despite the comparative advantages, countries are often reluctant to fully open up for trade because they want to protect their industries and employment opportunities, or they need time for a transition, or they are sensitive to lobbying. However, there are several stronger or weaker free-trade agreements in place now. The European Union, the US–Mexico–Canada (USMCA) Agreement in North America, and the World Trade Organization (WTO) at the global level are all good examples.

The relationship between trade and the environment has several aspects. First, trade leads to more growth, and growth may lead to more pollution and faster depletion of resources. This is the topic of Lecture 10. Second, free trade may imply that the production of goods and services which is heavily polluting moves to countries with lax environmental policies, so that pollution increases. This aspect is aggravated when countries start competing for economic activities by relaxing their environmental policies in a "race to the bottom". Third, trade increases the transportation of goods and services which leads to more pollution. These arguments imply that the environment may suffer from free trade. Furthermore, conflicts may arise between environmental policy and free trade. In 1991, Mexico brought a case to the General Agreement on Tariffs and Trade (GATT), the predecessor of the WTO. The USA had banned the import of tuna from Mexico because Mexico was using a fishing method that the USA did not allow. Dolphins could be trapped and killed in the nets that were used. The USA lost the case because the GATT ruled that under a free-trade agreement, the USA could not implement environmental regulations outside its territory. This means that the USA had the difficult choice to either abolish the environmental regulation or accept that their fishing industry had a disadvantage *vis-à-vis* their competitors.

A political debate arose from a quote in a memo at the World Bank in 1991 that was signed by Chief Economist Lawrence Summers: "Just between you and me, shouldn't the World Bank be encouraging more migration of the dirty industries to the LDCs (Less Developed Countries)?" This is economic logic because the LDCs have a comparative advantage in lower health costs, a lower pollution level, and a lower demand for a clean environment, but it feels, of course, politically very uncomfortable. A final argument in the discussion on trade and the environment is that strict environmental policy may be beneficial in the long run because it increases the competitiveness of the industry in that country (Porter, 1991). The firms may lose some market share in the short run because environmental policy forces them to invest and innovate, but these investments may pay out in the long run and increase their market share. There is empirical evidence for this, but the evidence is mixed (Porter and van der Linde, 1995).

This lecture focuses on two aspects of the relationship between trade and the environment. First, in a simple graphical analysis, this lecture considers the question of whether it is beneficial for a small economy to open up for trade by comparing their gains of trade with their environmental costs. Trade continues to be beneficial on the condition that environmental policy is in place, but otherwise, a trade-off may occur. Second, this lecture presents the main empirical results on the question of whether opening up for trade is good or bad for the environment. This empirical research partly tests the question of whether growth is necessarily bad for the environment (which is discussed in more detail in Lecture 10), and it partly tests the hypothesis that economic activities relocate to countries which have a lax environmental policy.

This lecture has two goals. The first is to show that environmental policy needs to be in place to guarantee positive net gains of trade. The second is to show by reporting the main results of empirical analyses that trade is not necessarily bad for the environment.

Section 3.2 presents the graphical analysis of the trade-off between the gains of trade and the external environmental costs. Section 3.3 discusses the empirical evidence on the hypothesis that trade may be bad for the environment. Section 3.4 concludes.

3.2 Trade, Environment, and Welfare

If a small economy opens up for trade, the prices are determined on the world market and therefore become exogenous to this economy. If the world market price of a good is higher than the price in autarky, the economy becomes an exporter of the good, and if this price is lower, the economy becomes an importer of the good. In both cases, there are gains of trade. However, if the production of the good leads to pollution and thus creates a negative environmental externality in the country, the environmental costs increase if the country becomes an exporter of this good and decrease if the country becomes an importer. It follows that the importing country has both gains of trade and lower environmental costs, but the exporting country faces a trade-off. Lecture 2 shows that a country can internalize an environmental externality by levying a Pigouvian tax. The following analysis shows that if the Pigouvian tax is in place, both the importing and exporting countries gain from opening up for trade (Anderson, 1992, Runge, 1995).

3.2.1 *Gains of trade*

Figure 3.1 gives a graphical representation of the gains of trade. Suppose that a country is in autarky and that this country produces and consumes one good. Figure 3.1 depicts the supply S and the demand D for this good, the equilibrium price p_a, and the quantity y_a that is produced and consumed in equilibrium. A measure for welfare is the sum of the producer surplus

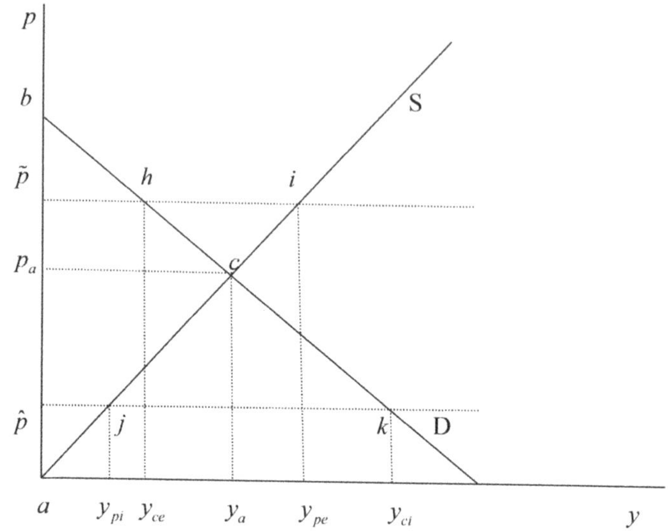

Figure 3.1. Gains of trade.

acp_a and the consumer surplus bcp_a which is equal to acb. If this country is a small economy and opens up for trade, supply and demand are determined by the price on the world market. If this price $\tilde{p}$ is larger than the price p_a in autarky, production increases to y_{pe} and consumption decreases to y_{ce}, so that the country becomes an exporter of the good. The export is equal to $y_{pe} - y_{ce}$. In this case, the producer surplus becomes $ai\tilde{p}$, the consumer surplus $bh\tilde{p}$, and welfare $aihb$. Welfare increases by $aihb - acb = chi$, which are the gains of trade. If the world market price $\hat{p}$ is smaller than the price p_a in autarky, production decreases to y_{pi} and consumption increases to y_{ci}, so that the country becomes an importer of the good. The import is equal to $y_{ci} - y_{pi}$. In this case, the producer surplus becomes $aj\hat{p}$, the consumer surplus $bk\hat{p}$, and welfare $ajkb$. Welfare increases by $ajkb - acb = cjk$, which are the gains of trade. Whether the country becomes an exporter or an importer, the country has positive gains of trade in both cases.

For example, if the supply is $S(y) = y$ and the demand $D(y) = 1 - y$, the price and quantity in autarky are $p_a = 0.5$ and $y_a = 0.5$, with the producer surplus $acp_a = 0.125$, consumer surplus $bcp_a = 0.125$, and total welfare $acb = 0.25$. If the world market price is $\tilde{p} = 0.75$, the production increases to $y_{pe} = 0.75$ and the consumption decreases to $y_{ce} = 0.25$, so that the country becomes an exporter of the good. The export is $y_{pe} - y_{ce} = 0.5$.

Table 3.1. Gains of trade.

	Price	Prod.	Cons.	Export/ import	Before trade	After trade	Gains of trade
Exporter	0.75	0.75	0.25	0.5	0.25	0.31	0.06
Importer	0.2	0.2	0.8	0.6	0.25	0.34	0.09

Producer surplus is $ai\tilde{p} = 0.28$, consumer surplus $bh\tilde{p} = 0.03$, and total welfare $aihb = 0.31$. Welfare increases by $chi = 0.06$, which are the gains of trade. If the world market price is $\hat{p} = 0.2$, the production decreases to $y_{pi} = 0.2$ and the consumption increases to $y_{ci} = 0.8$, so that the country becomes an importer of the good. The import is $y_{ci} - y_{pi} = 0.6$. Producer surplus is $aj\hat{p} = 0.02$, consumer surplus $bk\hat{p} = 0.32$, and total welfare $ajkb = 0.34$. Welfare increases by $cjk = 0.09$, which are the gains of trade; see Table 3.1.

3.2.2 *Pigouvian tax*

Figure 3.2 gives a graphical representation of the Pigouvian tax. It is a copy of Figure 2.2 in Lecture 2 but in terms of quantity y, depicting the marginal benefits MB and marginal costs MC of production, and the price p_b and quantity y_b before tax. Suppose that producing the good in this country leads to external environmental costs that should be added to the production costs. It follows that the marginal costs (MC) rotate to the marginal social costs (MSC). This drives a wedge between MC and MSC which is equal to the marginal external costs (MEC). If this country ignores the external environmental costs, the price and production are equal to p_b and y_b. If this country internalizes the external environmental costs, it decreases the production to y_a and raises the price to p_a by levying a tax τ. The Pigouvian tax is equal to the marginal external costs in the optimal level of production y_a, represented in Figure 3.2 by the solid part of the line cy_a. A measure for welfare is the producer surplus plus the consumer surplus minus the environmental costs. Before tax, welfare is equal to $aeb - aed = acb - cde$. After tax, the positive welfare components are the producer surplus agf, the consumer surplus bcp_a, and the tax revenues $fgcp_a$ that are returned to the economy. In total, this is equal to $agcb$. The environmental

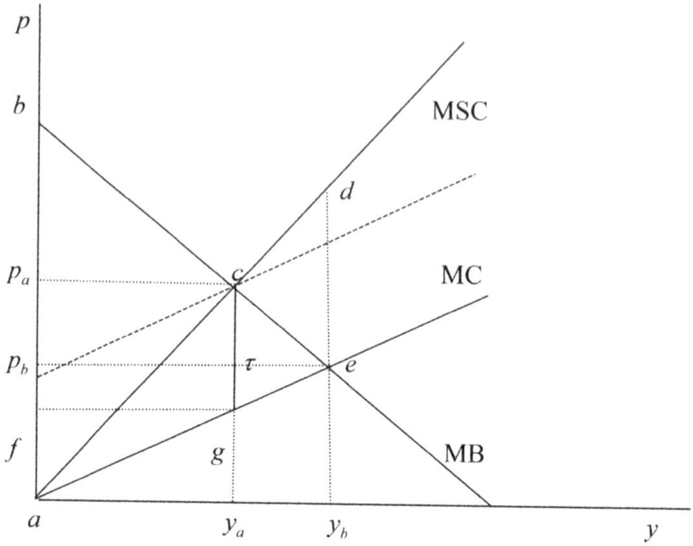

Figure 3.2. Pigouvian tax.

costs are agc. After tax, welfare is thus equal to $agcb - agc = acb$. It follows that by levying the Pigouvian tax τ, welfare increases by cde, which are the gains of internalizing the external environmental costs.

For example, if the marginal benefits (MB) are given by $1 - y$, MC by $0.5y$, MEC by $0.5y$, and MSC by y, then price and quantity before tax are $p_b = 0.33$ and $y_b = 0.67$. If this country internalizes the external environmental costs, it decreases the production to $y_a = 0.5$ and raises the price to $p_a = 0.5$ by levying the Pigouvian tax $\tau = 0.25$ that is equal to the marginal external costs in the optimal level of production $y_a = 0.5$. A measure for welfare is the producer surplus plus the consumer surplus minus the environmental costs. Before tax, welfare is equal to $aeb - aed = acb - cde = 0.22$. After tax, the positive welfare components are the producer surplus $agf = 0.06$, the consumer surplus $bcp_a = 0.125$, and the tax revenues $fgcp_a = 0.125$ that are returned to the economy. In total, this is equal to $agcb = 0.31$. The environmental costs are $agc = 0.06$. After tax, welfare is thus equal to $agcb - agc = acb = 0.25$. It follows that by levying the Pigouvian tax τ, welfare increases by $cde = 0.03$, which are the gains of internalizing the external environmental costs; see Table 3.2.

Table 3.2. Pigouvian tax.

	Price	Quantity	Producer surplus	Consumer surplus	Tax revenues	External costs	Welfare
No tax	0.33	0.67	0.11	0.22	0	0.11	0.22
Tax = 0.25	0.5	0.5	0.06	0.125	0.125	0.06	0.25

3.2.3 *Exporting country*

Figure 3.3 gives a graphical representation of the welfare consequences when the country opens up for trade with or without a Pigouvian tax in place. Figure 3.3 extends Figure 3.2 with the world market price $\tilde{p}$ that is larger than the price in autarky, so that the country becomes an exporter of the good. Note that the marginal benefit line MB is the demand line in Figure 3.1 and the marginal cost lines MC and MSC are the supply lines. Without a Pigouvian tax τ, so that MC is the supply line, production becomes y_{pe}, consumption y_{ce}, and export $y_{pe} - y_{ce}$. The gains of trade are $alhb - aeb = ehl$. However, because production increases from y_b to y_{pe}, the external environmental costs increase. In Figure 3.3, this increase in costs is given by the area between the marginal cost lines MC and MSC for the increase in production. Figure 3.3 does not show the intersection point of the line MSC with the line for the higher production level, but it will be clear that if the intersection point is m, the additional environmental costs are $delm$. It follows that the net gains of opening up for trade are $ehl - delm$. A direct way of calculating these net gains is as follows. Before trade, welfare is equal to $aeb - aed$. After trade, welfare is equal to $alhb - alm$. The net gains of trade become $alhb - alm - aeb + aed = ehl - delm$. These net gains can be positive or negative but are clearly negative for the case depicted in Figure 3.3. This will become clear in the example below. In the example, the additional environmental costs are higher than the gains of trade.

With a Pigouvian tax τ, production becomes $\tilde{y}_{pe}$, consumption y_{ce}, and export $\tilde{y}_{pe} - y_{ce}$. MSC is effectively the supply line. The Pigouvian tax τ is equal to the marginal external costs in the optimal level of production $\tilde{y}_{pe}$, and it is represented in Figure 3.3 by the solid part of the line $i\tilde{y}_{pe}$. The welfare analysis is a combination of the welfare analyses in Figures 3.1 and 3.2. The producer surplus for this level of production plus the tax revenues plus the consumer surplus minus the environmental costs is equal to

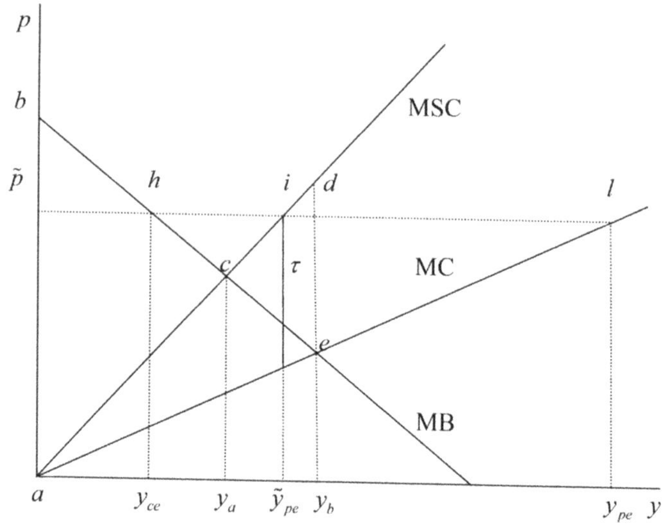

Figure 3.3. Exporting country.

$acb+chi$. This implies that if the country internalizes the external environmental costs with a Pigouvian tax, it has positive gains of trade chi because acb is the level of welfare in autarky with a Pigouvian tax. Note that after opening up for trade, but before levying a Pigouvian tax, welfare is equal to $alhb-alm$. Then the gains of internalizing the external environmental costs after opening up for trade are $acb + chi - alhb + alm = ilm$. Note that the Pigouvian tax τ changes when the country opens up for trade because the optimal level of production changes and thus its marginal external costs. The most important conclusion is that if the country has an environmental policy in place, in the form of a Pigouvian tax, the net gains of trade are always positive.

For example, suppose that MB are given by $1 - y$, MC by $0.5y$, MEC by $0.5y$, MSC by y, and that the world market price is $\tilde{p} = 0.6$, which is larger than the price in autarky so that the country becomes an exporter of the good. First, without a Pigouvian tax τ, so that MC is the supply line, production becomes $y_{pe} = 1.2$, consumption $y_{ce} = 0.4$, and export $y_{pe} - y_{ce} = 0.8$. The gains of trade are $alhb - aeb = ehl = 0.11$. However, because production increases from $y_b = 0.67$ to y_{pe}, the external environmental costs increase by $delm = 0.25$. It follows that the net gains of opening up for trade are $ehl - delm = -0.14$. Or, before trade, welfare is

Table 3.3. Exporting country.

	Price	Prod.	Cons.	Export	Before trade	After trade	Gains of trade
No tax	0.6	1.2	0.4	0.8	0.22	0.08	−0.14
Tax = 0.3	0.6	0.6	0.4	0.2	0.25	0.26	0.01

equal to $aeb - aed = 0.22$. After trade, welfare is equal to $alhb - alm = 0.08$. The net gains of trade become −0.14. Second, with a Pigouvian tax, production becomes $\tilde{y}_{pe} = 0.6$, consumption y_{ce}, and export $\tilde{y}_{pe} - y_{ce} = 0.2$. MSC is effectively the supply line. The Pigouvian tax is $\tau = 0.3$ or the marginal external costs in $\tilde{y}_{pe}$. Total welfare, or the producer surplus plus the tax revenues plus the consumer surplus minus the environmental costs, is equal to $acb + chi = 0.26$. This implies that if the country internalizes the external environmental costs with a Pigouvian tax, it has positive gains of trade $chi = 0.01$ because $acb = 0.25$ is the level of welfare in autarky with a Pigouvian tax. After opening up for trade, but before levying a Pigouvian tax, welfare is equal to $alhb - alm = 0.08$. The gains of internalizing the external environmental costs after opening up for trade are $ilm = 0.18$; see Table 3.3.

3.2.4 *Importing country*

Figure 3.4 extends Figure 3.2 with the world market price $\hat{p}$ that is smaller than the price in autarky, so that the country becomes an importer of the good. Without a Pigouvian tax τ, so that MC is the supply line, production becomes y_{pi}, consumption y_{ci}, and import $y_{ci} - y_{pi}$. The gains of trade are $ankb - aeb = enk$. Since production decreases from y_b to y_{pi}, the external environmental costs also decrease by $oned$. It follows that the total gains of opening up for trade are $enk + oned$. A direct way of calculating these total gains is as follows. Before trade, welfare is equal to $aeb - aed$. After trade, welfare is equal to $ankb - ano$. The total gains of trade become $ankb - ano - aeb + aed = enk + oned$. These total gains of trade are always positive.

With a Pigouvian tax τ, production becomes $\hat{y}_{pi}$, consumption y_{ci}, and import $y_{ci} - \hat{y}_{pi}$. MSC is effectively the supply line. The Pigouvian tax τ is equal to the marginal external cost for the optimal level of production

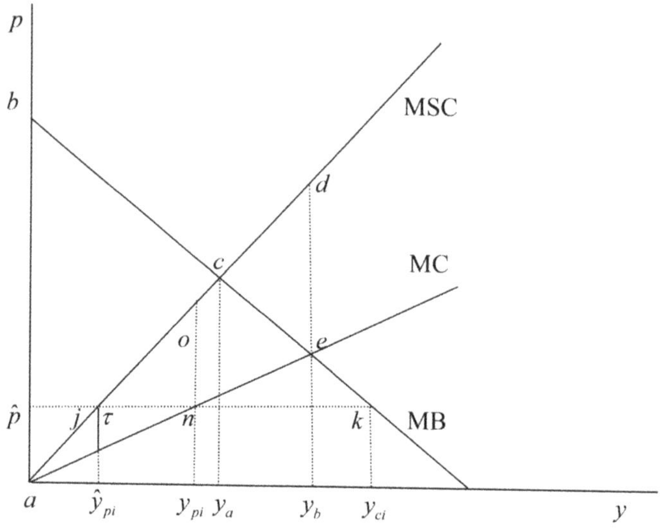

Figure 3.4. Importing country.

$\hat{y}_{pi}$, and it is represented in Figure 3.4 by the solid part of the line $j\hat{y}_{pi}$. The welfare analysis is a combination of the welfare analyses in Figures 3.1 and 3.2. The producer surplus for this level of production plus the tax revenues plus the consumer surplus minus the environmental costs is equal to $acb+cjk$. This implies that if the country internalizes the external environmental costs with a Pigouvian tax, it has positive gains of trade cjk because acb is the level of welfare in autarky with a Pigouvian tax. Note that after opening up for trade, but before levying a Pigouvian tax, welfare is equal to $ankb - ano$. Then the gains of internalizing the external environmental costs after opening up for trade are $acb+cjk-ankb+ano = jno$. Note that the Pigouvian tax τ changes when the country opens up for trade because the optimal level of production changes and thus its marginal external cost. The most important conclusion is that the importing country gains from lower environmental costs, as an importer, and from having an environmental policy in place in the form of a Pigouvian tax.

For example, the world market price is $\hat{p} = 0.2$, which is smaller than the price in autarky so that the country becomes an importer of the good. First, without a Pigouvian tax τ, so that MC is the supply line, production becomes $y_{pi} = 0.4$, consumption $y_{ci} = 0.8$, and import $y_{ci} - y_{pi} = 0.4$. The gains of trade are $ankb-aeb = enk = 0.03$. Since production decreases from

Table 3.4. Importing country.

	Price	Prod.	Cons.	Import	Before trade	After trade	Gains of trade
No tax	0.2	0.4	0.8	0.4	0.22	0.32	0.1
Tax = 0.1	0.2	0.2	0.8	0.6	0.25	0.34	0.09

$y_b = 0.67$ to y_{pi}, the external environmental costs decrease by $oned = 0.07$. It follows that the total gains of opening up for trade are $enk + oned = 0.1$. Or, before trade, welfare is equal to $aeb - aed = 0.22$. After trade, welfare is equal to $ankb - ano = 0.32$. The total gains of trade become 0.1. Second, with a Pigouvian tax, production becomes $\hat{y}_{pi} = 0.2$, consumption y_{ci}, and import $y_{ci} - \hat{y}_{pi} = 0.6$. MSC is effectively the supply line. The Pigouvian tax is $\tau = 0.1$ or the marginal external costs in $\hat{y}_{pi}$. Total welfare, or the producer surplus plus the tax revenues plus the consumer surplus minus the environmental costs, is equal to $acb + cjk = 0.34$. This implies that if the country internalizes the external environmental costs with a Pigouvian tax, it has gains of trade $cjk = 0.09$ because $acb = 0.25$ is the level of welfare in autarky with a Pigouvian tax. After opening up for trade, but before levying a Pigouvian tax, welfare is equal to $ankb - ano = 0.32$. The gains of internalizing the external environmental costs after opening up for trade are $jno = 0.02$; see Table 3.4.

3.2.5 *World market*

In general, trade on the world market evolves if the prices in autarky in some countries are higher than in other countries. This leads to exporting and importing countries and to a price on the world market that is somewhere in between the prices in autarky. If the pollution externalities of production are only local and do not cross borders, the welfare analyses in each of the exporting and importing countries are presented in the previous sections.

In special cases, most of the production occurs in the exporting countries and most of the consumption in the importing countries. Examples are the oil-producing countries and the wood-producing countries where the consumption mainly takes place in the developed countries which do not have much oil or forest. The environmental externality is climate change because burning oil leads to CO_2 emissions, and cutting trees diminishes

CO_2 storage. Suppose that the producing countries do not care about climate change, but the consuming countries care, so that they would like to internalize the external environmental costs and have a Pigouvian tax on production. Figure 3.2 gives an idea of what is at stake. This gives, of course, a very simplistic picture of the situation, abstracting from competitive issues on the world market and other tax options like consumption taxes or border tax adjustments, but it is interesting to consider this. Section 3.2.2 shows that the producing and consuming countries together gain cde, with a Pigouvian tax τ on production. The producing countries lose the producer surplus $fgep_b$ but gain the tax revenues $fgcp_a$, whereas the consuming countries lose the consumer surplus p_acep_b but gain lower environmental costs $cged$. It can happen that both the net gains $fgcp_a - fgep_b$ and $cged - p_acep_b$ are positive. By levying a tax on production, the producing countries lose producer surplus but have tax revenues that can be used for public goods, for example. The consuming countries face a higher price and thus lose consumer surplus, but they have lower environmental costs.

Figure 3.2 also depicts in some way a situation on the world market in which three blocks of countries are involved: the case of ivory trade. African countries are the producers, East-Asian countries are the consumers, and countries in Western Europe and North America are concerned about killing the elephants. Western Europe and North America succeeded in realizing a ban on ivory trade, so that the African and East-Asian countries lost their business. Section 3.2.2 shows that the three blocks of countries cooperating can gain, with a Pigouvian tax on production. It is possible that the three groups bargain for implementing a tax on ivory trade and have a producer surplus, a consumer surplus, tax revenues, and a lower threat to the existence of the elephants. The two examples here are special cases that fit the analysis in Section 3.2.2. Lectures 4 and 5 analyze international environmental policy and international environmental agreements in general.

3.2.6 *Summary*

The previous sections extend the standard graphical welfare analysis of trade with external local environmental costs of production. If a small economy opens up for trade and becomes an exporter because the world market price is higher than the price in autarky, it collects the standard gains of trade, but it also has higher environmental costs. The net gains of trade can go both ways. However, if the country has environmental policy in place, in the form of a Pigouvian tax, the net gains of trade are always positive. If a small economy opens up for trade and becomes an importer because the world market price is lower than the price in autarky, it collects the standard gains of trade and lower environmental costs. Environmental policy, in the form of a Pigouvian tax, further improves welfare. If a large economy opens up for trade, it affects the world market price, but the welfare analyses in exporting and importing countries do not change. If the countries are typical producing or consuming countries and value the environmental costs differently, bargaining and levying a Pigouvian tax can improve the welfare of each country.

3.3 Trade and Environmental Policy

Section 3.2 presents a simple but insightful exercise on the relation between trade and the environment, but that relation is, of course, more complicated. The discussion mainly focuses on two aspects. First, the standard argument is that trade leads to more growth, and growth leads to more pollution. Lecture 10 analyzes the last issue in detail, but for now, it is sufficient to note that economic growth and a decrease in pollution can go together because of changes in the technology and the composition of the economy (Grossman and Krueger, 1995). It follows that it is important to distinguish scale, technique, and composition effects. Second, there exists a concern that strict environmental policy will lower the competitiveness of the national industry on the world market. Some argue that the opposite holds because a strict environmental policy will induce the national industry to innovate, which will be beneficial in the long run (Porter, 1991), but the general idea remains that countries with a lax environmental policy attract more economic activities. Moreover, countries consider relaxing their environmental policy to benefit from the relocation of industries. This is called the *pollution haven hypothesis*. On the other hand, the Heckscher–Ohlin theorem for international trade predicts that trade is determined by differences in factor endowments. Polluting industries are usually capital-intensive and will therefore locate in countries which are relatively abundant in this factor of production. This is called the *factor endowment hypothesis*. Capital is both physical and human capital. The countries that are abundant in capital usually are developed countries which also have a relatively strict environmental policy. The question is what the data reveal. Does the scale effect dominate the technique and composition effects, or is it the other way around? Is there evidence for the pollution haven hypothesis or the factor endowment hypothesis? This section reports some empirical results on these issues.

3.3.1 *Empirical results*

Empirical analyses reject the pollution haven hypothesis in favor of the factor endowment hypothesis (Jaffe *et al.*, 1995). There is little evidence that environmental regulations have a large adverse effect on competitiveness. Estimates of the effect of environmental regulation on export, trade flows and plant-location decisions are either small or statistically insignificant. An important reason is that the cost of complying with the environmental regulation is just a small fraction of the total costs of production (about 2%). Saving on these costs does not outweigh the benefits of staying in the country where the industry is close to physical capital, human capital, technology, infrastructure, and markets.

Empirical analysis shows that growth due to trade has a "positive" scale effect on pollution in the sense that pollution increases, but a "negative" technique effect and an almost zero effect on the composition of the economy (Antweiler *et al.*, 2001). This analysis first develops a theoretical model, highlighting scale, technique, and composition effects, and then estimates these effects by using data on sulfur dioxide supplied by the World Health Organization. The technique elasticity dominates the scale elasticity. This empirical analysis thus concludes that free trade is good for the environment. Other empirical studies confirm this conclusion.

The list of empirical studies on trade and the environment is long, and this lecture does not intend to provide a full account of the results. However, the two studies that are briefly described here provide an answer to the main issues raised in the discussion on trade and the environment, namely trade leading to growth and the pollution haven hypothesis.

3.3.2 *Summary*

The theory and empirics on trade and the environment challenge the common wisdom that trade is bad for the environment. Environmental regulation implies a cost for polluting industries, but these industries are usually also capital-intensive. Since countries with strict environmental regulation are usually also abundant in capital as factor of production, the net effect on the location of polluting industries is ambiguous. It follows that environmental regulation can work because it does not necessarily imply that industries relocate to countries with lax environmental regulation. Empirical analyses on this issue reject the pollution haven hypothesis. An important reason is that the cost of complying with environmental regulation is relatively small. Another issue is that trade leads to growth and the scale effect of growth increases pollution. However, pollution may also decrease because of technological development and a change in the composition of the economy. The net effect is ambiguous. Empirical analyses show that the technique effect dominates the scale effect, with a zero effect on composition, so that trade is not bad for the environment. This section only reports some of the main empirical results. For interested people, a good textbook on trade and the environment is the one by Copeland and Taylor (2005).

3.4 Conclusion

Lecture 2 shows that environmental policy, in the form of a Pigouvian tax on production, increases welfare. Trade increases welfare as well. In the presence of external local environmental costs, however, opening up for trade may decrease welfare if the country becomes an exporter of the good and the gains of trade do not outweigh the larger environmental costs. This lecture shows that the net gains of trade are positive if the country has an environmental policy in place in the form of a Pigouvian tax. If the country becomes an importer of the good, it has both gains of trade and smaller environmental costs, but an importing country also benefits from levying a Pigouvian tax. The take-home message from the simple graphical analysis in this lecture is that levying this tax not only increases welfare but also guarantees positive net gains of trade.

The debate on trade and the environment usually focuses on two issues. First, trade leads to growth, and growth may lead to more pollution. This becomes an empirical question because technological development and changes in the composition of the economy counteract the scale effect of growth. The empirical analysis concludes that trade is good for the environment because the technique effect turns out to be stronger than the scale effect, and the composition of the economy hardly changes. Second, countries either have a strict or a lax environmental policy. The reason is that developing countries first want to develop and attract economic activities before paying more attention to the environment. Environmental policy can become a strategic instrument. The countries can speed up the process by further relaxing their environmental policy. Countries with a strict environmental policy may worry about the competitiveness of the national industry. Under the free-trade agreement WTO, they cannot use trade restrictions on imports of goods that are produced under a lax environmental policy (tuna and dolphins case). On the other hand, the countries with a strict environmental policy are usually also abundant in capital, and the polluting industries are usually capital-intensive. Trade theory implies that these industries locate in these countries. It follows that either the pollution haven hypothesis or the factor endowment hypothesis prevails. If the pollution haven hypothesis prevails, industries relocate and countries are tempted to relax their environmental policy, so that trade is bad for the environment. However, empirical analysis concludes that the pollution haven hypothesis must be rejected.

References

Anderson, K. 1992. The standard welfare economics of policies affecting trade and the environment. In *The Greening of World Trade Issues*, (eds.) Anderson, K. and Blackhurst, R. New York: Harvester Wheatsheaf, pp. 25–48.

Antweiler, W., Copeland, B.R., and Taylor, M.S. 2001. Is free trade good for the environment? *The American Economic Review* 91, 4: 877–908.

Copeland, B.R. and Taylor, M.S. 2005. *Trade and the Environment: Theory and Evidence*. Princeton: Princeton University Press.

Grossman, G.M. and Krueger, A.B. 1995. Economic growth and the environment. *The Quarterly Journal of Economics* 110, 2: 353–377.

Jaffe, A.B., Peterson, S.R., Portney, P.R., and Stavins, R.N. 1995. Environmental regulation and the competitiveness of U.S. manufacturing: what does the evidence tell us? *Journal of Economic Literature* 33, 1: 132–163.

Porter, M.E. 1991. America's green strategy. *Scientific American* 264, 4: 168.

Porter, M.E. and van der Linde, C. 1995. Toward a new conception of the environment-competitiveness relationship. *The Journal of Economic Perspectives* 9, 4: 97–118.

Ricardo, D. 1817. *On the Principles on Political Economy and Taxation*. London: John Murray.

Runge, C.F. 1995. Trade, pollution, and environmental protection. In *The Handbook of Environmental Economics*, (ed.) Bromley, D.W. Oxford: Blackwell, pp. 353–375.

Lecture 4

International Environmental Policy

4.1 Introduction

Lectures 1 and 2 consider the targets and instruments for environmental policy within a country. However, many environmental problems are not restricted to national borders, and can therefore not be handled by national policies alone. For example, pollutants emitted in country A may be partly transported by winds across the border to country B. This implies that focusing only on policy in country A will only control the part of the pollution that stays in country A. Moreover, country B cannot control the part of the pollution that originates in country A but ends up in country B. Country A may not worry about this, but country B will complain to country A. To solve this problem, international environmental policy is needed. The problem may also be reciprocal. For example, global pollution problems such as climate change have the property that each country by emitting greenhouse gases that cause the climate problem damages all the other countries in some way. National policies that only focus on the benefits and costs in the country itself do not take into account the damages to other countries.

International cooperation is needed for internalizing the transboundary externalities. In the absence of a mandate at the global level, a world government to implement environmental policy does not exist, and international cooperation is *voluntary*. This lecture discusses the possibilities and difficulties of international environmental policy with the purpose of handling global and cross-border pollution problems. As a conceptual framework, *game theory* is used to capture cooperative and non-cooperative behavior. It is one of the wicked problems of our time because it has proven to be difficult to establish successful international cooperation on important global environmental problems, such as climate change. The concern in these types of problems is that the lack of joint management of the common resource or the common environment may lead to a huge loss. The problem is often referred to as the *tragedy of the commons.* Hardin (1968) formulated this concept a long time ago, in a very intuitive but not in a precise way. This lecture starts with describing and discussing this concept and then moves to a precise formulation and analysis of these problems. The acid rain game is a classical example of a cross-border pollution problem and is presented at the end. Lecture 5 discusses the possibilities of partial international cooperation.

This lecture has two goals. The first is to explain why the environmental policy that is needed at the international level is essentially different from the environmental policy at the national level. The second is to develop a conceptual framework for analyzing this international environmental policy which is based on game theory.

Section 4.2 discusses the concept of the tragedy of the commons. Section 4.3 introduces game theory and shows how this conceptual framework can capture and analyze the problems at hand. Section 4.4 concludes.

4.2 Tragedy of the Commons

In 1968, ecologist Hardin wrote an influential paper in which he sketched a grim picture of the future of our commons. Commons are resources to which anybody has access, but nobody has property rights. He uses an old famous example of a pasture where cattle can graze. The herdsmen who use the pasture have a collective interest in keeping this resource available for the future. This implies that they must restrict the number of cattle grazing on the pasture to prevent it from being destroyed by over-grazing. However, an individual herdsman may have an incentive to let an extra animal graze because this will not destroy the pasture, but it gives extra benefits to the individual herdsman. The problem is that when every herdsman behaves in this way and adds an extra animal, over-grazing may occur, the pasture may be destroyed, and the herdsmen lose all future benefits. This mechanism is called the tragedy of the commons. A global environmental problem such as climate change has similar aspects. A country may have an incentive to emit a bit more greenhouse gases from its own perspective, but when all countries argue in this way and emit more greenhouse gases, the current climate conditions may be destroyed.

Hardin's statement received criticism on two important aspects. First, Hardin formulates a local problem, but such a tragedy will usually not occur at the local level since it is possible to regulate individual incentives. Within national borders, for example, the government has the mandate to regulate the behavior to prevent the destruction of the resource base (see Lecture 2). Furthermore, Ostrom (1990) reports on local communities in developing countries that succeeded in managing their local commons through various mechanisms of social control. However, Hardin could have formulated a global problem, and then the problem is more serious because a supranational government does not exist. Moreover, it is difficult to envisage how the mechanisms of social control could work at the global level.

The question remains whether a full tragedy of the commons will occur at the global level. Dasgupta (1982) criticizes Hardin on another aspect, namely that he is not precise in formulating his analysis. It is not clear that following the individual incentives always implies a destruction of the resource. It is possible that at some point an individual herdsman does not have an incentive to add another animal because the marginal benefits do not outweigh the marginal costs anymore. What is needed is a conceptual framework in which the individual and collective incentives and the behavior can be precisely formulated. Game theory provides such a framework. Game theory analyzes strategic behavior and provides non-cooperative and cooperative outcomes of strategic interaction. This lecture considers environmental problems that go beyond the national borders, and the number of agents is fixed, namely as the number of countries involved. The tragedy of the commons then refers to the loss of the benefits of cooperation in the case that the countries fail to act collectively. Whether this loss is really a tragedy in the sense of a full destruction remains to be seen. Global environmental problems, such as climate change, are commons problems. Cross-border environmental problems are somewhat different but can also be analyzed as a game. The following section introduces basic game theory which proves to be useful for the analysis of these types of environmental problems.

4.3 Game Theory

The essential characteristics of global and cross-border environmental problems are two-fold. One is that emissions of pollutants in one country cause damage in other countries and thus affect their welfare. The other one is that there is no government for internalizing these external effects because a state at the global level does not exist. Institutions at the global level such as the United Nations do not have the mandate to implement environmental policies within national borders. The United Nations is a platform where the countries can discuss their policies but in the end, each country decides which policy they implement in their own country. The situation can be a bit more complicated, like in the European Union where the countries have transferred part of their authority to a higher level, but essentially the countries choose their own policies and affect their own welfare and the welfare of other countries. This implies that the appropriate framework is a game. A well-known example of this game is the prisoner's dilemma. As the name indicates, the game originates from a situation in prison, but as is seen in the following, the structure is also very relevant for global environmental problems.

4.3.1 *Prisoner's dilemma*

The original story is as follows. Two prisoners are the suspects of a major crime, but the prosecutor can only prove that they committed a minor crime. The prosecutor offers each one of them a reduction in their sentence if they testify that the other one committed the major crime. Each prisoner has an incentive to testify but if they both do so, they are worse off than if they stay silent because the sentence for the major crime after reduction is still higher than the sentence for the minor crime. The same situation occurs in a simple game between two countries that have the choice to reduce their emission of pollutants or not. Suppose that the cost of emission reduction is 7 for each country and that the benefit of the emission reduction by one country is 5 for *both* countries. This reflects the transboundary (and positive) externality. Emission reduction not only benefits the country itself but also the other country. The possible outcomes are nicely represented in a so-called bi-matrix game (see Table 4.1).

If only one country reduces emissions, the net benefit for this country is -2, whereas the net benefit for the other country is 5. If both countries reduce their emissions, the net benefit for each country is 3. If both countries

Table 4.1. Net benefits in countries 1 and 2.

Prisoner's dilemma		
Emission reduction	**2: No**	**2: Yes**
1: No	(0, 0)	(5, −2)
1: Yes	(−2, 5)	(3, 3)

do not reduce their emissions, the net benefit for each country is 0. As in the prisoner's dilemma above, each country has an incentive to refrain from emission reduction: whatever the other country does, it is better not to reduce emissions ($0 > -2$, $5 > 3$). The reason is that from the perspective of one country, the cost of emission reduction is higher than the benefit. If both countries follow incentives, they are worse off than if they both reduce emissions: $0 < 3$. The problem is, however, that they have to trust each other when they decide to reduce emissions because each country has an incentive to deviate and thus to increase the net benefit from 3 to 5, in which case both countries end up with net benefit 0. They have to trust each other in suppressing this incentive, in order to realize the best outcome.

Game theory frames the analysis of the bi-matrix game in Table 4.1 as follows. If countries cooperate, they aim for the maximal joint net benefits. The sum of the net benefits is the highest when the countries both choose "yes" (i.e. to reduce emissions) because $6 > 3 > 0$. This implies that the full-cooperative solution is given by the set of actions ("yes", "yes"). If the countries do not cooperate, each country aims for its own maximal net benefits, but this depends of course on what the other country does. Non-cooperative behavior is characterized by the Nash equilibrium. The Nash equilibrium is the set of actions with the property that the action of one country is the best, given the action of the other country. A set of these best responses of one country to the other country is the Nash equilibrium. In Table 4.1, the best response of each country to whatever the other country does is "no" so that the Nash equilibrium is the set of actions ("no", "no"). In this case, the action "no" is a strictly dominant strategy in the sense that "no" is the best response to each action of the other country. However, the best responses may also differ, depending on the action of the other country. A Nash equilibrium may still exist, but may also not exist, or multiple Nash equilibria may exist. The problems in these lecture notes have unique Nash equilibria that are easy to derive. Note that each country is better off in the full-cooperative solution than in the Nash equilibrium ($3 > 0$) so that the full-cooperative solution is not only collectively the best but also individually preferred over the Nash equilibrium in this situation.

The last conclusion may not hold in an *asymmetric* prisoner's dilemma. Suppose that the cost of emission reduction is 6 for country 1 and 5 for country 2 and that the benefit of emission reduction by one of the countries is 5 for country 1 and 2 for country 2. For example, country 1 is more dependent on fossil fuel than country 2, and therefore the cost of the reduction of greenhouse gases is higher in country 1 than in country 2. On the other hand, country 1 is more vulnerable to climate change than country 2, and therefore the benefit of the reduction of greenhouse gases is higher in country 1 than in country 2. This results in the bi-matrix game in Table 4.2. The best response of each country to whatever the other country does is again "no" (for country 1: $0 > -1$, $5 > 4$, and for country 2: $0 > -3$, $2 > -1$). The intersection of the best responses ("no", "no") remains the Nash equilibrium. The full-cooperative solution is again ("yes", "yes") because the sum of the net benefits is highest: $3 > 2 > 1 > 0$. However, in this case, country 2 is worse off in the full-cooperative solution when compared to the Nash equilibrium ($-1 < 0$), so the full-cooperative solution is not better for country 2. The reason is that if both countries reduce emissions, country 2 has a lower total benefit than cost ($4 < 5$). To get country 2 on board, a transfer of at least 1 from country 1 to country 2 is needed. In game theory, this is called a side payment. In the international arena, monetary side payments are unusual. In the early 70s, the Netherlands paid money to France to induce France to cooperate and to prevent the release of waste from the salt mines in the Elzas on the river Rhine, but these payments are exceptional. However, a country can also "pay" another country by cooperating

Table 4.2. Net benefits in countries 1 and 2.

Asymmetric prisoner's dilemma		
Emission reduction	**2: No**	**2: Yes**
1: No	(0, 0)	(5, −3)
1: Yes	(−1, 2)	(4, −1)

on some other issue that is discussed between the countries. This action is called *issue linkage* (Cesar and de Zeeuw, 1996). For example, in the 1973 treaty on the Colorado River with Mexico, the USA agreed to pay the entire costs of mitigating the salinity of the river before it flows into Mexico, instead of splitting these costs in some way. Kneese (1988) argues that the reason must have been that the USA got something else in return, like a preferential position for the import of oil from Mexico.

In these simple bi-matrix games, the possible actions are emission reduction, yes or no. In practice, however, the question is up to which level countries reduce their emissions. The benefits and costs are functions of the levels of emission reduction. The following section provides a more general framework for game theoretic analysis.

4.3.2 *Non-cooperative and cooperative behavior*

To provide a more general framework, some notation is needed: n denotes the number of countries. There are two options: the game is formulated either in levels of emissions or in levels of emission reduction or abatement, as this is usually called. To show these two options, the global environmental problem is formulated in terms of the abatement levels $a_i, i = 1, 2, \ldots, n$, for country i, whereas the cross-border environmental problem is formulated in terms of the emission levels $e_i, i = 1, 2, \ldots, n$, for country i.

4.3.2.1 Global environmental problem

In the global environmental problem, each country i maximizes the net benefits

$$\max_{a_i} \left[B_i(a) - C_i(a_i)\right],$$

$$a = \sum_{j=1}^{n} a_j, \; i = 1, 2, \ldots, n, \tag{4.1}$$

where a denotes the total abatement, B a concave benefit function of total abatement, and C a convex cost function of a country's own abatement. It follows that the best responses of the n countries are given by the first-order conditions:

$$B_i'(a) = C_i'(a_i), \; i = 1, 2, \ldots, n, \tag{4.2}$$

which means, as usual, that marginal benefits are equal to marginal costs. The Nash equilibrium for non-cooperative behavior is given by the solution of the system (4.2), which is a system with n equations and n unknowns.

In a simple example, each benefit function is given by $B_i(a) = a$ so that $B_i'(a) = 1$, and each cost function is given by $C_i(a_i) = 0.5a_i^2$ so that $C_i'(a_i) = a_i$. It follows that the first-order conditions are $a_i = 1, i = 1, 2, \dots, n$, which is the Nash equilibrium.

The full-cooperative solution results from maximizing the total net benefits

$$\max_{a_1,\dots,a_n} \sum_{i=1}^{n} [B_i(a) - C_i(a_i)]. \tag{4.3}$$

The first-order conditions become

$$\sum_{j=1}^{n} B_j'(a) = C_i'(a_i), \; i = 1, 2, \dots, n, \tag{4.4}$$

which also means that marginal benefits are equal to marginal costs, but now each country takes account of the marginal benefits for all the countries. Since these marginal benefits are higher, abatement will be higher. This is precisely the same mechanism as in the Samuelson condition for the efficient provision of a public good (Samuelson, 1955). The full-cooperative solution is given by system (4.4), which is again a system with n equations and n unknowns. In the simple example with the benefit functions $B_i(a) = a$ and cost functions $C_i(a_i) = 0.5a_i^2$, these first-order conditions are $a_i = n$, $i = 1, 2, \dots, n$, which is the full-cooperative solution.

To illustrate the implications of this analysis, simple functional forms for the benefit and cost functions are chosen such that two parameters, β and γ, capture the essential incentives. For quadratic benefit functions $B_i(a) = \beta(a_0 a - 0.5a^2)$ and cost functions $C_i(a_i) = 0.5\gamma a_i^2$, marginal benefits $B_i'(a) = \beta(a_0 - a)$ and marginal costs $C_i'(a_i) = \gamma a_i$ are linear functions, and the slopes β and γ denote the respective intensities of the marginal change. The difference between the Nash equilibrium and the full-cooperative solution can be nicely illustrated in a graph. Note that this case is symmetric so that $a_i = a/n$. The marginal benefits and the marginal costs can be depicted in the same graph as functions of a_i. The marginal benefits in the Nash equilibrium then become $\beta(a_0 - na_i)$ and in the full-cooperative solution $n\beta(a_0 - na_i)$. It follows that the Nash equilibrium (denoted by superscript N) is $a_i^N = \beta a_0/(n\beta + \gamma)$, and the full-cooperative solution (denoted by superscript C) is $a_i^C = n\beta a_0/(n^2\beta + \gamma)$ (see Figure 4.1). It is easy to see that abatement in the full-cooperative solution is indeed higher than abatement in the Nash equilibrium because the line representing marginal benefits in the full-cooperative solution is steeper than the line representing the marginal benefits in the Nash equilibrium.

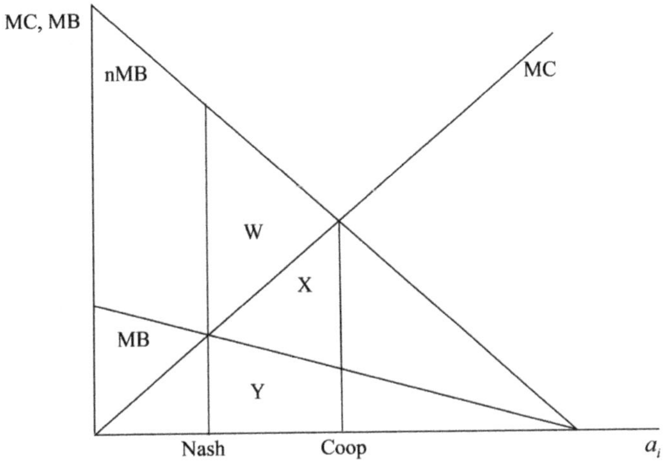

Figure 4.1. Gains of cooperation.

In Figure 4.1, the intersection of the marginal-cost line MC with the individual marginal-benefit line MB gives the Nash equilibrium, and the intersection of the marginal-cost line MC with the collective marginal-benefit line nMB gives the full-cooperative solution. For example, if MC is given by a_i, MB by $0.25(1 - a_i)$, and the number of countries is $n = 4$, the Nash equilibrium results from $0.25(1 - a_i) = a_i$ and is $a_i^N = 0.2$, and the full-cooperative solution results from $1 - a_i = a_i$ and is $a_i^C = 0.5$. Welfare is optimal in the full-cooperative solution. Similar to the graphical analyses in Lecture 1, the welfare loss of non-cooperation (or the welfare gains of cooperation) is identified in Figure 4.1. This is the triangle W, which is the difference between the loss in total benefits and the reduction in costs when abatement a_i is reduced to the level in the Nash equilibrium. When switching to non-cooperative behavior, each country reduces costs (area X + Y). This is beneficial from the perspective of that country (it is larger than the individual loss of benefits, i.e. area Y), but not from the perspective of the whole group of countries (it is smaller than the collective loss of benefits, i.e. area W + X + Y). In the example above, the triangle W is 0.09, the area X + Y is 0.15, and the area Y is 0.05. This is the same situation as the prisoner's dilemma presented in Table 4.1. In this analysis, the countries have the same benefit and cost functions so that the game is symmetric. However, countries are different so that we may end up with a similar situation as in the asymmetric prisoner's dilemma presented in Table 4.2. In the problem of climate change, for example, countries differ in their vulnerability to climate change and in their costs of reduction of emissions of greenhouse gases. In the asymmetric case, as discussed above, side payments or issue linkage may be needed to achieve full cooperation.

Barrett (1990) uses the graph in Figure 4.1 to relate the gains of cooperation to the slopes β and γ of the marginal benefits and marginal costs. The area W in Figure 4.1 is half times the product of the difference in abatement levels $a_i^C - a_i^N$ and the difference in marginal benefits at the Nash equilibrium a_i^N. It is easy to see that the difference in abatement levels $a_i^C - a_i^N$ becomes small if the slope γ becomes either large or small, and that the difference in the marginal benefits decreases if the slope γ decreases. This implies that the area W shrinks when the slope γ becomes small. In that case, the Nash equilibrium is close to the full cooperative solution. In this way, it is possible to provide a characterization of global environmental problems in terms of the potential gains of cooperation.

Example 4.1. Emissions of chlorofluorocarbon (or CFC) cause holes in the ozone layer so that too much ultraviolet radiation reaches the earth, which is an important cause of skin cancer. Skin cancer is a serious threat to life so that the benefits of reducing these emissions of CFC are substantial. On the other hand, the costs of reducing the emissions of CFC turned out to be small because of technological development: it proved to be possible to produce sprays and refrigerators that do not emit CFC. Thus, the gains of cooperation for this global environmental problem are small. This problem was the subject of an international agreement, called the Montreal Protocol. The first version was signed in 1987 by 46 countries and in 2016, almost all countries were part of this agreement. The Montreal Protocol was seen as a huge success, but it must be said that given the characterization above, the gains of cooperation were small, and non-cooperative behavior would probably have led to approximately the same outcome. Another example, namely climate change, leads to the opposite conclusion. Since climatologists indicate a serious risk of climate change with substantial damages, the benefits of reducing emissions of greenhouse gases are large again. However, the costs are substantial as well because the reduction requires a costly transition from the use of fossil fuels to the use of other energy sources. Therefore, the gains of cooperation for this global environmental problem are large, according to the model in Figure 4.1. This problem was the subject of a general agreement signed in Rio de Janeiro in 1992, namely the United Nations Framework Convention on Climate Change. All countries meet almost each year in what they call the Conference of the Parties (COP). In 1997, a large group of developed countries signed the Kyoto Protocol, which was the first attempt to establish an international environmental agreement for the reduction of emissions of greenhouse gases. Unfortunately, the Kyoto Protocol failed. In 2015, almost all countries signed the Paris Agreement. They agreed on limiting global warming, and they have committed to the first steps in reducing greenhouse gas emissions. However, the next steps are not yet clear. Comparing the global environmental problems above, it proves to be much harder to establish an international agreement in case the possible gains of cooperation are large than in case the possible gains are small. This is bad news. Lecture 5 continues and considers the problems of establishing an international environmental agreement.

4.3.2.2 Cross-border environmental problem

This problem is formulated in terms of emission levels $e_i, i = 1, 2, \ldots, n$, in country i. The costs of abatement or emission reduction are now formulated as a downward-sloping convex cost function C of emission levels, which is relevant in the range below the emission level resulting if damage due to emissions is ignored. The idea is as follows: the lower the emissions, the more the emissions are reduced, and the higher the costs. Damages occur in the country where the emissions end up, i.e. where the emissions are deposited. This means that a model is needed that connects the depositions d_i in country i with the emissions $e_j, j = 1, 2, \ldots, n$, originating from the country itself and possibly from all the other countries. If f_{ij} denotes the fraction of the emissions e_j originating in country j that is deposited in country i, it follows that

$$d_i = \sum_{j=1}^{n} f_{ij} e_j, \ i = 1, 2, \ldots, n, \tag{4.5}$$

which can be written in vector-matrix notation as

$$\begin{aligned} d &= Fe, \\ d &= [d_1, d_2, \ldots, d_n]', \\ F &= [f_{ij}], \\ e &= [e_1, e_2, \ldots, e_n]', \end{aligned} \tag{4.6}$$

where F denotes the transportation matrix of fractions of emissions that are transported from one country to the other, for example by winds, with f_{ii} the fraction deposited in the country itself. A very good example is the acid rain problem in Europe: see Section 4.3.2.3.

In a cross-border environmental problem, each country i minimizes the total costs

$$\min_{e_i} \left[C_i(e_i) + D_i(d_i)\right], d_i = \sum_{j=1}^{n} f_{ij}e_j, \; i = 1, 2, \ldots, n, \tag{4.7}$$

where C denotes a decreasing convex cost function of the emission levels, and D an increasing convex cost function of the depositions. It follows that the best responses of the n countries are given by the first-order conditions:

$$C_i'(e_i) + D_i'(d_i)f_{ii} = 0, d_i = \sum_{j=1}^{n} f_{ij}e_j, \; i = 1, 2, \ldots, n. \tag{4.8}$$

The Nash equilibrium in case of non-cooperative behavior is given by the solution of the system (4.8), which is a system with n equations and the n unknowns $e_i, i = 1, 2, \ldots, n$.

The full-cooperative solution results from collectively minimizing the total costs

$$\min_{e_1,..,e_n} \sum_{i=1}^{n} [C_i(e_i) + D_i(d_i)], d_i = \sum_{j=1}^{n} f_{ij}e_j. \tag{4.9}$$

The first-order conditions become

$$C_i'(e_i) + \sum_{j=1}^{n} D_j'(d_j)f_{ji} = 0, d_j = \sum_{k=1}^{n} f_{jk}e_k, \; i = 1, 2, \ldots, n. \tag{4.10}$$

In this case, each country takes account of the damages in other countries, which are caused by depositions originating from this country. Therefore, the emission levels will be lower. The full-cooperative solution is given by the system (4.10), which is again a system with n equations and the n unknowns $e_i, i = 1, 2, \ldots, n$. Note that the solution is expected to be asymmetric. Not only the cost functions are different, but also the location of the countries matters. When the countries are close to each other, the chances of cross-border externalities are higher. Furthermore, the winds that transport the emissions may have a dominant direction so that the cross-border externalities may be higher in one direction than in the other. The full-cooperative solution will lead to lower total costs and damages, but side payments may be needed to get all countries on board.

For example, if $n = 2$, $C_i(e_i) = 0.5(e_i - e_0)^2, i = 1, 2$, where e_0 indicates business-as-usual, and $D_i(d_i) = 0.5d_i^2, i = 1, 2$, marginal costs are $C_i'(e_i) = (e_i - e_0), i = 1, 2$, and marginal damages are $D_i'(d_i) = d_i, i = 1, 2$. Furthermore, if $f_{11} = 0.67$, $f_{12} = 0.25$, $f_{21} = 0.33$, and $f_{22} = 0.75$, it follows that $d_1 = 0.67e_1+0.25e_2$ and $d_2 = 0.33e_1+0.75e_2$. This means that the fractions 0.67 and 0.75 of the emissions in country 1 and country 2, respectively, stay in the country itself. The first-order conditions for the Nash equilibrium are $(e_i-e_0)+d_i f_{ii} = 0$, according to equation (4.8), and the first-order conditions for the full-cooperative solution are $(e_i - e_0) + d_1 f_{1i} + d_2 f_{2i} = 0$, according to equation (4.10). Note that in the full-cooperative solution, the damage in the other country and the effect that a country has on the damage in the other country are taken into account. The Nash equilibrium conditions yield $1.44e_1+0.17e_2-e_0 = 0$ and $0.25e_1+1.56e_2-e_0 = 0$ so that the Nash equilibrium becomes $(0.63e_0, 0.54e_0)$, and the conditions for the full-cooperative solution yield $1.56e_1+0.42e_2-e_0 = 0$ and $0.42e_1+1.63e_2-e_0 = 0$ so that the full-cooperative solution becomes $(0.51e_0, 0.48e_0)$. Both countries reduce their emissions when they cooperate but country 1 reduces emissions further than country 2 because country 1 does more damage to country 2 than the other way around. The costs and damages in the Nash equilibrium are $(0.225e_0^2, 0.292e_0^2)$ for the two countries, and the costs and damages in the full-cooperative solution are $(0.226e_0^2, 0.275e_0^2)$ for the two countries. The total costs and damages in the full-cooperative solution are lower than in the Nash equilibrium, $0.501e_0^2 < 0.517e_0^2$, but a small side payment of at least $0.001e_0^2$ from country 2 to country 1 is needed to get country 1 on board.

4.3.2.3 The acid rain game

Acid rain is the wet or dry deposition of sulfur dioxide and nitrogen oxides that causes the acidification of soils, and therefore a decrease in the productivity of soils. Nowadays, the problem is less urgent than it used to be because the emissions of sulfur dioxide are largely under control, but the emissions of nitrogen oxides are still a big issue. This section describes research that is a little bit outdated but has become the classical example of research on this type of problem. Note that winds can take the emissions across borders, and therefore emissions in one country can lead to damages in other countries. This turns the problem into a game. The acid rain game has become a classical example of a cross-border environmental problem.

The international discussion started when Norway realized that a large part of acid rain in Norway was due to emissions in the United Kingdom. Norway reached out to the other European countries and suggested the "30% club" (1985). In this agreement, the countries committed to reduce their emissions by 30% in a period of 8 years. Several countries stayed out of the agreement for the simple reason that damage in their country was minor because of their favorable location. For example, the United Kingdom heavily polluted Scandinavian countries but received little pollution from outside. The reason is that the winds blow mainly in the northeast direction. The reaction of economists to this situation was twofold. First, economists argued that the same reduction percentage in each country is probably not optimal from the cooperative perspective due to the many asymmetries. Second, economists argued that some form of side payments may be needed to get all the countries on board in an international agreement. The 30% club was followed by a series of protocols on acid rain in Europe (Helsinki Protocol, 1985; Sofia Protocol, 1988; Geneva Protocol, 1991; and more). All the protocols focused on a certain level of emission reduction for all participants but did not attend to the critique of economists. The protocols have been reasonably successful but again, like the Montreal Protocol, this was mainly due to relatively cheap technological improvements. The emissions of sulfur dioxide have now been significantly reduced. However, the emissions of nitrogen oxides are still a huge problem.

Mäler (1989) used the framework that was developed in Section 4.3.2.2. He considered the acid rain game in Europe. The Nash equilibrium between the countries involved is given by the set of equations (4.8), and the full-cooperative solution by the set of equations (4.10). Regarding the availability of data for the analysis, he had data on the cost functions C_i from the *RAINS* model that was developed at the research institute *IIASA* in Laxenburg, Austria, and on the transportation matrix F of fractions of emissions that are transported from one country to the other, as given in equations (4.5) and (4.6). This transportation matrix F originated from the *EMEP* program, with departments in Oslo and Moscow. This program had constructed a grid of measurement stations all over Europe for measuring the movements of sulfur dioxides and nitrogen oxides from one area to the other. However, a set of data on the damage functions D_i was not available. Mäler (1989) assumed that the emissions at the time represented the Nash equilibrium. Since these emissions, the cost functions C_i and the transportation matrix F were known, the set of equations (4.8) could be solved for the marginal damages $D_i'(d_i)$ of the depositions. However, for considering the full-cooperative solution, the marginal damages were needed over a larger range of depositions, and not only in the Nash equilibrium. Therefore, he assumed that the marginal damages were constant, $D_i'(d_i) = \gamma_i$, or that the damage functions D_i were linear so that (4.10) becomes

$$C_i'(e_i) + \sum_{j=1}^{n} \gamma_j f_{ji} = 0, \quad i = 1, 2, \ldots, n, \tag{4.11}$$

which yields the emission levels $e_i, i = 1, 2, \ldots, n$, in the full-cooperative solution.

By comparing the emission levels in the full-cooperative solution with the current emission levels, it follows which changes in emission levels in which countries were needed to achieve the optimal outcome for Europe as a whole. Moreover, this provides an estimate on the reductions in total costs for the countries separately and for Europe as a whole. First, it was interesting to find that the optimal reduction in total emissions of sulfur dioxide turned out to be 39%, which was close to the 30% Norway initially proposed. However, as was to be expected, the spread of emission reductions over the countries was very uneven. For example, the reduction needed to be high in Germany but could be low in Scandinavia. Germany is centrally located in Europe, and therefore Germany pollutes many other countries. Scandinavia, on the other hand, is located at the border of Europe. Furthermore, as was mentioned earlier, winds are predominantly northeast so that Scandinavia does not pollute other countries. The United Kingdom had to reduce emissions a lot as well. The UK is located at the border of Europe, but the UK heavily pollutes Scandinavia because of the direction of the winds. Therefore, the UK had high costs of emission reductions in the full-cooperative solution, but the UK did not have a large reduction in the costs of depositions. The net effect for the UK was even negative. This situation is an asymmetric prisoner's dilemma (Section 4.3.1) where one of the countries is worse off in the full-cooperative solution. To get the UK on board in an international agreement, a side payment to the UK is needed. More countries had a negative net effect so that more side payments were needed. Furthermore, the spread of the gains of cooperation over the countries was very uneven. One can argue that besides side payments to the countries with a negative net effect, more transfers between countries should be considered to smooth international cooperation. This research shows the way to tackle the problem, but more research is needed to achieve reliable quantitative recommendations.

4.3.3 *Summary*

The previous sections have characterized non-cooperative and cooperative behavior for two types of international environmental problems. The full-cooperative solution is best for the group of countries together but if the countries follow individual incentives, the Nash equilibrium results, and the countries are worse off. This does not have to result in a tragedy of the commons, but the emissions are higher, and it may also imply a larger risk for the preservation of the natural ecological system (see Lecture 8). In case of asymmetry, the full-cooperative solution may have the property that some countries are worse off than in the Nash equilibrium.

4.4 Conclusion

Global or cross-border environmental problems require international cooperation to reach the optimal outcome. The problem is that countries usually have an incentive to free ride on the efforts of other countries so that they will not join or not comply with international cooperation. Game theory provides a conceptual framework for this analysis. The incentive to free ride often breaks down cooperation, resulting in the non-cooperative Nash equilibrium with lower welfare. Full cooperation is optimal but may require side payments to some countries to get them on board.

References

Barrett, S. 1990. The problem of global environmental protection. *Oxford Review of Economic Policy* 6, 1: 68–79.

Cesar, H. and de Zeeuw, A. 1996. Issue linkage in global environmental problems. In *Economic Policy for the Environment and Natural Resources*, (ed.) Xepapadeas, A. Cheltenham: Edward Elgar, pp. 158–173.

Dasgupta, P. 1982. *The Control of Resources*. Cambridge, MA: Harvard University Press.

Hardin, G. 1968. The tragedy of the commons. *Science* 162, 3859: 1243–1248.

Kneese, A.V. 1988. Environmental stress and political conflicts: Salinity in the Colorado River. Paper presented at the conference Environmental Stress and Security, Stockholm.

Mäler, K.-G. 1989. The acid rain game. In *Valuation Methods and Policy Making in Environmental Economics*, (eds.) Folmer, H. and van Ierland, E. Amsterdam: Elsevier, pp. 231–262.

Ostrom, E. 1990. *Governing the Commons*. Cambridge: Cambridge University Press.

Samuelson, P.A. 1955. Diagrammatic exposition of a theory of public expenditure. *The Review of Economics and Statistics* 37: 350–356.

Lecture 5

International Environmental Agreements

5.1 Introduction

Global environmental problems such as climate change require international cooperation to internalize the externalities. Lecture 4 introduces game theory to compare the full-cooperative solution with the non-cooperative Nash equilibrium. The countries have an incentive to deviate from the full-cooperative solution, but when they deviate, they end up in the non-cooperative Nash equilibrium with lower welfare. This lecture considers whether it is possible to have stable partial cooperation or an international environmental agreement for a group of countries with the property that no country in the agreement has an incentive to leave. Leaving the agreement implies that a country can enjoy the free-rider benefits of being outside the agreement but loses the benefits of being part of the group of countries that internalizes each other's externalities. The usual analysis predicts small stable international environmental agreements, which explains the difficulties in achieving success at the international level but does not leave an optimistic conclusion. Alternative models exist with a more optimistic conclusion, but these models assume strategic behavior with threats, which are usually not seen in practice. The challenge in this literature is to investigate the design of stable and successful international agreements.

Lecture 8 discusses *tipping points* in ecological systems which are sudden changes in the system, and which imply a sudden loss in welfare. This lecture shows that in the case of possible tipping points (like climate tipping points) which lead to a sudden loss in welfare, cooperation may *not* be needed to avoid tipping. If the loss in welfare is sufficiently high, the non-cooperative Nash equilibrium already avoids tipping.

This lecture has two goals. The first is to explain why it is difficult to achieve large stable international environmental agreements. The second is to show options and situations for which it is possible to have an improvement over this rather grim picture.

Section 5.2 discusses several models for analyzing the stability and success of international environmental agreements. The basic model is a two-stage game in which countries first choose to join the agreement or not, and then play the abatement game. Section 5.3 concludes.

5.2 International Environmental Agreements

Global environmental problems such as climate change and the depletion of ozone require voluntary cooperation by sovereign states to internalize the negative externalities from emissions in each of the states. A global government with a mandate to choose and implement environmental policy does not exist. The United Nations can provide a platform to discuss the issues, but it cannot force states to implement cooperative policies. Game theory has shown that a prisoner's dilemma (Lecture 4) may arise meaning that individual incentives to free ride on the efforts of other countries erode the benefits of cooperation. Nevertheless, history has shown that successful international environmental agreements may occur. For example, almost all countries signed and implemented the Montreal Protocol on phasing out the emissions of CFC (see Section 4.3.2.1). However, the benefits of cooperation in this case were small so that the Montreal Protocol was a big success in terms of the number of signatories, but not so much in terms of the benefits of cooperation. The Kyoto Protocol, that was signed at a Conference of the Parties within the Framework Convention on Climate Change (see Section 4.3.2.1), looked like a promising first step in creating large benefits of cooperation, but this agreement failed in the stage of compliance or implementation. The last observation shows that an agreement needs to be stable in the sense that no country has an incentive to leave the agreement. On the other hand, no outside country should have an incentive to join the agreement either because it would mean that the agreement could have more signatories. These considerations imply that the game underlying an international environmental agreement becomes an extension of the game considered in Lecture 4. It is the so-called two-stage membership game. In the first stage, the countries have the choice to become a member of the agreement or not. In the second stage, the coalition of members and the individual outsiders choose their emission levels or their abatement levels. The Nash equilibrium of this two-stage membership game ensures that no country has an incentive to join or to leave the agreement. Partial cooperation is also feasible in this game. The countries weigh the benefits of partial cooperation against the benefits of free riding when choosing to become a member of the agreement or not. The equilibrium of this game can be seen as an equilibrium between these two incentives. The questions are how many countries will join the agreement and what the outcome will be.

5.2.1 *Two-stage membership game*

This game was first developed in industrial organization (d'Aspremont *et al.*, 1983), with the purpose of predicting the size of a stable cartel. The structure of that problem is similar: firms can decide to join the cartel or not, and then this cartel competes with the remaining firms on the market for goods or services. Note that for industrial organizations, small cartels are good news, but for an international environmental agreement, a small number of signatories is bad news. The two-stage membership game was used for developing the theory of international environmental agreements (Hoel, 1992; Carraro and Siniscalco, 1993; Barrett, 1994).

In the first stage, all the countries choose to become a signatory to the agreement or to stay outside. This choice depends on the net benefits they will have as a member of the coalition or as an outsider in the second stage. Therefore, the two-stage game is solved backward. It starts by solving the second stage, assuming s countries have signed the agreement, which means that the coalition of members has size s. The solution of the second stage yields the net benefits of the members and the outsiders as a function of s. Then the first stage of the two-stage game can be solved, which yields the number of signatories s. This number is the Nash equilibrium in the first stage, in which no country has an incentive to deviate. This means two things. A signatory will not be better off by stepping out and becoming an outsider to the coalition of size $s-1$ in the second stage, and an outsider will not be better off by signing and becoming a member of the coalition of size $s+1$ in the second stage.

The second stage is a combination of the non-cooperative and the cooperative behavior in Section 4.3.2.1. Combining the expressions (4.1) and (4.3), a coalition of s members and the $n-s$ individual outsiders, respectively, maximizes the net benefits

$$\max_{a_1,\dots,a_s} \sum_{i=1}^{s} [B_i(a) - C_i(a_i)],$$
$$\max_{a_i} [B_i(a) - C_i(a_i)], \quad i = s+1,\dots,n, \quad a = \sum_{j=1}^{n} a_j. \tag{5.1}$$

The first-order conditions become

$$\sum_{k=1}^{s} B_k'(a) = C_i'(a_i), \quad i = 1,\dots,s,$$
$$B_i'(a) = C_i'(a_i), \quad i = s+1,\dots,n, \tag{5.2}$$

which means that marginal benefits are equal to marginal costs, and each member country takes account of the marginal benefits for all the member countries. This is a system with n equations and n unknowns. In the simple example with the benefit functions $B_i(a) = a$ and cost functions $C_i(a_i) = 0.5a_i^2$, these first-order conditions become

$$a_i = s, \quad i = 1,\dots,s,$$
$$a_i = 1, \quad i = s+1,\dots,n, \tag{5.3}$$
$$a = s^2 + n - s.$$

For $s > 1$, the members of the coalition abate more because they take account of the externalities within the coalition. The game started as a symmetric game, but the structure of the game produced two types of countries: members and outsiders. The respective net benefits (denoted by W) in the second stage are

$$W^m(s) = s^2 + n - s - 0.5s^2,$$
$$W^o(s) = s^2 + n - s - 0.5, \tag{5.4}$$

where the superscript m denotes a member and the superscript o denotes an outsider. The net benefits of the members are lower because they abate more, whereas the outsiders partly free ride on the efforts of the coalition. Note that for $s = 1$, the Nash equilibrium in Section 4.3.2.1 results, and for $s = n$, the full-cooperative solution results.

Outsiders are better off than coalition members, so one may expect that no country wants to join the coalition in the first stage, but this is not the precise story. Joining the coalition means that the coalition becomes larger, and each coalition member will abate more. Therefore, the trade-off is to become a member of a larger coalition or to remain an outsider. A country will join the coalition of size s if $W^m(s+1) > W^o(s)$. Similarly, a country will leave the coalition of size s if $W^o(s-1) > W^m(s)$, which means that it is better to become an outsider to a smaller coalition than to remain a coalition member. A coalition is *stable* if no country has an incentive to join or to leave the coalition. The equilibrium conditions for the first stage are given by

$$\begin{aligned} W^m(s+1) &\leq W^o(s), \;\; s \leq n-1, \\ W^o(s-1) &\leq W^m(s), \;\; s \geq 2. \end{aligned} \tag{5.5}$$

The first condition in (5.5) is called *external stability* because no country has an incentive to join, and the second condition of (15) is called *internal stability* because no country has an incentive to leave. The net benefits in (5.4) for the simple example above yield the conditions

$$\begin{aligned} &0.5s^2 - s \geq 0, \\ &0.5s^2 - 2s + 1.5 \leq 0. \end{aligned} \tag{5.6}$$

The only values of s that satisfy both conditions (5.6) are $s = 2$ and $s = 3$ (see Figure 5.1). This means that only the coalitions of size 2 and size 3 are stable, independent of the total number of countries n. It means that the incentive to free ride quickly becomes stronger than the incentive to cooperate and that it is very hard to establish a high and stable level of cooperation. One may think that this pessimistic result is due to the simplicity of this example, but the result proved to be robust, and other models yield only small stable coalitions as well (Finus, 2003).

Section 4.3.2.1 concluded, when comparing the Montreal Protocol and the Kyoto Protocol, that it is apparently much harder to establish an international environmental agreement in case the gains of cooperation are larger than in case these gains are small. The question is whether the two-stage membership game supports this observation. The model in that section with quadratic benefit and cost functions is tedious to analyze in the context of a two-stage membership game. Moreover, it will again yield small stable coalitions so that it cannot provide an explanation for the Montreal Protocol. However, support for this observation results from analyzing the following extension of the prisoner's dilemma in Table 4.1. The n countries have a discrete choice to reduce emissions or not. The cost of emission

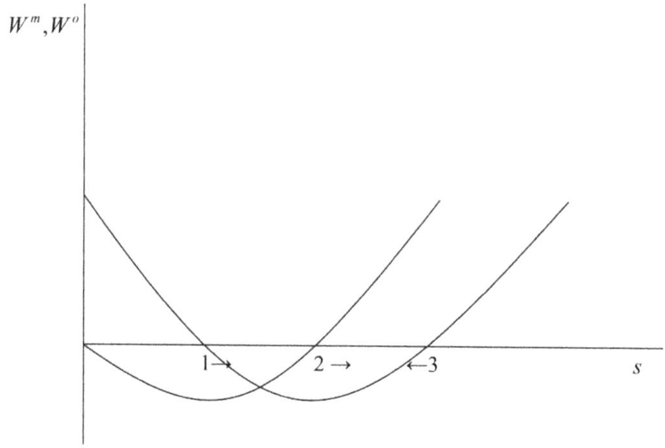

Figure 5.1. Stable coalitions.

reduction is γ for each country, and the benefit of emission reduction by a country is β for *all* n countries. Moreover, $\beta < \gamma$ so that each country has an incentive to refrain from the reduction of emissions. However, $n\beta > \gamma$ so that collectively the countries are better off by the reduction of emissions. In the two-stage membership game, it is only beneficial to form a coalition if it is large enough to make joint reduction of emissions beneficial, i.e. $s\beta > \gamma$, where s is the size of the coalition. Then the respective net benefits in the second stage are

$$\begin{aligned} W^m(s) &= s\beta - \gamma, \\ W^o(s) &= s\beta. \end{aligned} \tag{5.7}$$

An outsider does not have an incentive to join this coalition because the additional benefit does not outweigh the cost so that the first (or external) stability condition in (5.5) holds:

$$\beta < \gamma \Rightarrow (s+1)\beta - \gamma < s\beta. \tag{5.8}$$

A coalition member does not have an incentive to leave this coalition if this would imply that the coalition becomes too small to continue to make the choice to reduce emissions. It follows that the size of the stable coalition is the smallest s for which $s\beta > \gamma$. Note that the second (or internal) stability condition in (5.5) now holds because leaving the coalition means that the net benefits are reduced from $s\beta - \gamma > 0$ to 0. This result implies that the size of the stable coalition is large if the benefit β is much smaller than the cost γ, and that the size of the stable coalition is small if the benefit β lies close to the cost γ. This means that in case there is much to gain in an international environmental agreement by generating large benefits collectively, the size of the stable coalition is small. This is bad news again.

Additional support for the general statement that large stable coalitions imply small gains of cooperation arises by analyzing the asymmetric version of the simple example at the beginning of this section. Global environmental problems are usually asymmetric. For example, countries differ in their vulnerability to climate change and in their costs for the reduction of greenhouse gas emissions. For the asymmetric benefit functions $B_i(a) = \beta_i a$ and cost functions $C_i(a_i) = 0.5\gamma_i a_i^2$, the first-order conditions become

$$\begin{aligned} a_i &= \frac{\sum\limits_{j \in S} \beta_j}{\gamma_i}, \quad i \in S, \\ a_i &= \frac{\beta_i}{\gamma_i}, \quad i \notin S, \end{aligned} \tag{5.9}$$

where S denotes the coalition of size s. Countries abate more if their benefit (indicated by β_i) becomes larger or if their cost (indicated by γ_i) becomes smaller, and the members of the coalition abate more because they take account of the externalities within the coalition. It follows that the members of the coalition not only abate more if their own benefit is larger but also if the benefits of the other coalition members are larger. Therefore, it matters which type of countries join each other in the coalition. Pavlova and de Zeeuw (2013) distinguish two types of countries: one type with high benefit and low cost of abatement, and the other type with low benefit and high cost of abatement. They show that the two-stage membership game has two possible stable coalitions if these differences are sufficiently large. One coalition consists of three countries of the first type, and the other one consists of two countries of the first type and all the countries of the second type. Total abatement proves to be higher in the first situation than in the second situation. It is better if one country of the first type joins two other countries of the first type in a coalition than if all the countries of the second type join these two countries in a coalition. The reason is that a country of the first type, with the high benefit of abatement, increases the abatement of the other coalition members, according to (5.9). The conclusion is again that large stable coalitions do not go hand in hand with high levels of abatement.

The two-stage membership models again provide this grim picture: either the size of the stable coalition is small or if the size happens to be larger, the gains of cooperation are small. It is hard to achieve large gains of cooperation. However, there is a fundamental result in game theory, usually referred to as the folk theorem, which says that cooperation can be maintained if deviations are met with sufficient punishment. The basic idea is that the players use trigger strategies, which means that the players continue the cooperation if the other players also cooperate but switch to non-cooperative behavior if other players deviate (e.g. Friedman, 1986). If the discount factor is sufficiently high, the threat of ending up in the Nash equilibrium deters deviations and keeps the players in the full-cooperative solution. From this perspective, it shows that the threat in the two-stage membership game is not sufficiently strong. In the second stage, the coalition members do not take account of the deviator anymore, but this threat is apparently not big enough to suppress the free-rider incentive. The literature on this subject has developed two alternatives. In the first one, each country considers the possibility that deviating may trigger other countries to deviate as well, increasing the threat. This approach led to the concept of *farsighted stability* (Chwe, 1994). The second one originates from what is called cooperative game theory and uses threats that are similar to the trigger strategies in the folk theorem (Chander and Tulkens, 1995).

5.2.2 *Stronger threats*

In the two-stage membership game, the countries expect in the first stage that all the other countries do not change their position and remain either a coalition member or an outsider in the second stage. The outcome changes if the decision to leave the coalition triggers other countries to leave as well. In that case, the incentive to free ride decreases because the remaining coalition has fewer countries. This leads to the concept of *farsighted stability*. The basic idea is as follows. Suppose that the two-stage membership game has a stable coalition of size 3 and that the coalitions of larger size are not internally stable. This means that the net benefits of a member of the coalition of size 5 are smaller than the net benefits of an outsider to the coalition of size 4. For the simple example in the previous section,

$$W^m(5) = N + 7.5 < W^o(4) = N + 11.5$$

according to (5.4). It may happen, however, that the net benefits of a member of the coalition of size 5 are larger than the net benefits of an outsider to the coalition of size 3. This indeed holds in the simple example because

$$W^m(5) = N + 7.5 > W^o(3) = N + 5.5$$

according to (5.4). This implies that the country prefers to stay in the coalition of size 5 in case it expects that leaving the coalition will trigger another country to leave as well. It follows that using the concept of farsighted stability, larger stable coalitions result. In the context of this lecture, it is not possible to present a full analysis of the coalitions that are farsighted stable. In general, there is a set of farsighted stable coalitions, and the size of the largest one is close to the size n of the grand coalition. This is good news. It means that more cooperation results and more net benefits are achieved if the countries understand that leaving the international environmental agreement implies that other countries leave as well. Note that this model allows for having small and large stable coalitions. The underlying mechanisms are clear, but it does not mean that this is seen in practice. The prevailing experience is that it is hard to establish large and successful international environmental agreements.

In cooperative game theory, the idea is that the grand coalition of size n is stable if it is in the so-called *core* of a game, which means that a subset of players cannot block the agreement by deviating and doing better. An assumption has to be made on what the other players will do if a subset of players deviates. The other players can either punish the deviators by choosing strategies that are less favorable to them or they can simply switch to non-cooperative behavior. The grand coalition is in the so-called *γ-core* of the game if a subset of players cannot block the agreement under the second assumption. Chander and Tulkens (1995) use the γ-core concept for analyzing the stability of the grand coalition which means that they assume that the remaining countries switch to non-cooperative behavior in the case of a deviation. This is again a trigger strategy, as it was described at the end of the previous section. It is immediately clear that in the symmetric case, the grand coalition is in the core of the game. It is better to be a member of the grand coalition than to be a member of a smaller coalition when the other countries switch to outsiders. Using equation (5.4) again, this simply follows from

$$W^m(n) = 0.5n^2 > W^m(s) = 0.5s^2 + n - s, s < n.$$

It becomes more interesting in the asymmetric case. Chander and Tulkens (1995) show that the grand coalition is in the γ-core of the game when the countries share the total costs of the additional abatement under full cooperation according to their relative weights in the benefits of abatement. In the example in the previous section, the relative weights are $\beta_i / \sum \beta_j$. In the context of this lecture, it is not possible to present a precise proof, but it is intuitively clear that sharing the costs in this way mitigates the asymmetries so that the trigger strategies operate in a similar way as in the symmetric case. More importantly, however, the conclusion is that this model has an optimistic outcome in the sense that the grand coalition is stable, but it requires two behavioral assumptions. First, the countries should be willing to start cooperatively and switch to non-cooperative behavior in case other countries deviate. Second, the countries should be willing to use transfers between them in the asymmetric case to fulfill the requirement of sharing the additional costs of abatement according to the relative weights of the benefits. However, as mentioned earlier, both threats and transfers are not common practice in international environmental agreements.

5.2.3 *Tipping points*

The previous sections show that behavioral threats can induce cooperative behavior. In a way, threats from natural systems can induce cooperative behavior as well. Lecture 8 introduces tipping points in natural systems. Tipping, or crossing a threshold, causes a change in the system with a significant loss of welfare. It can be collectively optimal to reduce emissions more than in the absence of a tipping point, to prevent that tipping occurs. This is the full-cooperative solution in this case. If the loss of welfare from tipping is sufficiently large, a deviation by one individual may also not be beneficial when it causes tipping. Cooperation and non-cooperation then coincide. Coordination on this Nash equilibrium mimics cooperative behavior (Barrett, 2013).

In order to show the effect of a tipping point on the outcome of the game, the example in Section 4.3.2.1 is extended by changing the benefit functions into $B_i(a) = a - l$, if $a < a^{tp}$, and into $B_i(a) = a$, if $a \geq a^{tp}$, with cost functions $C_i(a_i) = 0.5a_i^2$ (Barrett, 2013). It means that if the total level of abatement a stays below the critical level a^{tp}, emissions are still so high that they cause the natural system (like the climate system) to cross a threshold and to tip into a state with a loss of benefits l for each country. The conclusion in Section 4.3.2.1 was that in the absence of such a possibility, the full-cooperative solution is $a_i = n, i = 1, 2, \ldots, n$, with total abatement $a = n^2$ and net benefits $0.5n^2$ for each country. If the total abatement is not high enough to prevent tipping, i.e. $n^2 < a^{tp}$, losses l will occur so that the net benefits become $0.5n^2 - l$ for each country. However, the countries could consider abating up to the critical level a^{tp}, to prevent tipping and the loss l for each country. Each country abates a^{tp}/n. This is indeed better for the countries collectively if the net benefits for each country are higher than in case they let tipping occur, i.e.

$$a^{tp} - 0.5\left(\frac{a^{tp}}{n}\right)^2 > 0.5n^2 - l \quad \text{or} \tag{5.10}$$

$$l > 0.5\left(\frac{a^{tp}}{n} - n\right)^2. \tag{5.11}$$

Inequality (5.11) means that the countries collectively choose to abate up to the critical level a^{tp} if the loss l of tipping is larger than the decrease in net benefits from increasing abatement.

Section 4.3.2.1 also concluded that in the absence of the possibility of a tipping point, the Nash equilibrium is $a_i = 1, i = 1, 2, \ldots, n$, with total abatement $a = n$ and net benefits $n - 0.5$ for each country. This level of total abatement is lower than the critical level a^{tp}, since $n < n^2 < a^{tp}$, so that tipping with the corresponding losses l will occur, and the net benefits become $n - 0.5 - l$ for each country. However, the countries could consider abating more. In the non-cooperative setting, the question becomes whether $a_i = a^{tp}/n, i = 1, 2, \ldots, n$, can also be a Nash equilibrium so that tipping and the corresponding loss l to each country are prevented in a Nash equilibrium. This requires that an individual country does not have an incentive to deviate, in case the other $n-1$ countries choose the abatement level a^{tp}/n. If an individual country deviates, it will choose the abatement level $1 < a^{tp}/n$, as in the case without the possibility of tipping, but it also has to accept the loss l because tipping will occur. It follows that a country will not deviate, and $a_i = a^{tp}/n, i = 1, 2, \ldots, n$, will be a Nash equilibrium if

$$a^{tp} - 0.5\left(\frac{a^{tp}}{n}\right)^2 > 1 + \frac{n-1}{n}a^{tp} - 0.5 - l \quad \text{or} \tag{5.12}$$

$$l > 0.5\left(\frac{a^{tp}}{n} - 1\right)^2. \tag{5.13}$$

The right-hand side in (5.13) is larger than in (5.11), which is to be expected since it will require a larger loss to suppress free riding than to induce the countries to collectively avoid tipping.

For example, suppose that the number of countries is $n = 10$ and that the critical abatement level is $a^{tp} = 150$. Condition (5.11) shows that if $l > 12.5$, it is collectively optimal to abate up to the critical level. Condition (5.13) shows that if $l > 98$, the set of abatement levels $(15, 15, \ldots, 15)$ is a Nash equilibrium that abates up to the critical level. In the range $12.5 < l < 98$, it is collectively optimal to avoid tipping, but this cannot be achieved in a Nash equilibrium. If $l > 98$, however, it is collectively optimal to avoid tipping, and this can be achieved in a Nash equilibrium. Finally, if $l < 12.5$, it is best to let tipping occur because the costs to avoid tipping are too high as compared to the relatively low loss of tipping.

The important conclusion is that if condition (5.13) holds, it is not only collectively optimal to choose $a_i = a^{tp}/n, i = 1, 2, \ldots, n$, but this is also a Nash equilibrium. Only in the range of l, for which condition (5.11) holds but condition (5.13) does not hold, it is collectively optimal to prevent tipping, but this cannot be achieved in a Nash equilibrium. Note that $a_i = 1, i = 1, 2, \ldots, n$, remains a Nash equilibrium in the presence of a tipping point if it is not beneficial for an individual country to increase abatement up to a^{tp} by itself. If a game has two Nash equilibria, it becomes a so-called coordination game. If it is collectively optimal to choose $a_i = a^{tp}/n, i = 1, 2, \ldots, n$, and if the two Nash equilibria exist, the countries do not have to cooperate, but they can coordinate on the Nash equilibrium $a_i = a^{tp}/n, i = 1, 2, \ldots, n$. It follows that if condition (5.13) holds, the full-cooperative outcome and the best non-cooperative Nash equilibrium coincide. In this case, there is no need to worry about the possible gains of cooperation that are vulnerable to free riding. It is simply best for an individual country to choose $a_i = a^{tp}/n$ if the other countries do the same, and this is also collectively optimal. The tipping point in the natural system, with a sufficiently large loss l of tipping, allows the countries to coordinate on a non-cooperative Nash equilibrium with the same result as when they would cooperate.

As stated earlier, behavioral threats are not common practice in international environmental agreements. However, threats in natural systems from tipping may also induce optimal behavior, but the tipping points have to be recognized and the expected loss in welfare has to be sufficiently big. An example is the expectation of substantial damage due to climate change, for a temperature increase of more than two degrees Celsius. Up to now, this has not led to emission reductions that will prevent tipping, and it remains difficult to establish an international agreement. Apparently, the expected loss in welfare is not sufficiently high. Otherwise, the model above predicts that the countries will coordinate on an international environmental agreement respecting the threshold. In such a case, the free-rider incentives are suppressed by the expected large loss of tipping, as is formalized in condition (5.13).

5.2.4 *Summary*

The previous sections first introduced the two-stage membership game to give a possible explanation, by using game theory, for the difficulty of establishing an international environmental agreement with a large number of signatories. The requirement that a coalition is internally and externally stable leads to very small stable coalitions or to larger stable coalitions with only small gains of cooperation. Moreover, two alternative models were introduced, one based on farsighted stability, and one based on the core in cooperative game theory. These models yield large stable coalitions, but they require that the countries are willing to formulate and execute threats to deviate if other countries deviate. The problem is that this does not seem to be common practice in the international political arena. In one of the amendments, the Montreal Protocol formulated trade sanctions on countries that were not part of the agreement, which can be viewed as a threat for not joining the agreement. However, these trade sanctions were never implemented because, as said earlier, technological development solved the issue. The Conferences of the Parties following the Kyoto Protocol also discussed fines on non-compliance, but these fines were never implemented either. The conclusion is that the two-stage membership game fits better with reality. This means that from the perspective of game theory, the grim conclusion of small coalitions or small gains of cooperation remains. A better design of international environmental agreements is needed to solve the basic difficulty of free riding in a prisoner's dilemma. The effect of tipping in natural systems provides some relief to this grim conclusion. If the welfare loss of tipping is sufficiently large, the countries can coordinate on a non-cooperative equilibrium that avoids tipping.

5.3 Conclusion

This lecture shows that partial cooperation may be stable in the sense that no country has an incentive to leave the agreement, but the number of cooperating countries will be small. This number becomes larger if it is expected that in case a country leaves the agreement, more countries will leave so that the free-rider benefits decrease. This threat may deter free riding and lead to what is called the farsighted stability of an agreement. In the situation that the agreement completely falls apart in case of a deviation, such a threat will hold all countries together in an agreement. The last idea is based on the γ-core concept in cooperative game theory. Other possible threats are, for example, that countries lose the benefits of trade with other countries in the agreement in the case of leaving. Up to now, these behavioral threats have not functioned in the practice of international environmental agreements. Nature can provide a threat as well. If so-called tipping can occur in an ecological system, like the climate system, free riding is suppressed if it would cause the system to tip with a sufficiently large loss of welfare. Coordination on a non-cooperative Nash equilibrium can then prevent tipping so that cooperation is not needed.

References

Barrett, S. 1994. Self-enforcing international environmental agreements. *Oxford Economic Papers* 46, 1: 878–894.

Barrett, S. 2013. Climate treaties and approaching catastrophes. *Journal of Environmental Economics and Management* 66, 2: 235–250.

Carraro, C. and Siniscalco, D. 1993. Strategies for the international protection of the environment. *Journal of Public Economics* 52, 3: 309–328.

Chander, P. and Tulkens, H. 1995. A core-theoretic solution for the design of cooperative agreements on transfrontier pollution. *International Tax and Public Finance* 2, 2: 279–293.

Chwe, M.S.-Y. 1994. Farsighted coalitional stability. *Journal of Economic Theory* 63, 2: 299–325.

d'Aspremont, C., Jacquemin, A., Gabszewicz, J., and Weymark, J. 1983. On the stability of collusive price leadership. *Canadian Journal of Economics* 16, 1: 17–25.

Finus, M. 2003. Stability and design of international environmental agreements: The case of transboundary pollution. In *The International Yearbook of Environmental and Resource Economics 2003/2004*, (eds.) Folmer, H. and Tietenberg, T. Cheltenham: Edward Elgar, pp. 82–158.

Friedman, J.W. 1986. *Game Theory with Applications to Economics.* Oxford: Oxford University Press.

Hoel, M. 1992. International environmental conventions: The case of uniform reductions of emissions. *Environmental & Resource Economics* 2, 2: 141–159.

Pavlova, Y. and de Zeeuw, A. 2013. Asymmetries in international environmental agreements. *Environment and Development Economics* 18, 1: 51–68.

Lecture 6

Renewable Resources

6.1 Introduction

Lectures 1 and 2 develop targets and instruments for policy to reduce pollution which is a by-product of production or consumption and harms the environment. This lecture switches to the other relationship with the natural environment, namely the use of resources. Some resources are easily *renewable*, such as fish and energy from the sun, but other resources such as oil and minerals take a lot of time to replenish. If the time to renew is very long on a human timescale, the resources are referred to as *non-renewable*, and they are analyzed as if the available stock on earth is fixed. If the resource is renewable, it is easy to formulate a sustainability requirement. The stock of the resource stays intact if the extraction equals the replenishment. However, if the resource is non-renewable, it is more difficult to keep this resource available. Either a substitute for the resource has to be found, or production technologies have to be developed that substitute away from using this resource (see Lecture 10). This lecture considers renewable resources, and Lecture 7 considers non-renewable resources.

This lecture has a link with Lectures 1 and 2 on pollution. Pollution starts to harm when it exceeds the assimilative capacity of the natural environment. Similarly, extraction starts to deplete the resource if it exceeds the regenerative capacity of the ecological system. These are dynamical processes. This lecture introduces techniques for analyzing dynamical models. Another important issue is the property rights on the resource. In case no property rights have been assigned, everyone has *open access* to the resource. This lecture compares this situation to the situation in which an economic agent owns the resource and manages it optimally, from an economic perspective. Both situations require an integrated bio-economic analysis. For example, a high-seas fishery is often open access, and the analysis combines the dynamics of the fish stock and the economic dynamics of entry and exit in and out of the fishery. If the fishery is under control, harvesting follows a path that takes the biological dynamics of the fish stock into account and yields the optimal net benefits from using the fishery. Resources under open access are usually referred to as *common-property* or *common-pool* resources. This lecture shows that a lack of joint management of a common-pool resource leads to substantial losses (see also Lecture 4).

This lecture has two goals. The first is to present the typical way of modeling a renewable resource. The second is to compare how the renewable resource will develop under open access and under optimal management.

Section 6.2 presents the typical model for the growth of a fish stock with biological dynamics and human intervention by harvesting fish. Section 6.3 analyzes the bio-economic model for the fishery under open access and under optimal management. Dynamical aspects of optimization are discussed for a simple model, with a formal analysis in an appendix. Section 6.4 concludes.

6.2 The Fishery Model

To be able to analyze a fishery, it is important to understand the development of the fish population over time. In 1838, Verhulst developed a model to describe the growth of a population in general. Based on his data, he needed a model where growth is initially low, because the number of individuals is small, but where growth becomes low again after a period of high growth, because the size of the population becomes a restrictive factor (for lack of food or other resources). The standard growth model is exponential, with increasing growth forever. That model assumes that at each time t, the marginal change in the size of the population $\dot{s}(t)$ is equal to a constant fraction g of the size of the population $s(t)$, i.e. $\dot{s}(t) = gs(t)$. The solution to this model is the time path $s(t) = s(0)e^{gt}$, where $s(0)$ denotes the initial size of the population. The proof for this is simply that differentiating $s(t)$ with respect to time t gives $\dot{s}(t) = gs(0)e^{gt} = gs(t)$. However, the solution to this growth model is an exponential curve that increases slowly in the beginning but increases forever and does not level off so that it does not fit to what Verhulst had observed in the data on the population dynamics. It follows that the standard growth model with a constant growth rate

$g = \dot{s}(t)/s(t)$ does not work. Therefore, he added a term to the growth model that captures the restrictive effect of a large size of the population:

$$\dot{s}(t) = gs(t)\left(1 - \frac{s(t)}{s_{\max}}\right). \tag{6.1}$$

When the size of the population $s(t)$ is still small, the term between brackets in (6.1) is close to 1, and the model behaves as the standard model, with initially low growth. However, if the size of the population $s(t)$ is close to the maximum size $s_{\max}$, this term is close to 0, and growth is small again. Growth is large in between, due to the quadratic form of the right-hand side of equation (6.1). The solution to (6.1) is the so-called *logistic growth curve* (see Appendix B). The curve starts with low growth, accelerates, levels off, and finally converges asymptotically to the level $s_{\max}$. This maximum size of the population is the size that the ecological environment can sustain. This maximum is called the *carrying capacity.*

Research on many different fisheries all over the world has shown that model (6.1) captures what is observed on fish stocks in practice quite well. This model has become the standard basic model for a fishery and even for a renewable resource in general. The parameter for the carrying capacity $s_{\max}$ plays a crucial role in equation (6.1). If the size of the fish stock $s(t)$ is smaller than $s_{\max}$, the right-hand side of (6.1) is positive and thus the fish stock grows. If the size of the fish stock $s(t)$ is larger than $s_{\max}$, the right-hand side of (6.1) is negative and the fish stock decreases. In that case, the ecological environment of the fish does not support a larger fish stock. The stock $s_{\max}$ is a *steady state* which means that for $s(t) = s_{\max}$, the right-hand side of (6.1) is 0 and the fish stock does not change. Without human intervention, the fish stock is in this steady state or returns to this steady state after disturbances. Lecture 8 considers the situation that the ecological system structurally changes and tips with a shock to the carrying capacity of the fish.

It is time now to add human intervention by harvesting fish for commercial purposes. With a *fixed* harvesting rate h, model (6.1) changes into

$$\dot{s}(t) = gs(t)\left(1 - \frac{s(t)}{s_{\max}}\right) - h := G(s(t)) - h, \quad s(0) = s_0, \tag{6.2}$$

with G denoting the growth function. Figure 6.1 pictures this growth function, as a function of the fish stock s, together with the harvesting rate h. It is immediately clear that if the harvesting rate is larger than the maximum of G, the fish stock will decline, and the fish will become extinct.

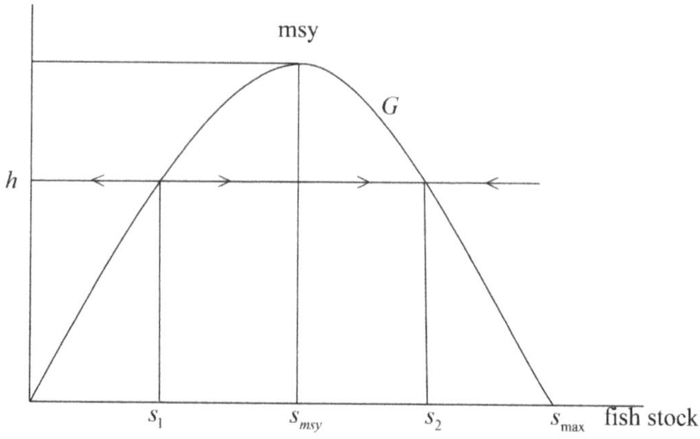

Figure 6.1. Growth and harvesting.

It is possible to harvest at the maximum of G, but this is risky, and as is seen later, this is not the outcome of economic behavior. This maximum is called the *maximum sustainable yield.* The corresponding fish stock s_{msy} equals half the fish stock $s_{\max}$ that results in the absence of human intervention. If the harvesting rate h lies between 0 and this maximum, model (6.2) has two steady states, s_1 and s_2, the intersection points of h and G. Steady state s_1 is not stable. In case of a disturbance to the left, the fish will become extinct. In case of a disturbance to the right, the fish stock will grow to s_2 because growth G is larger than harvesting h between s_1 and s_2.

6.3 The Gordon–Schaefer Model

It is time to consider the economics of the fishery. The harvested fish is sold at a market. It is assumed that the price p is constant and given. Harvesting requires an effort u in terms of labor and the use of boats and fishing gear. It is assumed that the total price w of this effort is constant and given. The success of fishing strongly depends on the density of the fish. Therefore, Schaefer (1957) suggested making the level of the harvesting rate h dependent on the stock of the fish s, the level of effort u, and a technology coefficient α in the following way:

$$h(s) = \alpha u s. \tag{6.3}$$

A better technology α, more effort u, and a bigger fish stock s yield a larger harvesting rate h. In the sequel, a distinction is made between this fishery under open access and this fishery under optimal management.

6.3.1 *Open access*

In 1954, Gordon considered the situation that everyone has access to the fishery so that economic agents will enter if profits are positive but exit if profits are negative. This means that in equilibrium, each agent has zero profits. Using harvesting rule (6.3), zero profits yield

$$ph = p\alpha us = wu \Rightarrow s = \frac{w}{\alpha p}, \tag{6.4}$$

where total revenues are given by ph and total costs are given by wu. This basic result already allows for an interesting conclusion. The stock of fish s is driven up by a high price w per unit of effort, but it is driven down by a high price p per unit of fish and by a good catching technology α. Indeed, fish stocks are under threat all over the world in case of high prices, cheap labor, and modern boats and fishing gear.

The dynamical process of entry and exit in and out of the fishery is formulated as

$$\dot{u}(t) = \varphi(ph(t) - wu(t)) = \varphi(\alpha ps(t) - w)u(t). \tag{6.5}$$

This simply means that effort u increases if the profits $ph - wu$ are positive and decreases if the profits are negative. The parameter φ indicates the speed of adjustment. In a steady state where the effort does not change, the right-hand side of (6.5) is 0 and the level of the fish stock is given by equation (6.4). Replacing the fixed harvesting level in equation (6.2) by the Schaefer harvesting rule (6.3), the combination of equations (6.2) and (6.5) is a *bio-economic* dynamical system that describes the development of a fishery, under open access. In a steady state where the fish stock does not change, the right-hand side of (6.2) is 0. With (6.3), this implies that

$$gs\left(1 - \frac{s}{s_{\max}}\right) = \alpha us \Rightarrow u = \frac{g}{\alpha}\left(1 - \frac{s}{s_{\max}}\right). \tag{6.6}$$

Equations (6.6) and (6.4) indicate the steady states of the equations (6.2) and (6.5), respectively, and are depicted as lines in the (s, u)-plane in Figure 6.2.

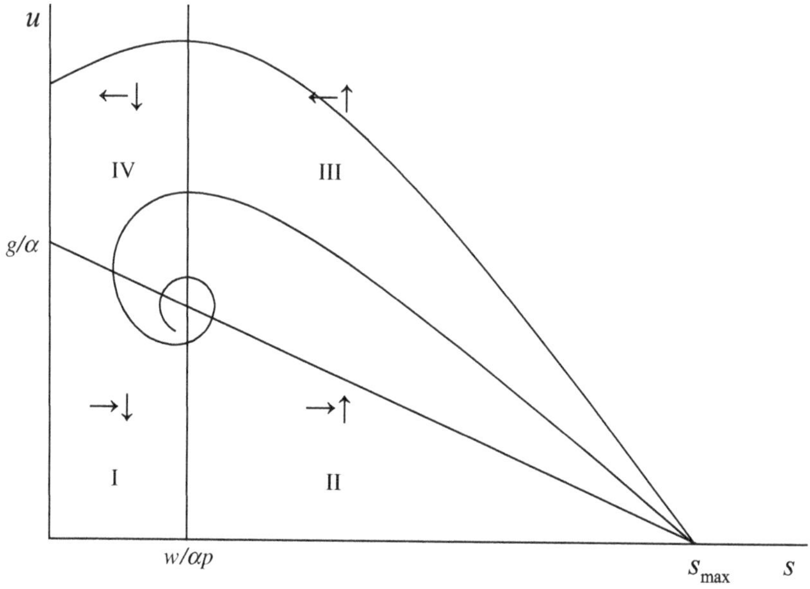

Figure 6.2. Bio-economic dynamics.

For example, if $g = 0.05$, $s_{\max} = 10$, $p = 1$, $w = 0.02$, and $\alpha = 0.01$, the lines representing equations (6.4) and (6.6) become $s = 2$ and $u = 5 - 0.5s$, respectively, so that the steady state of the bio-economic system becomes $(2, 4)$. Section 6.3.2 contains a numerical example, including optimal management, with real-world data.

Figure 6.2 is a so-called *phase diagram*. The two lines divide the plane into four areas, I, II, III, and IV. Area I is below the line representing the steady states of the equation (6.2) so that the right-hand side of (6.2) is positive and thus the fish stock s is increasing. Furthermore, area I is to the left of the line representing the steady states of equation (6.5) so that the right-hand side of (6.5) is negative and thus the effort u is decreasing. Similarly, in area II, the fish stock increases but the effort increases as well. In area III, the fish stock decreases but the effort increases, and in area IV, the fish stock and the effort decrease. This already provides much information on the path of (s, u). Figure 6.2 sketches two possible paths, starting in the natural steady state $(s_{\max}, 0)$ before harvesting (see Smith, 1968). When the curves cut the vertical steady-state line, exit out of the fishery occurs and the effort decreases. For the lower curve, the effort is sufficiently low, and the adjustment is sufficiently fast so that the curve then cuts the line representing the steady-state fish stocks. The fish stock recovers, and the curve starts to curl around and to converge to the steady state of the bio-economic system (6.2) and (6.5). However, for the upper curve, the effort is high, and the adjustment is not fast enough to prevent the fish from becoming extinct because the fish stock becomes zero. It is beyond the scope of these lecture notes to present a precise solution of the bio-economic system and a precise analysis of the curves that can occur, but it is possible to draw some general conclusions about this model for an open-access fishery.

The bio-economic model above predicts that if the fish becomes commercially attractive, the fish stock declines from the natural steady state $s_{\max}$ to the new steady state given by $w/\alpha p$, with corresponding steady-state levels of effort and harvest. The path will "overshoot" the new steady state, in the sense that the fish stock becomes lower before it finally converges to the new steady state. This means that there is a risk that the fish stock gets close to zero and that the fish thus becomes extinct, although a precise analysis is beyond the scope of these lecture notes. The new steady state is low when the cost of effort is low, the price of the fish is high, and the fishing technology is advanced. To verify the model, empirical data are needed. One of the first and most famous examples is the very old data set on the fur seal hunt in the North Pacific. At the end of the 19th century, this seal hunt started because their fur became commercially attractive. It was an open-access renewable resource before the countries that were involved in the hunt started negotiations and reached an agreement on regulating this resource in the North Pacific Fur Seal Treaty in 1911. The seal is not a fish, but the analysis is the same. Figure 6.3 shows that the data during the open-access period quite well follow the prediction of the bio-economic model (which uses different notation and has a slightly different set-up but is essentially the same as the model above). The figure was already produced in 1976, but it was not published until recently (Wilen, 2018). It has become the standard example for verification of this bio-economic model.

6.3.2 *Optimal management*

The open-access fishery model in the previous section is the appropriate model in case no property rights are assigned in the fishery. However, under the 1982 United Nations Convention on the Law of the Sea, countries have the right to manage an exclusive economic zone, 200 nautical miles out of their coast. This means that countries can try to regulate the fishery to

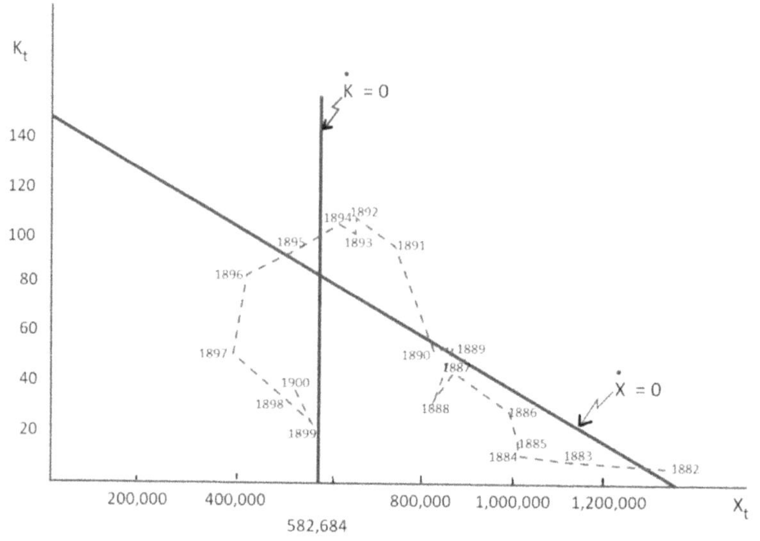

Figure 6.3. North Pacific fur seal hunt (Wilen, 2018).

achieve optimal management. In this way, it is possible to generate positive profits from the fishery, the fish stock will be higher, and the risk of extinction is under control. The exclusive economic zones can also be open-access fisheries when the countries do not regulate the fishery. On the other hand, outside these exclusive economic zones, the countries can regulate the fishery as well if they manage to reach an agreement with each other and to comply with this agreement, as in the North Pacific Fur Seal Treaty in the previous section (see also Lecture 5).

Optimal management of a fishery that is governed by the dynamical equation (6.2) requires dynamical optimization techniques. The aim is to determine the path of effort $u(t)$, resulting in a path for harvest $h(t)$ and for stock of fish $s(t)$ using equations (6.2) and (6.3), in order to maximize total (discounted) net profits. Section 6.3.4 and Appendix D return to the dynamical analysis of a simpler fishery model, but this section takes a shortcut and considers static optimization first. This section assumes that the fishery is in a sustainable steady state, where harvest $h = \alpha es$ is equal to growth $G(s)$, so that the equation (6.6) holds. Using the key assumption $h = G(s)$, it is easy to express the net profits $\Pi(s)$, which is the difference between total revenues $ph = pG(s)$ and total costs wu, in terms of the fish stock s:

$$\Pi(s) = pG(s) - wu = pgs\left(1 - \frac{s}{s_{\max}}\right) - w\frac{g}{\alpha}\left(1 - \frac{s}{s_{\max}}\right). \tag{6.7}$$

It is assumed that $w/\alpha p \leq s_{\max}$ because otherwise net profits $\Pi(s)$ are negative and no fishing will occur. The first-order condition for maximization of net profits $\Pi(s)$ yields

$$\Pi'(s) = pg\left(1 - \frac{2s}{s_{\max}}\right) + \frac{wg}{\alpha s_{\max}} = 0. \tag{6.8}$$

The second-order condition $\Pi''(s) = -2pg/s_{\max} < 0$ is fulfilled so that equation (6.8) yields the level of the fish stock for which the net profits are maximal. Rewriting equation (6.8) as

$$pg\left(1 - \frac{2s}{s_{\max}}\right) = \frac{-wg}{\alpha s_{\max}}, \tag{6.9}$$

shows that this condition simply means that the marginal total revenues (left-hand side) are equal to the marginal total costs (right-hand side). The optimal level of the fish stock is

$$s^* = 0.5\left(s_{\max} + \frac{w}{\alpha p}\right), \tag{6.10}$$

which lies midway between the carrying capacity $s_{\max}$ and the steady-state level of the fish stock under open access. Using (6.6), the optimal effort level u^* and harvest level h^* follow.

It is easy to provide a graphical representation of the maximization of net profits $\Pi(s)$. The graph of the total revenues $ph = pG(s)$ has the same shape as the graph of the growth function $G(s)$, and total costs wu are represented by a downward-sloping line, according to equation (6.6). Figure 6.4 shows the situation. The net profits are the difference between the parabola for the total revenues and the downward-sloping line for total costs. The net profits are maximal at $s = s^*$. This is precisely the point where the line tangent to the parabola is parallel to the downward-sloping line. This is another way of saying that the marginal total revenues are equal to the marginal total costs in the point $s = s^*$. The slope of the line that is tangent to the parabola is the derivative of the total revenues $pG(s)$ and is thus equal to the marginal total revenues, given by the left-hand side of condition (6.9). The slope of the downward sloping line is the derivative of the total costs wu and is thus equal to the marginal total costs, given by

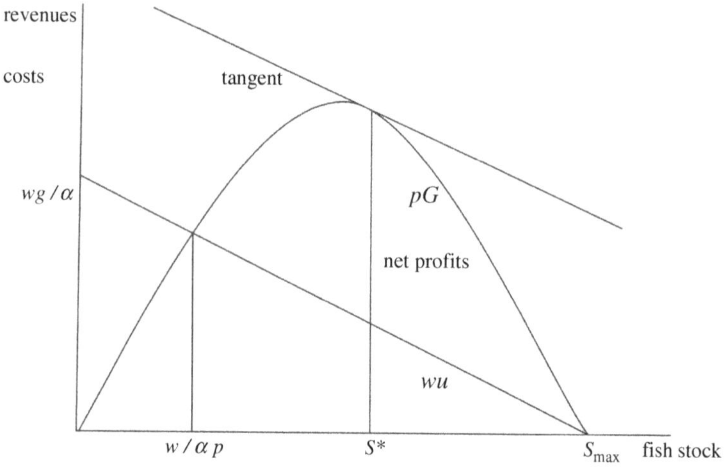

Figure 6.4. Maximization of net profits.

the right-hand side of (6.9). Note that zero profits in Figure 6.4 result at the intersection of the parabola and the downward-sloping line at $s = w/\alpha p$. This corresponds to equation (6.4) in Section 6.3.1.

Example 6.1. The blue whale (a mammal, not a fish) was abundant in all the oceans until the end of the 19th century, but it became commercially attractive, and it was hunted down close to extinction. International cooperation resulted in the International Whaling Commission. This institution adopted a moratorium on commercial whaling in 1982. Several countries, such as Japan and Norway, oppose a moratorium arguing that it is possible to hunt whales and keep the stock of blue whales at a safe sustainable level. The discussion has three positions. The first one is open access, with the risk of extinction, but no country supports this position. The second position is a moratorium, which means that the blue whale is given a high existence value and is left undisturbed in its natural environment. The third one is optimal management, which means that commercial options are accepted but existence at a sustainable level is guaranteed. It is interesting to look at some numbers. The models above are simple, but the numbers illustrate these different positions. Biologists have estimated the parameters g and $s_{\max}$ of the growth function $G(s)$ for blue whales in the Antarctic, and they have found $g = 0.05$ and $s_{\max} = 400{,}000BWU$, where BWU stands for blue-whale units. This means that without human intervention, the stock of blue whales in the Antarctic converges to $400{,}000BWU$. If u

denotes the number of whale-catching ships, a reasonable technology coefficient in the catching rule (6.3) is $\alpha = 1.25(10)^{-3}$. It is assumed that the price p is 6,000 euro per BWU, and the cost w is 600,000 euro for a whale catcher. Under open access, using (6.4), the stock of blue whale converges to $w/\alpha p = 80{,}000 BWU$ in the long run, with the risk of extinction, as was shown in Section 6.3.1. Under optimal management, the stock of blue whales is kept at $s^* = 240{,}000 BWU$ using (6.10), and the number of whale catchers is reduced from 32 in the open-access steady state to $u^* = 16$, using (6.6). Net profits from whaling increase from zero to $p\alpha u^* s^* - wu^* = 19.200.000$ euro.

6.3.3 *Regulation*

Each country can regulate an open-access fishery in their exclusive economic zone, 200 nautical miles out of their coast. Furthermore, the countries together can regulate an open-access fishery at the high seas if they manage to reach an agreement and to comply with this agreement. The benchmark of regulation is the outcome under optimal management, in which the profits are maximal, and the fish stock is higher than under open access. The number of fishing boats has to decrease, but each one of them will have a positive profit. Note that the benchmark changes if a value is attached to the fish stock for other than commercial reasons. Lecture 2 discusses policy options, and it distinguishes command-and-control, taxes, and tradable permits. It is interesting to see how these policy options work out in the context of a fishery.

Command-and-control in the context of a fishery usually means reducing fishing effort, for example, by restrictions on the boat size, the fishing gear, and the periods and the areas for fishing. This effectively means reducing the technology coefficient α in the harvesting rule (6.3). It has the ecological advantage that the fish stock resulting under open access increases, as follows from (6.4). However, restrictions on fishing technology are not advantageous from an economic perspective because the profits remain zero. Using a tax is also not a good idea in the context of a fishery. By introducing the tax, it is possible to decrease the (net) price p of fish or to increase the price w of effort so that the fish stock resulting under open access can be increased up to the optimal level s^*, as follows from (6.4). However, the fishery remains open access in this case, with zero profits for each of the economic agents. Due to these complications, taxes are hardly used for regulating a fishery in practice.

Tradable permits, or tradable quotas as it is called in the context of a fishery, are the best policy instrument for regulating this situation. The idea is to set the *total allowable catch* (TAC) at the optimal level h^* and to turn this restriction into *individual transferable quotas* (ITQs). It is not allowed to catch fish without ITQs. The total allowable catch (TAC) assures the optimal management of the fishery and tradability of the individual transferable quotas (ITQs) assures cost efficiency and dynamic efficiency. Countries like Canada, Iceland, New Zealand, Australia, and the USA already use this system successfully.

6.3.4 *Dynamics*

Dynamical optimization of the Gordon–Schaefer model is very complicated. Appendix C introduces a dynamical optimization technique, but applying this to the Gordon–Schaefer model is not easy. Section 6.3.2 takes a shortcut, assumes a sustainable or steady state where harvest equals growth, and applies static optimization without discounting. This section takes another shortcut by simplifying the fishery model to be able to look at dynamical aspects. This fishery model skips the Schaefer rule (6.3), so that harvest h becomes the choice variable, and assumes zero cost of harvesting. The objective is to maximize discounted total revenues ph over time, subject to the net growth of the fishery, given by equation (6.2). Appendix D provides the precise solution for this fishery model, using the dynamical optimization technique presented in Appendix C, but the remaining part of this section focuses on the basic ideas.

Resource models are dynamical models. It means that the economics of resource models should take into account that harvesting now affects the resource in the future. More specifically, the marginal benefit of harvesting a unit of the resource now should be compared with the marginal cost, i.e. with the marginal benefit of leaving this unit in the current stock of the resource $s(t)$. The price p is fixed, but harvesting a unit of fish now yields an interest of rp in the next period, whereas leaving this unit in the fish stock yields fish growth $G'(s(t))$, with the value $pG'(s(t))$. The earnings of harvesting a unit now or leaving it in the fish stock $s(t)$ may differ and lead to a different harvest. If $G'(s(t)) > r$, harvest h will be 0 and if $G'(s(t)) < r$, harvest h will be as large as possible. If harvest h is 0, the fish stock s grows and if harvest h is as large as possible, the fish stock s decreases. These dynamical processes meet at the point where the fish stock s is in the steady state s^*, given by $G'(s^*) = r$. In this steady state, harvest h is equal to the fish growth $G(s^*)$. The earnings rp of harvesting a unit of fish and $pG'(s^*)$ for leaving this unit in the fish stock are the same in the steady state s^*. If the initial fish stock $s_0 < s^*$, so that $G'(s_0) > r$, the optimal harvest $h^* = 0$ until the fish stock s reaches the steady state s^*, followed by the steady-state harvest $h^* = G(s^*)$. Otherwise, if $s_0 > s^*$, so that $G'(s_0) < r$, the optimal harvest h^* is as large as possible until the fish stock s reaches the steady state s^*, followed by the steady-state harvest $h^* = G(s^*)$. This solution is called a *most rapid approach path* in the theory on dynamical optimization because it is optimal to move to the steady state as quickly as possible. The steady-state condition $G'(s^*) = r$ is called the *golden rule* of the fishery, similar to the golden rule of the Ramsey growth model (Lecture 10). It is interesting to compare the result with the optimization in Section 6.3.2. First, note that the cost of harvesting in this section is assumed to be 0, whereas the cost of the harvesting effort w in Section 6.3.2 is positive. For $w = 0$, equation (6.10) shows that the optimal fish stock is $s^* = 0.5s_{\max}$. This would also be the solution of the golden rule $G'(s^*) = r$ in the case $r = 0$. The fishery model in this section shows that a positive interest rate r drives the optimal steady-state fish stock down. The analysis of the Gordon–Schaefer model in Section 6.3.2 shows that a positive cost of the harvesting effort w drives the optimal steady-state fish stock up. A dynamical optimization of the Gordon–Schaefer model is tedious, but it would yield the outcome in equation (6.10) as the optimal steady-state fish stock for $r = 0$. A positive interest rate r would drive the optimal steady-state fish stock down again.

6.3.5 *Summary*

The previous sections consider a renewable resource that is commercially attractive but is harvested under different property rights. The process of regeneration of the resource is modeled as logistic growth. This captures the generally observed phenomenon that growth starts at a low level, then accelerates, but levels off because of lack of food or other resources. The focus of the analysis is the fishery that fits the model of logistic growth quite well. However, examples in these sections show that the analysis also applies to other species. An important concept in a model of logistic growth is the carrying capacity of the natural environment.

The analysis compares the open-access regime with the regime of optimal management. Under open access, there are no property rights to the resource so that everyone has access and, as a result, profits are dissipated.

Moreover, the steady state of the renewable resource is low, and an open-access regime runs the risk of driving the resource to extinction. When property rights are assigned, or when an agreement is reached to jointly manage the resource, the situation improves considerably. Under optimal management, profits are large, and the steady state of the renewable resource is high so that the risk of extinction practically disappears. The best way to regulate such an open-access resource is to set up a system of individual transferable quotas that add up to a total allowable catch at the level of the optimal harvest.

Growth is a dynamical process, and the analysis of renewable resources therefore requires dynamical models and techniques. The model for an open-access fishery is a dynamical system that is relatively easy to analyze with the help of a phase diagram, without the need for a precise solution. However, the analysis of a renewable resource under the optimal-management regime requires dynamical optimization techniques, which are more complicated. The previous sections focus on the static steady-state optimization. For a simpler fishery model, the last section shows the main result for the dynamics. The golden rule for the fishery, i.e. the marginal growth of the fish stock is equal to the interest rate, determines the optimal steady state of the fish stock. It is optimal to move to this steady state as quickly as possible.

6.4 Conclusion

Renewable resources are resources that have the capacity to grow and renew the available stock of the resource. The standard example is a fishery, but many more resources have the same characteristics. In principle, it is possible to have sustainable development by harvesting the same amount as growth adds to the stock. The typical growth function for a fishery is the *logistic growth* function, which starts low, accelerates, levels off, and converges to the *carrying capacity*, which is the largest level of the fish stock that the natural environment can support.

This lecture distinguishes *open access*, the situation without property rights or regulation, and *optimal management*, the situation with property rights or regulation. Under open access, the resulting steady-state stock of the resource is low and close to depletion, and the profits are zero. Under optimal management, the resulting steady-state stock of the resource is high and far away from depletion, and the profits are positive. The analysis of the situation with open access uses a dynamical system in which the stock of the resource and the level of effort simultaneously change. The analysis of the situation under optimal management uses optimization techniques. Under the sustainability requirement, the optimization becomes static and relatively simple.

A full dynamical analysis of the optimal management of a resource requires a dynamical optimization technique. The dynamical analysis uses a simpler fishery model, with zero cost of harvesting. The golden rule determines the steady-state stock of the resource, analogously to the golden rule of capital accumulation in the Ramsey growth model. The optimal path is a most rapid approach path that moves to the steady state as quickly as possible.

Resource economics is a very old and broad field. This lecture only presents the basics of the analysis of renewable resources. Lecture 7 presents the basics of the analysis of non-renewable resources. For interested people, good and broad textbooks in resource economics are Dasgupta (1982), Conrad and Clark (1987), and Hartwick and Olewiler (1986).

References

Conrad, J.M. and Clark, C.W. 1987. *Natural Resource Economics: Notes and Problems*. Cambridge: Cambridge University Press.

Dasgupta, P. 1982. *The Control of Resources*. Cambridge, MA: Harvard University Press.

Gordon, H.S. 1954. The economic theory of a common-property resource: The fishery. *Journal of Political Economy* 62, 2: 124–142.

Hartwick, J.M. and Olewiler, N.D. 1986. *The Economics of Natural Resource Use*. New York: Harper & Row.

Schaefer, M.B. 1957. Some consideration of population dynamics and economics in relation to the management of the commercial marine fisheries. *Journal of the Fisheries Research Board of Canada* 14, 5: 669–681.

Smith, V.L. 1968. Economics of production from natural resources. *The American Economic Review* 58, 3: 409–431.

Verhulst, P.-F. 1838. Notice sur la loi que la population suit dans son accroissement. *Correspondence Mathématique et Physique* 10: 113–121.

Wilen, J.E. 2018. Common property resources and the dynamics of overexploitation: The case of the North Pacific fur seal. *Marine Resource Economics* 33, 3: 217–243. (this paper appeared in 1976 as a working paper at the University of British Columbia.)

Lecture 7

Non-Renewable Resources

7.1 Introduction

Lecture 6 considers resources that are easily *renewable*, with fish as the best example. This lecture considers resources for which the time to renew is very long on a human timescale, such as oil and minerals. These resources are referred to as *non-renewable*. The main difference is that renewable resources have the capacity to grow on a human timescale, but non-renewable resources grow so slowly that the analysis assumes the stock to be fixed. New discoveries of oil and minerals give some relief but in the end, the available amount on earth is limited. It follows that renewable resources can last forever as long as harvest does not exceed growth, but non-renewable resources will be depleted at some point. When a non-renewable resource is depleted, the economy has to switch to a substitute for the resource or has to do without it. Moreover, if a substitute is available at a better price, the economy will choose to switch. In any case, the main problem is to determine the optimal extraction path for the non-renewable resource.

In the early 70s of the last century, the limited availability of non-renewable resources gave rise to a big societal concern. At that time, a large group of prominent people had formed the *Club of Rome*, who had commissioned a group of scientists at MIT in Cambridge MA, USA, to investigate environmental concerns. These scientists produced the famous report *The Limits to Growth* (Meadows *et al.*, 1972). Although this report considered the environmental issues in a broad sense, the discussion focused on the limited availability of non-renewable resources, with a warning for the future. Many economists were not so much concerned because they expected that the mechanisms of scarcity, a higher price, lower use, and the search for alternatives would solve the problem. This view received support from the outcome of the famous bet between the biologist Paul Ehrlich and the economist Julian Simon (Sabin, 2013). Ehrlich could choose five minerals and set a future time, and Simon bet that the inflation-adjusted prices of these minerals at that time would not have increased, indicating that these resources had not become scarce. Simon won the bet. This does not mean that the possible depletion of non-renewable resources is not a problem. It only means that economic mechanisms delay the problem. Moreover, in the meantime, the issue has shifted. In the case of oil or other fossil fuels, for example, the issue is not so much how to optimally extract the available oil from the ground, but how to keep the oil in the ground to prevent climate change.

The main part of this chapter focuses on the optimal price path and extraction path of a non-renewable resource, in the presence of a possible substitute for the resource. This substitute is called a *backstop technology*, which is available at a certain price called the *choke price*. The non-renewable resource is used as long as the price is lower than this choke price. The core of the analysis is the *Hotelling rule* that yields the price path for a non-renewable resource. This lecture presents a model to discuss the effect of changes in the stock of the resource, the demand for the resource, the discount rate, the choke price, and the extraction costs. Most of the non-renewable resources are used in production. Given the discussion on the limits to growth, it is interesting to consider how a non-renewable resource in production affects growth (see Lecture 10).

This lecture has two goals. The first is to introduce the Hotelling rule. The second is to analyze a non-renewable resource as an asset that has to be extracted in an optimal way, and to analyze the effect of changes in the economic parameters.

Section 7.2 presents the Hotelling rule, which is the core of the analysis of non-renewable resources. Section 7.3 uses a model for the optimal extraction path of a non-renewable resource to discuss the effect of changes in important parameters. Section 7.4 concludes.

7.2 The Hotelling Rule

In 1931, Hotelling presented the basic idea for the price path of a non-renewable resource which has remained the core of the analysis ever since. He simply argued that at the margin, the owner has the choice to extract one more unit of the resource, sell this at a price p, and invest the income, or to leave this unit of the resource in the ground for later. The condition of no-arbitrage between extracting the unit now or extracting it in the future implies that the increase in the price of the resource must be the same as the result of extracting a unit now and investing the income at the interest rate r. This yields a price path where the change in the price, $\dot{p}(t)$, at each time t is equal to that result, $rp(t)$. Under perfect competition, any price path which does not satisfy this no-arbitrage condition cannot be part of an equilibrium because the owners of the resources would have an incentive to either bring forward or delay the extraction. Hotelling also showed that the welfare analysis of the optimal extraction of a non-renewable resource gives rise to the same price rule (Section 7.2.2). Similar to the basic growth model in Section 6.2, the solution to this no-arbitrage condition, $\dot{p}(t) = rp(t)$, is the price path $p(t) = p(0)e^{rt}$. This is easy to show by differentiating the right-hand side with respect to time t. The price path is called the *Hotelling rule*. The idea is very intuitive. It means that the price grows at the rate of interest. The no-arbitrage condition is similar to the condition for the golden rule of the fishery in Section 6.3.4. In that case, the price is fixed but in the steady state for the fish stock, the earnings rp of harvesting a unit of fish and $pG'(s^*)$ for leaving this unit in the fish stock are the same in the steady state s^*.

7.2.1 *Perfect competition*

This idea of Hotelling applies immediately in a perfectly competitive market. It may help to start with a two-period problem. The stock of the resource is denoted by s and the quantity of extraction by q. The initial stock of the resource is s_0. After extraction of q_0 in the first period, the stock in the second period is $s_1 = s_0 - q_0$. If the resource does not have a value anymore in the future, the entire stock s_0 will have been extracted at the end of the second period. It follows that the owner of the resource has to decide how much to extract in the first period, q_0, and how much to leave for extraction in the second period, $q_1 = s_1 = s_0 - q_0$. At the end of the second period, the value of a unit of the resource extracted in the first period is equal to $(1+r)p_0$, which is the price p_0 augmented with the interest r that can be earned on the income. In equilibrium, this value has to be equal to the price p_1 in the second period because otherwise the owner of the resource has an incentive to bring forward or to delay extraction. It follows that

$$p_1 = (1 + r)p_0, \tag{7.1}$$

which is the Hotelling rule for a two-period problem. Equation (7.1) implies that the price grows at the rate of interest. The initial price p_0 and the extraction path (q_0, q_1) follow by adding the demand equations.

Suppose that demand is represented by the linear inverse demand function $p = M - bq$. It follows that the equilibrium is given by the Hotelling rule (7.1), demand equations $p_0 = M - bq_0$ and $p_1 = M - bq_1$, and the condition that the whole stock s_0 is extracted, i.e. $q_0 + q_1 = s_0$. Demand becomes

$$q_0 = [M - p_0]/b,$$

$$q_1 = [M - (1 + r)p_0]/b,$$

so that the extraction of the whole stock s_0 implies

$$2M - (2 + r)p_0 = bs_0.$$

It follows that the initial price p_0 becomes

$$p_0 = (2M - bs_0)/(2 + r). \tag{7.2}$$

The Hotelling rule (7.1) for the price p must hold. The price path (p_0, p_1) increases with the rate of interest r, and thus the extraction path (q_0, q_1) decreases. The price path (p_0, p_1) adjusts until demand yields an extraction path (q_0, q_1) that depletes the resource. The interpretation of the initial price p_0 in (7.2) is straightforward. If the parameter M increases or the parameter b decreases, the demand schedule shifts out and the price path must shift up. If the initial stock s_0 is high, the prices must be low. If the interest rate r is high, the price increase is stronger, and thus the initial price p_0 must be lower to deplete the resource.

For example, if $s_0 = 100$, $r = 0.05$, $M = 30$, and $b = 0.2$, the Hotelling rule yields for the price in the second period $p_1 = 1.05p_0$. The demand in the first and in the second periods becomes $q_0 = 150 - 5p_0$ and $q_1 = 150 - 5.25p_0$, respectively, so that extraction of the whole stock $s_0 = 100$ implies that the initial price becomes $p_0 = 19.51$. The price path is $(p_0, p_1) = (19.51, 20.49)$, and the extraction path is $(q_0, q_1) = (52.45, 47.55)$. If $M = 35$ or $b = 0.1$, so that demand increases, the initial price goes up to $p_0 = 24.39$. If the initial stock $s_0 = 120$ or the interest rate $r = 0.06$, the initial price goes down to $p_0 = 17.56$ or $p_0 = 19.42$, respectively.

It is assumed here that the extraction costs are zero so that the owners of the resource earn interest rp on the gross price p for each unit of extraction. It is easy to extend the analysis for a constant marginal extraction cost

γ. The argument of Hotelling applies to the net price $p - \gamma$ so that the Hotelling rule (7.1) becomes $p_1 - \gamma = (1+r)(p_0 - \gamma)$, or $p_1 = (1+r)p_0 - r\gamma$. It follows that the price increase is less strong than in the case with zero extraction costs. In order to extract the whole stock s_0, the initial price p_0 must increase so that the price path (p_0, p_1) starts higher but is flatter than in the case with zero extraction costs. In the example above, if $\gamma = 2$, the price and the demand in the second period become $p_1 = 1.05p_0 - 0.1$ and $q_1 = 150.5 - 5.25p_0$, respectively, so that the initial price becomes $p_0 = 19.56 > 19.51$, with the price path $(p_0, p_1) = (19.56, 20.44)$, and with the extraction path $(q_0, q_1) = (52.2, 47.8)$. Furthermore, it is assumed that the stock of the resource s_0 is fixed. According to equation (7.2), a higher stock s_0 lowers the initial price p_0, and thus the price path (p_0, p_1). In the example, the initial stock $s_0 = 120$ yields the initial price $p_0 = 17.56$. This is the effect of an unexpected new discovery of the resource.

It is straightforward to extend the analysis to a multi-period problem. In equilibrium, it should not be beneficial for the owner of the resource to swap one unit of extraction from period 0 to period t, or vice versa. This implies that the price $p(t)$ at period t must be the same as the price $p(0)$ at period 0, augmented with compound interest, i.e.

$$p(t) = (1+r)^t \, p(0), \;\; t = 1, 2, \ldots, \tag{7.3}$$

which is the Hotelling rule for a multi-period problem. The price p grows at the rate of interest r. Given a demand schedule, the initial price adjusts so that the resource will be fully depleted. Section 7.3 investigates this issue in more detail. Appendix E shows how the Hotelling rule in continuous time follows from equation (7.3). This results in $p(t) = p(0)e^{rt}$.

7.2.2 *Welfare analysis*

Hotelling (1931) also showed that the welfare analysis of the optimal extraction of a non-renewable resource gives rise to the same price rule. It may help to start with a two-period problem and the linear inverse demand function again. At the time t, the quantity is q_t and the price is $M - bq_t$. A measure for utility U at the level of extraction q_t is the area under the inverse demand curve, which is equal to $Mq_t - 0.5bq_t^2$. It follows that the derivative $U'(q_t)$ or the marginal utility $M - bq_t$ is equal to the price. Hotelling (1931) uses the integral, i.e. the opposite of the derivative, to indicate the area under the inverse demand curve, $U(q_t) = \int_0^{q_t} p(q)dq$, so that $U'(q_t) = p(q_t)$ or the marginal utility is equal to the price. Based on this property, it is easy to connect the optimal extraction of the non-renewable resource to the price path in the two-period problem. The initial stock of the resource is s_0. If the resource does not have a value anymore at the end of the second period, the only question is how much to extract in the first period because the remainder of the resource is extracted in the second period.

Total discounted utility becomes

$$U(q_0) + \frac{1}{1+r}U(q_1), \quad q_1 = s_0 - q_0, \tag{7.4}$$

where q_0 and q_1 denote the extractions in the first and second period, and r denotes the discount rate (equal to the interest rate here). Maximization yields the first-order condition with respect to q_0. Since $dq_1/dq_0 = -1$, this yields

$$U'(q_0) + \frac{1}{1+r}U'(q_1)\frac{dq_1}{dq_0} = U'(q_0) - \frac{1}{1+r}U'(q_1) = 0. \tag{7.5}$$

Since the marginal utility is equal to the price, it follows that (7.1) holds again.

It is straightforward to extend this analysis to a multi-period problem. If $q(0), q(1), \ldots$ is the optimal path of extraction, it is not beneficial to swap one unit of extraction from period 0 to period t, or vice versa. This implies that the discounted marginal utilities are the same, i.e.

$$U'(q(0)) = \frac{1}{(1+r)^t}U'(q(t)), \quad t = 1, 2, \ldots. \tag{7.6}$$

Since the marginal utility is equal to the price, it follows that (7.3) holds. Appendix F shows the precise derivation by using a Lagrange parameter.

7.2.3 *Monopoly*

If the market structure is a monopoly, the single owner of the resource does not take the price as given but can control price and demand by taking the inverse demand function, $p(q)$, into account. The objective of the monopolist is to maximize total income

$$(1+r)p(q_0)q_0 + p(q_1)q_1, \quad q_1 = s_0 - q_0, \tag{7.7}$$

where the price p_0 is replaced by the inverse demand $p(q_0)$ and the price p_1 by $p(q_1)$. Since $dq_1/dq_0 = -1$, the first-order condition with respect to q_0 becomes

$$(1+r)[p'(q_0)q_0 + p(q_0)] = p'(q_1)q_1 + p(q_1). \tag{7.8}$$

For the monopolist, $p'(q_0)q_0 + p(q_0)$ is the marginal revenue of the extraction in the first period, and $p'(q_1)q_1 + p(q_1)$ is the marginal revenue of the extraction in the second period. Equation (7.8) is the same as equation (7.1), with the prices p_0 and p_1 replaced by the marginal revenues for the monopolist in the two periods. The conclusion is that the Hotelling rule holds again in case of a monopoly, not for prices but for marginal revenues.

Suppose that demand is represented by the linear inverse demand function $p = M - bq$. Marginal revenue is equal to $p'(q)q + p(q) = M - 2bq$. The first-order condition (7.8) becomes

$$(1 + r)(M - 2bq_0) = M - 2bq_1.$$

Using $q_1 = s_0 - q_0$, the optimal extraction in the first period is equal to

$$q_0 = (2bs_0 + rM)/2b(2 + r),$$

so that in case of a monopoly, the initial price $p_0 = M - bq_0$ is

$$p_0 = [(2 + 0.5r)M - bs_0]/(2 + r). \tag{7.9}$$

For the example in Section 7.2.1, the marginal revenue is $30 - 0.4q$, and the first-order condition $1.05(30 - 0.4q_0) = 30 - 0.4q_1$. Using $q_0 + q_1 = 100$, it follows that $q_0 = 50.61$ and $p_0 = 19.88$.

Comparing equation (7.9) with equation (7.2) shows that the initial price p_0 in case of a monopoly is higher than that in case of perfect competition so that extraction q_0 is lower in case of a monopoly than in case of perfect competition. Section 7.3.3 returns to this issue.

7.2.4 *Summary*

The Hotelling rule is the core of the analysis of the optimal extraction of a non-renewable resource. It simply says that the marginal revenue of extracting the resource grows at the rate of interest r. In case of perfect competition with zero extraction costs, this holds for the price p, but in case of monopoly, this holds for the marginal revenue. Moreover, if the extraction costs are considered, the Hotelling rule holds for the net price and not for the gross price.

Sections 7.2.1–7.2.3 derive the results for a two-period or a multi-period problem. The analysis of the general dynamical problem in continuous time requires a dynamical optimization technique. Appendix C presents Pontryagin's *maximum principle*. The technique is hard to prove, but easy to apply. By using this technique, Appendix F generalizes and extends the analysis in Sections 7.2.1–7.2.3 to the general dynamical problem.

An important issue is whether the actual prices of non-renewable resources confirm this theory and follow the prediction of the Hotelling rule. The results of empirical tests of this rule are mixed (Berck, 1995). Note, however, that the basic Hotelling rule is based on several strong assumptions, such as perfect competition, zero extraction costs, perfect foresight, and a fixed stock of the resource. The previous sections discuss some modifications to the assumptions of perfect competition, zero extraction costs, and a fixed stock of the resource. Although it remains difficult to provide precise explanations for the empirical observations, the Hotelling rule continues to be useful in providing explanations. The theory has survived for almost a century.

7.3 Optimal Extraction Path

This section assumes that at a certain point, such a resource becomes obsolete. There can be several reasons for this. Technological development can make resources obsolete. It can also happen that a substitute becomes available that is better or cheaper than the resource that is used. The reason can be that a resource is not a low-hanging fruit anymore but becomes expensive to extract so that a potential substitute becomes more attractive. Policies can make resources more expensive with the aim of lowering the use of these resources because of the pollution they generate. For example, a tax makes the use of fossil fuels more expensive to lower emissions of CO_2, which lead to climate change. Substitutes such as solar energy and wind energy become more attractive. The purpose of such a tax is to stimulate the substitution and to leave fossil fuels in the ground. However, the owners of the resource will react because the value of the remaining assets will be zero (*stranded assets*). They will change their strategies to prevent this from happening. This is a good example of the tension between a societal interest, such as avoiding climate change, and a private interest, such as maximizing profits from owning a resource.

7.3.1 *Hotelling model*

The assumption is that at a certain level of the price, called the *choke price*, the demand for the resource becomes zero. At the level of the choke price, it becomes cheaper to use a substitute for the resource or to use a substitute for the technology that does not need this resource anymore. The substitute is called a *backstop technology*. It is not in the interest of the owners to keep some of the resources after substitution has taken place because it has no value anymore. Assuming that the owners are forward-looking, they will force lower prices to sell more and deplete the resource at the time the demand for the resource becomes zero. The Hotelling rule implies that the price p grows at the rate of interest r, but the initial price $p(0)$ still has to be determined. Lowering the initial price $p(0)$ lowers the whole price path, $p(t) = p(0)e^{rt}$, and thus increases the demand for this resource over the whole extraction period up to the time T where the price reaches the choke price. In this way, the price path $p(t)$ respects the Hotelling rule and induces a total demand for the resource that is equal to the initial stock of the resource s_0.

Figure 7.1 presents the model. It has four quadrants. In the first quadrant, the price p is depicted, as a function of time t. The price path starts at $p(0)$ and reaches the choke price M at time T. The second quadrant shows the demand curve: quantity q as a function of the price p. Demand becomes zero at the choke price M. Demand is met by extraction of the resource, which is depicted in the third quadrant, as a function of time t. Extraction starts high, meeting demand for price $p(0)$, and becomes zero when demand becomes zero at time T. The fourth quadrant is empty. The area under the extraction path in the third quadrant must be equal to the total extracted quantity. If the initial stock of the resource s_0 is higher than the total extracted quantity, moving the path of extraction out in the third quadrant increases the total extracted quantity, until at some point it fully depletes the resource. This can be achieved by moving the price path down

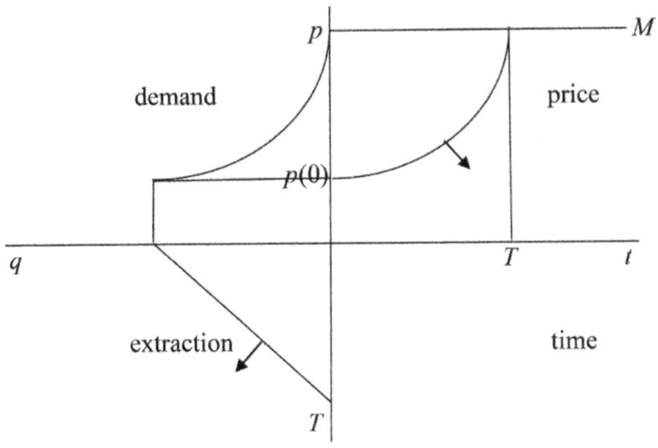

Figure 7.1. Price, demand, and extraction.

in the first quadrant, i.e. by lowering the initial price $p(0)$ and increasing the time T.

7.3.2 *Analysis*

An algebraic analysis may further clarify the model above. The question is as follows: what is the initial price $p(0)$ so that the total extraction is equal to the initial stock of the resource s_0? It is convenient to change the linear inverse demand function to (Heijman, 1990)

$$p = Me^{-bq}, \tag{7.10}$$

where b is a parameter indicating the steepness of the curve. The function (7.10) has the property that the price p is equal to the choke price M when demand q is equal to zero. For this function, a very high demand at a very low price is possible, but this is outside the range of analysis and will not play a role. The graph of the function (7.10) is depicted in the second quadrant of Figure 7.1. The price p as a function of time t follows the Hotelling rule and is depicted in the first quadrant of Figure 7.1. The price path, $p(t) = p(0)e^{rt}$, hits the choke price M at time T, which gives an equation connecting the choke price M and the time of depletion T:

$$p(0)e^{rT} = M. \tag{7.11}$$

Using the inverse demand function (7.10) in order to connect the price path $p(t)$ to the extraction path $q(t)$, and using (7.11) to substitute M, yields

$$p(0)e^{rt} = p(t) = Me^{-bq(t)} = p(0)e^{rT}e^{-bq(t)} = p(0)e^{rT-bq(t)}. \tag{7.12}$$

The extraction path $q(t)$ follows from (7.12):

$$rt = rT - bq(t) \Rightarrow q(t) = r(T-t)/b. \tag{7.13}$$

The extraction path is a line and runs from rT/b to zero. It is depicted in the third quadrant of Figure 7.1. The area under the extraction path, $0.5T(rT/b)$, is equal to the total extracted quantity, which has to be equal to the initial stock of the resource s_0. It follows that

$$0.5T(rT/b) = s_0 \Rightarrow T = \sqrt{2bs_0/r}. \tag{7.14}$$

The last step of the analysis combines (7.11) and (7.14) to solve for the initial price $p(0)$:

$$p(0) = Me^{-rT} = Me^{-\sqrt{2rbs_0}}. \tag{7.15}$$

For example, if $M = 30$, $b = 0.1$, $r = 0.05$, and $s_0 = 100$, according to equation (7.13) the extraction path becomes $q(t) = 0.5(T-t)$. The area under the extraction path is $0.25T^2$, and this is equal to the initial stock $s_0 = 100$ so that the time of depletion becomes $T = 20$. It follows that the initial price is $p(0) = 30e^{-1} = 11.04$. The price path becomes $p(t) = 11.04e^{0.05t}$, which indeed hits the choke price $M = 30$ at $t = 20$.

A higher choke price M increases $p(0)$, and this moves the price path (and the demand path) up in Figure 7.1: the substitutes for the resource are more expensive, and this allows higher prices for the resource. Equations (7.14) and (7.15) show what happens in Figure 7.1 when the parameters in the model change. The three parameters r, b, and s_0 affect the initial price $p(0)$ and the time T at which the resource is depleted. First, a higher rate of interest r lowers both the initial price $p(0)$ and the time of depletion T. The price p grows at a higher rate and starts at a lower value. In Figure 7.1, this means that the price path in the first quadrant starts lower, crosses the old price path, and reaches the choke price M in a shorter time T. Consequently, the path of extraction in the third quadrant starts higher, crosses the former extraction path, and depletes the resource in a shorter time T. Figure 7.2 depicts this effect. In the example, if $r = 0.06$, according to equation (7.13) the extraction path now becomes $q(t) = 0.6(T - t)$. The area under the extraction path is $0.3T^2$, and this is equal to the initial stock $s_0 = 100$ so that the time of depletion becomes $T = 18.26$. It follows that the initial price is $p(0) = 30e^{-1.1} = 9.99 < 11.04$. The price path becomes $p(t) = 9.99e^{0.06t}$, which indeed hits the choke price $M = 30$ at $t = 18.26 < 20$.

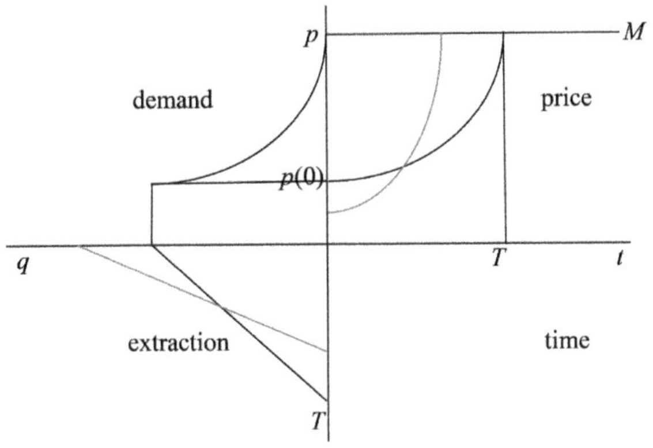

Figure 7.2. The effect of a higher interest rate r.

Second, a steeper demand curve (a larger b), which implies a drop in the demand, decreases the whole price path $p(t)$ and increases the time T, in order to deplete the resource. In the example, if $b = 0.2$, according to equation (7.13) the extraction path becomes $q(t) = 0.25(T - t)$. The area under the extraction path is $0.125T^2$, and this is equal to the initial stock $s_0 = 100$ so that the time of depletion becomes $T = 28.28$. It follows that the initial price is $p(0) = 30e^{-1.4} = 7.4$. The price path becomes $p(t) = 7.4e^{0.05t}$, which indeed hits the choke price $M = 30$ at $t = 28.28$. Finally, a larger initial stock of the resource (a larger s_0) has the same effect: it decreases the whole price path $p(t)$ and increases the time T. In the example, if $s_0 = 120$, the area under the extraction path is still $0.25T^2$ so that the time of depletion becomes $T = 21.91$. It follows that the initial price is $p(0) = 30e^{-1.1} = 9.99$. The price path becomes $p(t) = 9.99e^{0.05t}$, which indeed hits the choke price $M = 30$ at $t = 21.91$. Note that the initial price is the same as for an increase in the interest rate to $r = 0.06$, but the price path is less steep for the lower interest rate and hits the choke price later. The last result predicts that new unexpected discoveries of a non-renewable resource shift the price path down. This is indeed observed in the actual behavior of oil prices, for example.

The introduction of Section 7.3 presents the problem that a carbon tax with the purpose of stimulating a switch from fossil fuels to substitutes, such as solar energy and wind energy, may not work. The carbon tax raises the price of fossil fuels, and the idea is that the price will hit the choke price earlier so that part of the fossil fuels stays in the ground. However, the model above shows that the owners of the resource will react and force the price to change to prevent stranded assets. This is called the *green paradox* (Sinn, 2012). A carbon tax may even induce the owners of fossil fuels to accelerate the extraction.

An alternative environmental policy is to fix the maximal amount of carbon that can be emitted into the atmosphere. Climatologists argue that exceeding this carbon budget will lead to unacceptable damage (tipping point, Lecture 8). Taking account of the natural assimilation, this effectively means that the policy must limit the total amount of fossil fuels that can be extracted. It follows that such a policy reduces the initial stock of the resource s_0, which increases the price path $p(t)$ and decreases the time T where the initial stock and thus the carbon budget is exhausted, as shown in the model above. To achieve efficiency, this carbon budget (or the maximal amount of fossil fuels that can be extracted before tipping occurs) can be divided into permits or extraction rights which can be traded on a market for permits (Lecture 2).

7.3.3 *Monopoly and extraction costs*

Sections 7.2.1 and 7.2.3 present extensions of the Hotelling rule to the cases with extraction costs and with a monopoly. In case of a marginal extraction cost γ, the net price $p - \gamma$ grows at the rate of interest r. The question is what happens to the gross price path in the first quadrant of Figure 7.1. In case of monopoly, the marginal revenue $p'(q)q + p(q)$ grows at the rate of interest r. The question is what happens to the price path. The analysis starts with the first case, with a marginal extraction cost.

In the case of a constant marginal extraction cost γ, Hotelling's argument implies that the net price grows at the rate of interest. As in the two-period model in Section 7.2.1, the price path in the first quadrant of Figure 7.1 for this case follows immediately, namely

$$p(t) - \gamma = (\tilde{p}(0) - \gamma)e^{rt} \Rightarrow p(t) = (\tilde{p}(0) - \gamma)e^{rt} + \gamma. \tag{7.16}$$

The question is how the price path (7.16) relates to the price path $p(t) = p(0)e^{rt}$ that results in the case of zero extraction costs. Substituting $t = 0$, the price path $(\tilde{p}(0) - \gamma)e^{rt} + \gamma$ starts in $\tilde{p}(0)$. However, the initial price $\tilde{p}(0)$ cannot be equal to the initial price $p(0)$. The reason is that the curve $(p(0) - \gamma)e^{rt} + \gamma$ rewritten as $p(0)e^{rt} - \gamma(e^{rt} - 1)$ is *flatter* for $\gamma > 0$ than the curve $p(0)e^{rt}$ because $e^{rt} - 1 > 0$. If the initial prices $\tilde{p}(0)$ and $p(0)$ were the same, the price path (7.16) would start at the same point as the price path in Figure 7.1, but it would be flatter and lie below that price path. It follows that the extraction path in the third quadrant of Figure 7.1 would start at the same point as in the case of zero extraction costs, but it would be flatter with higher extractions. This implies that the resource would be depleted earlier, while the price path would hit the choke price M later. This cannot be the solution. Thus, the initial price $\tilde{p}(0)$ in (7.16) must be higher than the initial price $p(0)$ in the case of zero extraction costs. This confirms the result with the two-period model in Section 7.2.1. In Figure 7.1, the price path (7.16) starts higher in the first quadrant, crosses the price path in the case of zero extraction costs, and reaches the choke price M at a later time $\tilde{T}$. The extraction path in the third quadrant starts lower, crosses the old extraction path, and depletes the resource at the time $\tilde{T}$. This effect is opposite to the effect of a higher interest rate r depicted in Figure 7.2. Intuitively, this is clear because now the marginal costs γ are increased, whereas the higher interest rate r implies an upward pressure on the price p.

Returning to the example in Section 7.3.2, if $M = 30$, $b = 0.1$, $r = 0.05$, and $s_0 = 100$, the initial price with zero extraction costs is $p(0) = 11.04$.

If the extraction costs are $\gamma = 2$, the algebra is not so elegant as in Section 7.3.2 and does not lead to a linear extraction path, but the reasoning above shows that the initial price $\tilde{p}(0)$ must be higher than $p(0)$. To give an idea, suppose that $\tilde{p}(0) = 11.6$. The price path becomes $9.6e^{0.05t} + 2$, which indeed reaches the choke price $M = 30$ at a later time $\tilde{T} = 21.41 > 20$. At the choke price, demand and extraction are zero, but the initial extraction $\tilde{q}(0)$ is lower than $q(0) = 10$ because the initial price is higher. According to equation (7.10), $\tilde{q}(0) = 9.5$. The total extracted amount is approximately equal to $0.5\tilde{q}(0)\tilde{T} = 101.7$. The extraction path $\tilde{q}(t)$ starts lower but runs longer to deplete the resource.

In the case of a monopoly, Hotelling's argument applies to the marginal revenue given by $p'(q)q + p(q)$. To find the effect of a monopoly on the price path $p(t)$, it is convenient to switch back to the linear inverse demand function, i.e. $p(q) = M - bq$. In that case, the marginal revenue becomes $-bq + p$, i.e. $2p - M$, so that Hotelling's argument yields

$$2p(t) - M = (2p_m(0) - M)e^{rt} \Rightarrow p(t) = (p_m(0) - 0.5M)e^{rt} + 0.5M. \quad (7.17)$$

The question is how the price path (7.17) compares to the price path $p(t) = p(0)e^{rt}$ in the case of perfect competition. The price path (7.17) is the same as the price path (7.16), with γ replaced by $0.5M$. This implies that the conclusions carry over. The assumption of a linear inverse demand curve in the monopoly case means that the extraction path in the third quadrant of Figure 7.1 has a different curvature, but this does not change the story. The conclusion is that the price path for a monopoly starts at a higher initial price $p(0)$, crosses the price path of perfect competition, and reaches the choke price M at a later time T_m. This confirms the result with the two-period model in Section 7.2.3. It implies that the extraction path starts lower, and the depletion of the resource takes longer. Since monopoly depletes a resource more slowly than perfect competition, one might say that the monopolist is the conservationist's friend. As Solow (1974) wrote, "No doubt they would both be surprised to know it"!

7.3.4 *Summary*

The previous sections show the optimal extraction path of a non-renewable resource where the price path follows the Hotelling rule. The idea is that the growth rate of the price is given, but the initial price is still a degree of freedom that can shift the price path up and down. The demand curve connects this price path to the extraction path. By introducing the price level (*choke price*) where a substitute for the resource takes over and demand becomes zero (*backstop technology*), the optimal extraction path follows from choosing the level for the initial price such that the non-renewable resource is depleted. A higher choke price allows for higher resource prices, but a lower choke price forces the prices down to deplete the resource.

A larger initial stock of the resource lowers the initial price and thus the whole price path and extends the time of depletion. A steeper demand curve has the same effect because the increase in prices leads to lower demand and extraction so that lower prices and more time are needed to deplete the resource. A higher rate of interest increases the growth rate of the resource price. It follows that the prices are initially lower but at some point, the prices become higher so that the resource is depleted in a shorter time. The introduction of a constant marginal extraction cost has the opposite effect. The Hotelling rule applies to the net price, but the gross price follows a different path: the gross prices are initially higher but at some point, these prices become lower so that the resource is depleted in a longer time.

In case the market structure switches to a monopoly, the effect is the same as the case of adding a constant marginal cost of extraction: the prices are initially higher but at some point, the prices become lower so that the resource is depleted in a longer time. Therefore, the monopolist conserves the resource longer than perfect competition but of course, this does not mean that the welfare is higher. This lecture shows that maximizing welfare and maximizing profit under perfect competition both lead to the Hotelling rule.

Finally, the basic analysis of a renewable resource in Lecture 6 and the basic analysis of a non-renewable resource in this lecture use an argument of arbitrage between now and the future. In Lecture 6, the price of the renewable resource was fixed, and the interest on revenue from the harvest was compared with the value of natural growth in the resource. In this lecture, the interest on revenue from the extraction is compared with an increase in the price. In the analysis of this lecture, a price increase is needed to realize an equilibrium, in which the owner of the resource is indifferent between extraction now or in the future. It is not difficult to extend the analysis of this lecture to a renewable resource. The no-arbitrage condition $\dot{p}(t) = rp(t)$, which is the Hotelling rule for a non-renewable resource, changes into $\dot{p}(t) = (r - G'(s(t))p(t)$. The last part of Appendix G, equations (G.10)–(G.12), yields a formal proof. The marginal increase in the price is smaller because leaving a unit of the resource in the stock s at time t provides growth $G'(s(t))$ with the value $G'(s(t))p(t)$ so that the interest on revenue $rp(t)$ must be equal to this additional value plus the marginal increase in the price, i.e. $G'(s(t))p(t) + \dot{p}(t)$, which yields $\dot{p}(t) = (r - G'(s(t))p(t)$ as the rule for a renewable resource.

7.4 Conclusion

Non-renewable resources, such as oil and minerals, do not renew on a human timescale, so the availability is limited. Therefore, these resources are depleted at some point, which means that the economy has to substitute these resources or continue without them. This lecture focuses on the optimal extraction path under the assumption that at a certain level of the price, a substitute will be available. The core of the analysis is the *Hotelling rule*, which yields the price path of the resource. The analysis shows how the price path and optimal extraction path change, for changes in some important economic parameters. A higher initial stock of the resource or a lower demand pushes the price path down and extends the time of depletion. A higher interest rate leads to lower prices initially, but the prices increase faster, and the time of depletion comes earlier. A constant marginal extraction cost or a monopoly for the owner of the resource leads to higher prices initially, but the price path is flatter, and the time of depletion comes later.

References

Berck, P. 1995. Empirical consequences of the Hotelling principle. In *The Handbook of Environmental Economics*, (ed.) Bromley, D.W. Oxford: Blackwell.
Heijman, W. 1990. Natural resource depletion and market forms. *Wageningen Economic Papers* 90–1, Wageningen Agricultural University.
Hotelling, H. 1931. The economics of exhaustible resources. *Journal of Political Economy* 39, 2: 137–175.
Sabin, P. 2013. *The Bet: Paul Ehrlich, Julian Simon, and Our Gamble Over Earths Future.* New Haven: Yale University Press.
Sinn, H.-W. 2012. *The Green Paradox.* Cambridge, MA: The MIT Press.
Solow, R.M. 1974. The economics of resources or the resources of economics. *The American Economic Review* 64, 2: 1–14.

Lecture 8

Ecological Systems and Tipping Points

8.1 Introduction

Lecture 6 considers renewable resources such as fish in isolation, but resources are usually part of a larger ecological system. Lecture 6 shows that aggressive harvesting of fish threatens the availability of the fish and may drive the fish to extinction but affecting the ecological system, in which the fish functions, threatens the availability of the fish as well. An important concept in a fishery is the carrying capacity, which is the largest level of the fish stock that the ecological system can support. Pollution of that ecological system affects the carrying capacity and thus the options for the fishery. In general, an ecological system provides a set of ecosystem services. For example, a lake provides fish, water, and amenities for enjoying the lake, and a coral reef provides fish and colorful corals to watch. For such an ecological system, the problem is that pollution or overfishing or climate change may threaten the health of the ecological system and thus the availability of the ecosystem services that it provides.

Ecological systems often have the property that the switch from a healthy to a non-healthy state occurs suddenly, is big, and is difficult or impossible to restore. This is called a regime shift, and such a shift occurs at a so-called *tipping point* (Scheffer *et al.*, 2001). An example is the lake where at some point a small increase in the release of phosphorus on the lake shifts the lake from a so-called "oligotrophic" state to a so-called "eutrophic" state with a sudden big loss of ecosystem services (Carpenter *et al.*, 1999). Another example is the sudden "bleaching" of a coral reef (the corals turn white, and the coral reef starts dying), when the temperature of the ocean just exceeds the maximal temperature that is normal for the ocean, leading to a big loss of ecosystem services that the coral reef provides (Hughes *et al.*, 2003).

Lecture 1 yields the analysis of balancing the benefits of polluting activities and the costs of pollution. If the costs are the loss of ecosystem services, the possibility of a tipping point in the ecological system complicates the optimal management. This lecture presents the lake model with a potential tipping point that shifts up the costs of polluting the lake. Optimal management of the lake requires a dynamical optimization technique. A precise analysis is beyond the scope of these lecture notes, but this lecture discusses the results that are quite intuitive.

Lecture 6 yields the analysis of the fishery with a fixed carrying capacity. In the following analysis, the fishery model has a carrying capacity that can get a shock from tipping of the ecological system in which the fish functions. This can be modeled as a probabilistic event where the fishery shifts to a fishery with a lower carrying capacity. A precise analysis is again beyond the scope of these lecture notes, but the results are also quite intuitive. A fishery is a type of growth model and similar issues arise in other growth models, such as the Ramsey model of economic growth. In that model, a tipping point in the climate system can give a shock to the total factor productivity, which is a parameter in the production and thus in the accumulation of capital.

This lecture has two goals. The first is to introduce ecological systems with tipping points. The second is to consider optimal management of both ecological systems with tipping points and economic models with parameters that are subject to possible tipping.

Section 8.2 discusses ecological systems with tipping points. Section 8.3 presents optimal management of the lake model and considers possible tipping in growth models, such as the fishery and the Ramsey model of economic growth. Section 8.4 concludes.

8.2 Ecological Systems

The focus of ecology has shifted from studying specific species to studying the ecological system in which these species function. Resource economics is changing in the same direction. Section 6.2 studies the dynamics of the stock of fish. The natural environment in the form of the carrying capacity is important but fixed, and not subject to a possible change. The only threat to the fish is a high level of harvesting. However, the ecological system in which the fish functions may change and affect the carrying capacity. Pollution may be the cause of such a change in the ecological system but also climatic conditions or actions that affect the food chain of the system. The classical example is the pollution of a lake by the release of phosphorus from agricultural activities that decreases the availability of the ecosystem services that the lake provides, such as fish, water, and several amenities (Carpenter *et al.*, 1999). Resource economics then changes from managing a specific species to managing the ecological system. Another example is a coral reef which is a habitat for fish and provides fish and amenity values in the form of colorful corals (Hughes *et al.*, 2003). Three factors threaten the coral reefs: too high temperatures of the water because of climate change, pollution from agricultural activities on nearby lands, and overfishing in the food chain. These are examples of outside factors that threaten the ecological system but naive management of a species, such as creating an abundance of lobster in the Gulf of Maine (Steneck *et al.*, 2011), also creates a risk for the existence of the current system. A disturbance of an ecological system makes it more vulnerable and increases the risk of collapse.

8.2.1 *Tipping points*

Many ecological systems have *tipping points* (Scheffer *et al.*, 2001). For example, in the release of phosphorus on a lake, exceeding a specific level just a little bit shifts the lake into very different conditions. The original stability is lost, and the new conditions imply a sudden big loss of ecosystem services. Furthermore, reducing the level of phosphorus will not immediately shift the conditions of the lake back to the original situation. A large reduction is needed, or the shift may even be irreversible. It means that pollution of an ecological system not only leads to gradual damage, but it may at some point *tip* the system leading to a big loss of resources. The coral reef is the other example. At some point, a small increase in the temperature of the water in the ocean, due to climate change, shifts the coral reef from a healthy state to a state in which the corals turn white (this is called bleaching) and the coral reef starts dying. The website www.regimeshifts.org provides more examples. Climatologists argue that the biggest threat in climate change is a tipping point that may occur at a yet unknown level of accumulated carbon in the atmosphere, with drastic consequences for the climate on earth (Lenton and Ciscar, 2013).

8.3 The Economics of Tipping Points

Optimal management of the ecosystem services provided by an ecological system requires taking account of possible tipping points or regime shifts. There are two strands of literature. The first line of research focuses on the typical model for an ecological system with tipping points and considers the trade-off between the benefits of the activities that cause pollution of the ecosystem and the costs of losing ecosystem services, including the possibility of tipping. The second line of research considers the potential shift of a parameter in a standard economic model (such as the carrying capacity in the fishery or the productivity in an economic growth model) as a probabilistic event that is caused by tipping in the larger ecological system. The following sections discuss examples for each of these two lines of research.

8.3.1 *Tipping in the lake model*

Limnologists have studied lakes extensively and have formulated a model that captures the dynamical behavior of lakes quite well, with parameter values that reflect the differences between lakes. One of the main findings is that the accumulation of phosphorus in the lake can give rise to a tipping point (Carpenter *et al.*, 1999). The lake model is complicated, but a stylized version of the model already shows what a tipping point precisely is.

The simplified version of the lake model is given by the dynamical equation

$$\dot{P}(t) = L(t) - \left(bP(t) - \frac{P^2(t)}{P^2(t)+1}\right) := L(t) - M(P(t)), \quad P(0) = P_0, \quad (8.1)$$

where P denotes the stock of phosphorus, L denotes the loading of phosphorus on the lake, and M captures the terms describing the behavior of the lake. The terms between brackets reflect the outflow and sedimentation minus the recycling of phosphorus back into the lake. This formulation is the core of an estimated model that fits the data when modeling the dynamics of phosphorus in a lake. The parameter b differs across lakes but in the sequel, it has a value that fits the dynamics in lakes that have potential tipping points. The steady states of the phosphorus stock occur if the right-hand side of equation (8.1) is 0, or $L = M(P)$.

Figure 8.1 depicts the steady states in the (P, L)-plane for a value of the parameter b that yields a curve like this ($0.5 < b < 0.65$, see Mäler *et al.*, 2003). In Figure 8.1, $b = 0.52$, and tipping occurs at $(P, L) = (0.31, 0.074)$,

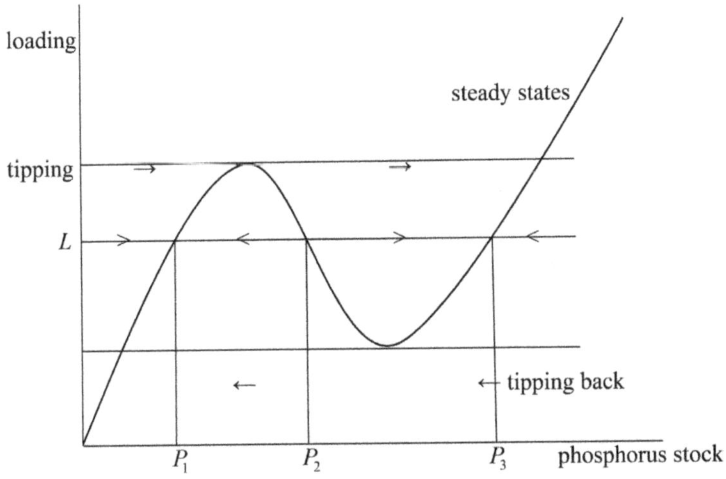

Figure 8.1. Lake model.

and tipping back occurs at $(P, L) = (0.96, 0.02)$. For a fixed level of loading $L = 0.6$, the steady state $P_1 = 0.17$ is stable because the stock of phosphorus increases to the left of P_1 and decreases to the right of P_1. Similarly, the steady state $P_3 = 1.37$ is also stable. However, the steady state $P_2 = 0.5$ in the middle is unstable. If the initial level of the phosphorus stock P_0 is smaller than P_2, the lake will end up in the steady state P_1: the level of the phosphorus stock is low, and the lake provides a high level of ecosystem services. However, if the initial level of the phosphorus stock P_0 is larger than P_2, the lake will end up in the steady state P_3, with a low level of ecosystem services.

Suppose that the lake is in the steady state P_1 and the loading L is increased. The steady state moves up along the curve, increasing the damage to the lake, but this increase is only gradual. However, when the loading reaches the top of the curve, a slight increase tips the lake to the steady state $(P, L) = (1.44, 0.074)$ with a high stock of phosphorus. This implies that at this tipping point, a small increase in the loading of phosphorus on the lake leads to a big loss of ecosystem services. Restoring the good conditions of the lake is not easy, as can be seen from Figure 8.1. The loading L has to be substantially decreased, from $L = 0.074$ to $L = 0.02$ in Figure 8.1, before the lake tips back to the steady state $(P, L) = (0.04, 0.02)$ with a low stock of phosphorus.

Ecologists have also estimated a dynamical equation for the loading of phosphorus L on the lake, with observed past data. However, normative economic models consider the question: what is the optimal path of loading $L(t)$, given the benefits of agricultural activities (that lead to the release of the phosphorus) and the costs of losing ecosystem services? The aim is to determine the path of loading $L(t)$ to maximize total discounted net benefits given by

$$\int_0^\infty e^{-\rho t}\left(B(L(t)) - \gamma D(P(t))\right) dt, \tag{8.2}$$

subject to equation (8.1), where B denotes the benefits that correspond to the loading L, D the damage costs that correspond to the level of the phosphorus stock P, ρ the discount rate, and γ the relative weight of the costs as compared to the benefits. Generally, if γ is small, the damage is not considered to be very important, so the outcome is close to business-as-usual. However, if γ is large, the damage is important and especially if tipping may occur, the agricultural activities have to be decreased or innovated in order to lower the release of phosphorus. Maximization of (8.2) subject to (8.1) is a dynamical optimization problem.

Appendix C shows how to solve this problem. By using the so-called Hamilton function $H(P, L, \lambda) = B(L) - \gamma D(P) + \lambda(L - M(P))$, the problem can be handled by solving the first-order condition $B'(L) = -\lambda$ plus the dynamical system (C.13). The first-order condition means that the marginal benefits of loading $B'(L)$ are equal to the marginal costs $-\lambda$ of increasing the stock of phosphorus. Since the analysis of the dynamical system (C.13) is complicated in this case, the full solution is beyond the scope of these lecture notes. For the specific functional form of the net benefits $\ln L - 0.5\gamma P^2$, Mäler *et al.* (2003) provide the solution. That paper shows what the effect is of the presence of a tipping point. If γ is large so that the damage of the stock of phosphorus is relatively important, the solution has one steady state in the clean area of the lake, and the optimal path of loading $L(t)$ moves the lake to this clean steady state. The combination of potential tipping with attaching high importance to the damage that can occur makes it optimal to avoid tipping or to put in the effort to move back to the clean area of the lake. If γ is small so that the damage is relatively unimportant, the solution has two steady states, one in the clean area of the lake and one in the polluted area of the lake. What will happen depends on the initial conditions of the lake. If the lake is already very dirty, it is too costly to move the lake back to the clean area, so the lake ends up in the polluted steady state. If the lake is not so dirty yet, the optimal path of loading $L(t)$ moves the lake to the clean steady state. It follows that the optimal solution is to clean up the lake except when γ is small (so that damage is considered less important) and the lake is very dirty. This also means that if ecosystem services are considered essential for life on earth, so the value of the parameter γ is effectively high, it is optimal to avoid tipping or to move back to the clean state, if possible. For example, if tipping of the climate is expected to make life on earth very difficult, it is best to stay away from a potential tipping point. This is an important motivation for the target to stay below the temperature increase of 2 degrees in the Paris Agreement in 2015. Lecture 4 shows the difficulty of international cooperation because there are incentives to deviate, so the countries end up in the non-cooperative Nash equilibrium, but Lecture 5 shows that a Nash equilibrium already avoids tipping if the costs of tipping are sufficiently high. In such a case, the high costs of tipping are a blessing in disguise.

8.3.2 *Tipping in growth models*

The second strand of literature considers standard economic models in which one of the parameters can shift, due to a tipping point in the natural environment. An example is the fishery model where the carrying capacity can shift due to tipping of the ecological system in which the fish functions (Polasky *et al.*, 2011). The carrying capacity is a parameter in the growth function for fish (see Lecture 6). Another example is the Ramsey model of economic growth where the total factor productivity can shift due to tipping of the climate with consequences for the productivity (van der Ploeg and de Zeeuw, 2019). The total factor productivity is a parameter in the production and thus in the capital accumulation.

Figure 8.2 depicts the growth functions for the fishery. If the carrying capacity shifts from $s_{\max 1}$ to $s_{\max 2}$, due to tipping in the ecological system that carries this fish, the growth function of the fishery shifts from G_1 to G_2 (Lecture 6). The tipping point is unknown, but such a shift can be modeled as a probabilistic event by means of a *hazard rate*. The hazard rate is a function of time. It denotes the conditional probability that a shift takes place, given that the shift has not taken place before. Suppose the shift is irreversible and occurs only once. It follows that optimal management has to take the probability into account that the fishery at some point shifts

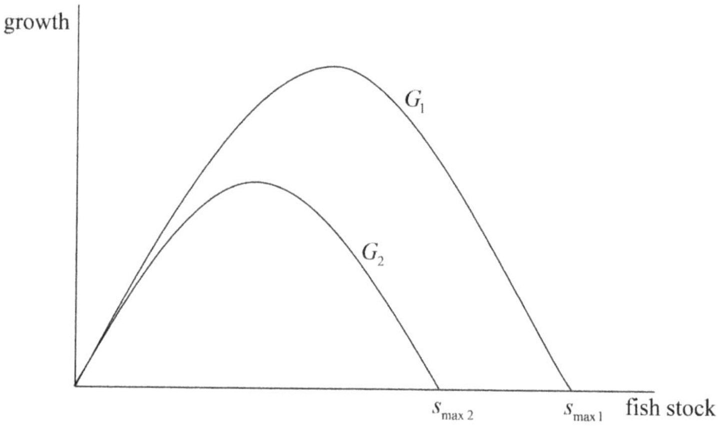

Figure 8.2. Tipping of the carrying capacity $s_{\max}$.

from a situation with a high growth G_1 of the fish stock to a situation with a low growth G_2.

The dynamics of the fish stock in equation (6.2) in Lecture 6 change into

$$\begin{aligned} \dot{s}(t) &= G_1(s(t)) - h(t), \ t < T, \ s(0) = s_0, \\ \dot{s}(t) &= G_2(s(t)) - h(t), \ t \geq T, \end{aligned} \tag{8.3}$$

where s denotes the stock of fish, h the harvesting rate, and T the tipping point. Section 6.3.4 in Lecture 6 and Appendix D show that in the absence of tipping, the optimal solution is to move as quickly as possible to the steady state of the fishery $s_1{}^*$ given by the golden rule $G_1'(s_1{}^*) = r$, where r is the interest rate. Note that after tipping has occurred, the optimal solution is to move as quickly as possible to the steady state of the fishery $s_2{}^*$ given by the golden rule $G_2'(s_2{}^*) = r$. Polasky *et al.* (2011) provide the optimal solution for the fishery in case tipping can occur. The precise analysis is complicated, but the solution is easy to understand. Before tipping occurs, it is optimal to target for the steady state $s_1{}^*$, as if there is no risk of tipping. When tipping occurs, it is optimal to adjust instantaneously to the lower $s_2{}^*$ by harvesting $s_1{}^* - s_2{}^*$ and to continue with the steady-state harvesting $h = G_2(s_2{}^*)$ after tipping.

This solution assumes that the hazard rate is fixed and thus exogenous to the problem. In that case, it is optimal to behave as usual and to adjust when tipping occurs. However, it is realistic to assume that the ecological

Table 8.1. Tipping in the fishery.

	Exogenous hazard rate	**Endogenous hazard rate**
Total collapse	Increased exploitation	Ambiguous
Regime shift	Business-as-usual	Precaution

system is more vulnerable to a regime shift in case of high harvesting and a low stock of fish. This implies that the hazard rate or the probability of tipping is endogenous and depends negatively on the stock of fish. The analysis with an endogenous hazard rate shows that before tipping, it is optimal to aim for a steady state that is larger than ${s_1}^*$. Behavior becomes precautionary: the harvest and thus the fish stock and the risk of tipping are reduced, which gives a rigorous justification of the so-called precautionary principle.

It is interesting to compare the solution in case of a shift in the carrying capacity with the solution in case of a total collapse of the fish stock. In the last case, a fixed exogenous hazard rate is the same as a discount rate in its interpretation as a risk of mortality. Indeed, the analysis shows that the hazard rate simply augments the discount rate, and the optimal solution becomes increased exploitation of the fishery. However, an endogenous hazard rate which depends negatively on the stock of fish also works the other way, and the optimal solution becomes ambiguous. Table 8.1 summarizes the optimal solution for the fishery by distinguishing the total collapse and the regime shift as well as the exogenous and the endogenous hazard rates. Nature usually recovers in some way from a shock to the system and settles into a new but different equilibrium. Therefore, the analysis with a tipping point or regime shift is more realistic than the analysis with a total collapse. In case a quick adjustment to the new situation is possible, like in the fishery, just reducing the risk of tipping becomes the optimal policy.

Another type of growth model is the Ramsey economic growth model, with the trade-off in balancing consumption c and investment in the capital stock k. The aim is to determine the path of consumption $c(t)$ to maximize the present value of utility U:

$$\int_0^\infty e^{-\rho t} U(c(t))dt, \text{ subject to } \dot{k}(t) = f(k(t)) - c(t),\ k(0) = k_0, \quad (8.4)$$

where ρ denotes the discount rate, f the production net of depreciation, and k the capital stock, with k_0 as the initial stock. The structure of the problem is the same as the structure of the fishery. Consumption is like harvesting. The stock of capital is like the stock of fish, and it grows with the production net of depreciation minus consumption. In the steady state, the consumption is equal to the net production. The steady-state capital stock k^* is also given by the golden rule $f'(k^*) = \rho$ which is standard macroeconomics (see Lecture 10). The use of fossil fuels in production leads to emissions of CO_2 that accumulate into a stock of carbon in the atmosphere, and this causes climate change. The DICE (Dynamic Integrated Climate-Economy) model integrates climate change into the Ramsey growth model by adding a module where the emissions of CO_2 lead to an increase in the temperature that causes climate change and, in this way, affects the total factor productivity in the production function (Nordhaus, 1992). Climatologists predict that at some point, the climate system will tip, and this will lead to a shock in the total factor productivity. The structure of this problem is the same as for the fishery. Tipping in the larger natural system causes a shift in one of the parameters of the economic model.

As for the growth function in the fishery, the Ramsey growth model with potential climate tipping has two production functions, $f_1(k)$ with the higher total factor productivity before climate tipping and $f_2(k)$ with the lower total factor productivity after climate tipping. Figure 8.3 depicts the production functions. In the absence of climate tipping, the steady-state capital stock ${k_1}^*$ is given by the golden rule $f_1({k_1}^*) = \rho$. After climate tipping, the steady-state capital stock ${k_2}^*$ is given by the golden rule $f_2({k_2}^*) = \rho$. There is, however, a difference with the fishery model. The behavior before climate tipping is not the same as the behavior in the absence of climate tipping. The reason is that in the Ramsey growth model, when climate tipping occurs, the adjustment to the new steady state takes time and is not instantaneous as in the fishery model. For a *CRRA* utility function with a reasonable value for the elasticity of intertemporal substitution, the steady-state capital stock before tipping is larger than ${k_1}^*$ (van der Ploeg and de Zeeuw, 2019). The reason is consumption smoothing: the optimal path prepares for a downward jump in consumption at the tipping point. The dashed line in Figure 8.3 depicts the consumption path toward the steady state after climate tipping. If the targeted steady-state capital stock before tipping is larger than ${k_1}^*$, the downward jump in consumption is smaller. The additional saving before climate tipping is a form

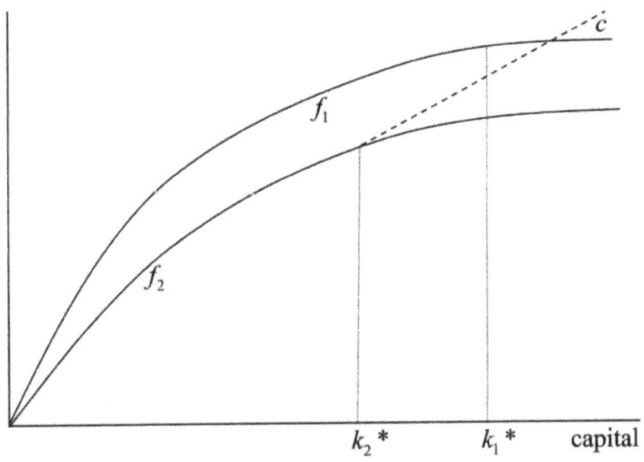

Figure 8.3. Tipping of the total factor productivity.

of precaution, but this is different from the precautionary behavior in the fishery that lowers the risk of tipping. Moreover, the higher capital stock leads to more production, and thus to more emissions and a higher risk of climate tipping.

For example, if $\rho = 0.04$, $f_1(k) = 0.4\sqrt{k}$, and $f_2(k) = 0.34\sqrt{k}$, meaning that tipping shifts the total factor productivity from 0.4 to 0.34, the golden rule $0.2(k_1{}^*)^{-0.5} = 0.04$ yields $k_1{}^* = 25$, and $0.17(k_2{}^*)^{-0.5} = 0.04$ yields $k_2{}^* = 18$. After tipping, the consumption path converges back to the steady state $(k_2{}^*, f_2(k_2{}^*) = (18, 1.44)$. It passes below the steady state $(k_1{}^*, f_1(k_1{}^*) = (25, 2)$, which implies that the jump down to this consumption path is smaller if the targeted capital stock before tipping is larger than $k_1{}^* = 25$. The reason for lowering the jump is consumption smoothing, and the additional saving is a form of precaution.

The emissions of CO_2 and the accumulated stock of carbon in the atmosphere matter when the hazard rate is endogenous and depends positively on the stock of carbon. In that case, lowering emissions lowers the stock of carbon and thus lowers the risk of climate tipping. It follows that besides the additional saving, the optimal policy before tipping requires an additional tax on CO_2 emissions to reduce the risk of climate tipping. Calibrated models of the economy show that the additional saving is small, but the additional tax is large as compared to the regular tax that corrects for the gradual damage of climate change. The structural change that results from climate tipping is so damaging that a high tax is required to reduce this risk.

8.3.3 *Summary*

A new development in resource economics is to consider ecological systems as a whole or when considering specific species, to take account of possible changes in the ecological systems. This also connects pollution and resources. Ecological systems often have tipping points, where a small increase in pollution causes a non-marginal loss of ecosystem services. This section shows what a tipping point is by using a stylized version of the lake model.

Since the models of ecological systems with tipping points are complicated, the analysis of optimal management is complicated as well. This section only reports some typical results. In general, an ecological system can be in a healthy state with a high level of ecosystem services or in a non-healthy state with a low level of ecosystem services. Tipping shifts the ecological system from a healthy state to a non-healthy state. Tipping back to a healthy state may be possible but it requires a large reduction of pollution. It is optimal to stay below the tipping point, or to tip back to a healthy state, if the damage of the loss of ecosystem services is considered important compared to the benefits of the activities that cause the pollution. If the damage is considered less important, the ecological system stays clean if it starts clean. However, if in this case the ecological system is already heavily polluted, a clean-up is not the best thing to do.

Another development in research is to consider the effect in standard economic analyses of possible tipping in the natural environment. An example in renewable resource economics is the carrying capacity in a fishery that can shift due to a tipping point in the ecological system. An example in macroeconomics is the total factor productivity in the Ramsey growth model that can shift due to a climate tipping point. Tipping in these analyses is a probabilistic event. The analysis is complicated, and this section only reports general results. When the hazard rate is endogenous, the optimal steady-state fish stock is larger than in the absence of a tipping point because it reduces the risk of tipping: harvesting becomes precautionary. The optimal steady-state capital stock in the Ramsey growth model is larger, for exogenous and endogenous hazard rates, but the reason is different: the additional saving reduces the downward jump in consumption at the climate tipping point. When the hazard rate is endogenous in the Ramsey model, the optimal tax on emissions is much larger than in the absence of a climate tipping point because a lower stock of carbon in the atmosphere reduces the risk of climate tipping.

8.4 Conclusion

Renewable resource economics follows ecology and extends the focus from managing a specific species to managing the larger ecological system. This approach also connects pollution and resources. An important concept in the analysis of ecological systems is a *tipping point* where a small increase in pollution leads to a big loss of ecosystem services. It is difficult and it may be even impossible to restore the healthy state of the ecological system. In one strand of the literature, an explicit model exists for the ecological system with a tipping point (e.g. the lake model). If the costs of losing ecosystem services are considered important, optimal management of the ecological system is to prevent tipping or to restore the healthy state. If an explicit model for the ecological system does not exist, tipping can be modeled as a probabilistic event. In this strand of literature, optimal management of a fishery, for example, takes the probability into account that the carrying capacity can shift to a lower level. If the probability of tipping is fixed and exogenous, harvesting behavior does not change but adjusts when tipping occurs. However, if the probability of tipping is lower for a higher fish stock, behavior becomes precautionary. In case of a total collapse of the fish stock, harvesting increases. Tipping can also occur in the climate system and lead to a shock in the total factor productivity in the Ramsey growth model. Even if the probability of tipping is fixed and exogenous, additional saving targets for a higher steady-state capital stock than in the absence of climate tipping, to smooth consumption. If the probability of climate tipping is higher for a higher stock of carbon in the atmosphere, optimal policy requires a significantly higher tax on emissions than in the absence of climate tipping.

References

Carpenter, S.R., Ludwig, D., and Brock, W.A. 1999. Management of eutrophication for lakes subject to potentially irreversible change. *Ecological Applications* 9, 3: 751–771.

Hughes, T.P., *et al.* 2003. Climate change, human impacts, and the resilience of coral reefs. *Science* 301, 5635: 929–933.

Lenton, T.M. and Ciscar, J.-C. 2013. Integrating tipping points into climate impact assessments. *Climate Change* 117, 3: 585–597.

Mäler, K.-G., Xepapadeas, A., and de Zeeuw, A. 2003. The economics of shallow lakes. *Environmental & Resource Economics* 26, 4: 603–624.

Nordhaus, W.D. 1992. The DICE model: Background and structure of a dynamic integrated climate-economy model of the economics of global warming. *Cowles Foundation Discussion Papers* 1009, Yale University.

van der Ploeg, F. and de Zeeuw, A. 2019. Pricing carbon and adjusting capital in order to fend off climate catastrophes. *Environmental & Resource Economics* 72, 1: 29–50.

Polasky, S., de Zeeuw, A., and Wagener, F. 2011. Optimal management with potential regime shifts. *Journal of Environmental Economics and Management* 62, 2: 229–240.

Scheffer, M., Carpenter, S., Foley, J.A., Folke, C., and Walker, B. 2001. Catastrophic shifts in ecosystems. *Nature* 413: 591–596.

Steneck, R.S., *et al.* 2011. Creation of a gilded trap by the high economic value of the Maine lobster fishery. *Conservation Biology* 25, 5: 904–912.

Lecture 9

Stock Pollution

9.1 Introduction

Lectures 1 and 2 provide a static analysis of pollution targets and instruments. This means that the analysis applies to flow pollution where the emissions such as noise are instantaneous and immediately disappear. However, most pollution problems are stock-pollution problems where emissions accumulate into a stock of pollution which causes damage. A good example is the emission of greenhouse gases that accumulate into a stock of greenhouse gases in the atmosphere which causes climate change with damaging consequences such as the melting of ice, the different precipitation patterns, and the increased occurrence of storms and flooding. Lecture 7 considers the optimal extraction of non-renewable resources such as oil and other fossil fuels, which renew slowly and therefore have a limited supply. Societal concern has shifted attention over time from the limited availability of these resources to the threat of climate change, so the analysis of stock pollution has become important.

Production that uses fossil fuels causes emissions of CO_2 that accumulate in the atmosphere and lead to climate change. In its simplest form, the analysis maximizes the benefits of production minus the damage of the stock pollution. The analysis requires the use of a dynamical optimization technique, but considering the steady state already provides the main result. The optimum results when the marginal benefits are equal to the marginal damages, which are now the present value of all future marginal damages because the emissions stay in the stock of pollution until they are fully assimilated by nature. The tax rate that the government has to levy now to correct for the pollution externalities is equal to the total marginal damage. The dynamical optimization technique provides a dynamical system in the stock of pollution and the total marginal damage. The solution of this dynamical system yields the time path toward the steady state. Note that production is the central concept in economic growth. Since the emissions of CO_2 are an output of production and the use of fossil fuels is an input into production, the main results of Lectures 7 and 9 return in the analysis of economic growth and the environment (Lecture 10).

Climate change is a global stock-pollution problem. This means that the countries have to levy the worldwide optimal tax to correct for all the externalities. However, the countries have an incentive to lower the tax rate to only correct for the externalities within the country and not for the externalities to the other countries. This is another example of the game called the prisoner's dilemma (Lecture 4). The cooperative outcome yields a higher tax rate than the non-cooperative Nash equilibrium. The production is lower, with lower benefits, but the stock of pollution is much lower, so the net benefits are higher in case the countries cooperate.

This lecture has two goals. The first is to present the dynamical analysis of stock-pollution problems. The second is to return to game theory, with non-cooperative and cooperative behavior, for the analysis of global stock-pollution problems.

Section 9.2 analyzes the local stock-pollution problems. Section 9.3 analyzes global stock-pollution problems. Section 9.4 concludes.

9.2 Stock Pollution

While in the early 70s of the last century the limited availability of oil and other fossil fuels was a big societal concern, attention shifted in the late 80s of the last century to climate change as the consequence of the use of oil and other fossil fuels. Climate change is a problem of stock pollution. The emissions of CO_2 accumulate in the atmosphere and block the return of solar radiation, which causes warming and several climate effects such as the melting of ice, the different precipitation patterns, and the increased occurrence of storms and flooding. There are two sides to the problem: the threat of depletion of non-renewable resources, such as oil and other fossil fuels, and the threat of pollution, such as climate change. Lecture 7 focused on the resource side. This section focuses on the pollution side.

9.2.1 *Emissions and stock pollution*

The use of oil and other fossil fuels leads to the emissions of CO_2 that accumulate in the atmosphere. Accumulation is the opposite of extraction. The extraction of fossil fuels gradually decreases an initial stock of fossil fuels, whereas the emissions of CO_2 from burning fossil fuels gradually increase the stock of carbon in the atmosphere. The natural environment assimilates part of the stock. The CO_2 emissions net of assimilation add to the stock of carbon, which is the cause of climate change. This means that production not only is affected by the availability of non-renewable resources but also leads to the external effect of emissions as a by-product of production y. In the social optimum, a trade-off is made between the benefits of production and the damages of climate change (e.g. Keeler *et al.*, 1972; Nordhaus, 1992).

Emissions are also denoted by y, assuming a one-to-one relation to production y, with a proper choice of dimensions. Accumulation of pollution means that at each time t, the increase in the stock of pollution is equal to the flow of emissions net of assimilation:

$$\begin{aligned} \dot{x}(t) &= y(t) - \delta x(t), \\ x(0) &= x_0, \end{aligned} \tag{9.1}$$

where x denotes the stock of pollution, δ the rate of assimilation by the natural environment, and x_0 the initial stock of pollution. Equation (9.1) is in a way the opposite of equation (6.2) for the growth of a fish stock in Lecture 6. The fish stock grows if the natural growth is larger than the human harvesting. The stock of pollution x grows if the human emissions y are larger than the natural assimilation δx. The objective is to balance the benefits B of the production y and the damages D of the resulting stock of pollution x. As in Lecture 6 for a fishery and in Lecture 7 for the optimal extraction of a non-renewable resource, the problem can be solved with a dynamical optimization technique. Appendix I provides the analysis with the dynamical equation (9.1) for the stock of pollution x, but the main text develops the results for the multi-period version of (9.1), i.e. $x(t+1) - x(t) = y(t) - \delta x(t), t = 0, 1, 2, \ldots$.

9.2.2 *Multi-period analysis*

Suppose that the benefits are given by $B(y) = \beta y - 0.5y^2$, and the damages are given by $D(x) = 0.5\gamma x^2$. In the case of flow pollution, damages depend instantaneously on emissions or production y, so $x = y$. The optimality condition that marginal benefits $\beta - y$ are equal to marginal damages γy yields $y = \beta/(1+\gamma)$. Production y will decrease from its "bliss point" β to $\beta/(1+\gamma)$, taking account of the damages caused by the emissions y. However, in the case of stock pollution, emissions y increase the stock of pollution x and remain part of this stock as far as natural assimilation δy does not remove the increase. Marginal benefits $\beta - y$ stay the same, but marginal damages γx change in the case of stock pollution and become the sum of a series of marginal damages over time. In each period, natural assimilation lowers the increase in the stock by a factor $1-\delta$, and discounting lowers the marginal damages by the discount factor $1/(1+\rho)$. The optimality condition that the marginal benefits $\beta - y(0)$ at time $t = 0$ are equal to the sum of a series of marginal damages $\gamma x(t), t = 1, 2, \ldots$ yields

$$\beta - y(0) = \frac{1}{1+\rho}\gamma x(1) + \frac{1-\delta}{(1+\rho)^2}\gamma x(2) + \frac{(1-\delta)^2}{(1+\rho)^3}\gamma x(3) + \cdots. \tag{9.2}$$

In the steady state (y^*, x^*), equation (9.2) becomes

$$\beta - y^* = \left(\frac{1}{1+\rho} + \frac{1-\delta}{(1+\rho)^2} + \frac{(1-\delta)^2}{(1+\rho)^3} + \cdots\right)\gamma x^* = \frac{1}{\rho+\delta}\gamma x^*, \tag{9.3}$$

where the calculation of the sum of the series between brackets uses the formula for the sum of a geometric series (Appendix H). It cannot be optimal to accumulate pollution forever, so the accumulation must come to a stop in a steady state. An interpretation of the optimality condition (9.3) is very easy. The instantaneous marginal benefits $\beta - y^*$ are equal to the present value of all future marginal damages γx^* discounted by the discount rate ρ plus the assimilation rate δ. If the discount rate ρ is high, the future damages weigh less in the optimization. If the assimilation rate δ is high, nature assimilates a large part of the emissions preventing future damages. Using the steady-state condition $y^* = \delta x^*$, the optimal steady state (y^*, x^*) becomes

$$y^* = \frac{\beta\delta(\rho+\delta)}{\gamma+\delta(\rho+\delta)}, \quad x^* = \frac{\beta(\rho+\delta)}{\gamma+\delta(\rho+\delta)}. \tag{9.4}$$

This optimal production y^* differs from the optimal production $y = \beta/(1+\gamma)$ in the case of flow pollution, unless $\delta = 1$ (meaning that nature assimilates all pollution as in the case of noise) and $\rho = 0$ (meaning that damage is instantaneous). Future damages depend on the discount rate ρ and the assimilation rate δ. In the steady state, emissions y^* are equal to the natural assimilation δx^*. The stock of pollution accumulates up to x^*. Section 9.2.4 considers the dynamics.

For example, if $\beta = 0.2$, $\gamma = 0.005$, $\delta = 0.05$, and $\rho = 0.03$, the optimality condition in the steady state for stock pollution is $0.2 - y^* = 0.005x^*/0.08 = 0.0625x^*$. The marginal damages are the sum $0.005x^*/1.03 + (0.95)0.005x^*/1.06 + \cdots$. Using the steady-state condition $y^* = 0.05x^*$, the optimal steady state becomes $(y^*, x^*) = (0.089, 1.78)$.

9.2.3 *Taxes*

Lecture 2 shows that a tax on emissions (which in the simple model of Section 9.2 is a tax on production) can lower production y to the optimal level when taking the damage of pollution into account. The benefits after tax become $B(y) = \beta y - 0.5y^2 - \tau y$, where τ denotes the tax rate. The optimality condition becomes $\beta - y = \tau$, i.e. the marginal benefits are equal to the tax rate. The idea is that when the tax rate is equal to the marginal damage at the optimal level of emissions, the production will adjust to the optimal level. Such a tax is called the *Pigouvian* tax, which was introduced in Lecture 2. Figure 9.1 depicts the situation. The previous section shows that in the case of flow pollution, the optimal level of production is $y = \beta/(1 + \gamma)$, and the marginal damage at the optimal level of emissions is

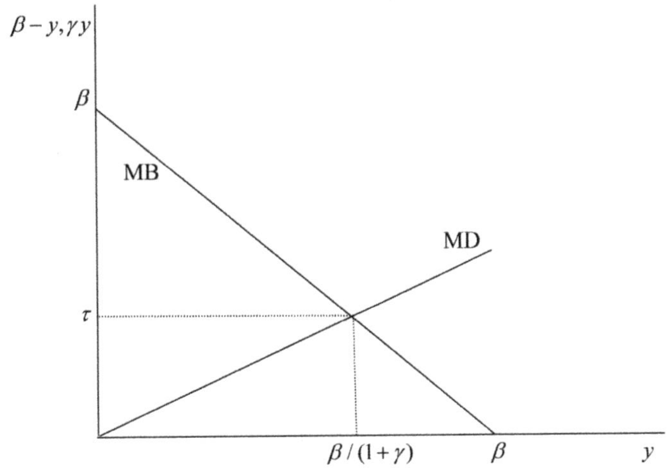

Figure 9.1. Pigouvian tax rate for flow pollution.

$\gamma\beta/(1+\gamma)$. If the government levies this tax rate, the optimality condition for private production is $\beta - y = \gamma\beta/(1+\gamma)$, which realizes $y = \beta/(1+\gamma)$.

In the case of stock pollution, the idea is essentially the same. The only difference is that the marginal damage is the present value of a stream of all future marginal damages. In the steady state (y^*, x^*), equation (9.3) shows that total marginal damage is equal to $\gamma x^*/(\rho+\delta)$. Using the optimal level of the stock of pollution x^* in (9.4), the tax rate τ^* becomes

$$\tau^* = \frac{\beta\gamma}{\gamma + \delta(\rho+\delta)}. \tag{9.5}$$

If the government levies the tax rate τ^*, the optimality condition is $\beta - y = \tau^*$, which realizes y^* in (9.4) as the optimal level of production. In the example, $\tau^* = 0.111$, so $y^* = 0.089$.

9.2.4 *Time path*

Before the steady state (y^*, x^*) is reached, the analysis is complicated. The issue is how to determine the total marginal damage or the tax rate (and thus the optimal level of production or emissions) on the time path toward the steady state. The problem is that the total marginal damage on the right-hand side of (9.2), determining the optimal level $y(0)$, is forward-looking. It requires knowing the future values of the stock of pollution $x(t), t = 1, 2, \ldots$, to be able to calculate the future marginal damages $\gamma x(t), t = 1, 2, \ldots$. The solution results by casting this into a backward recursive process, starting with the steady state values for the stock of pollution x^*, given by equation (9.4), and for the total marginal damages, denoted by μ^* and given by the tax rate τ^* in equation (9.5). Using the state equation, it is possible now to calculate the state x and the total marginal damages μ one step before the steady state is reached. Step by step, backward in time, this process yields the time path $(x(t), \mu(t))$, which at some time t hits the initial condition for the stock of pollution $x(0) = x_0$ in equation (9.1). The resulting $\mu(0)$ is the tax rate $\tau(0)$ at time 0, and $y(0) = \beta - \tau(0)$ is the optimal level of the production or emissions. Turning the time again, the path of the tax rate $\tau(t) = \mu(t)$ that was found yields the paths for the optimal production or emissions $y(t)$ and for the stock of pollution $x(t)$. In practice, it is difficult to change the tax rate all the time. Therefore, it is common practice to levy the steady-state tax rate τ^* in equation (9.5), which becomes optimal when the steady state is reached.

It is time to return to Section 9.2.1, with the accumulation of the stock of pollution (9.1) in continuous time. Appendix I derives the results using a dynamical optimization technique and provides the dynamical system in the state x and the total marginal damages μ

$$\dot{x}(t) = \beta - \mu(t) - \delta x(t), \quad x(0) = x_0,$$
$$\dot{\mu}(t) = (\rho + \delta)\mu(t) - \gamma x(t). \tag{I.5}$$

The steady-state conditions for the system (I.5) yield the same (x^*, μ^*) as in equations (9.4) and (9.5) (note that $\tau^* = \mu^*$). The variable x has the initial condition x_0, but the variable μ does not have an initial condition. However, optimality requires that the optimal path $(x(t), \mu(t))$ converges to the steady state (x^*, μ^*). It is possible again to find this optimal path by starting close to the steady state and by working backward in time until the path hits the initial condition $x(0) = x_0$. This yields the initial condition $\mu(0)$, which is a similar process as finding $p(0)$ in Section 7.3 in Lecture 7. Note that in the process backward in time, the time derivatives $\dot{x}(t)$ and $\dot{\mu}(t)$ change sign. In this specific case, where the equations of (I.5) are both linear, it is possible to simplify the problem by postulating a linear relationship between the variables x and μ, but it is beyond the scope of these lecture notes to provide a complete analysis. However, a simple graphical analysis may help to understand the result.

Section 6.3.1 in Lecture 6 uses a so-called *phase diagram* to depict solutions of a dynamical system. Figure 9.2 depicts the phase diagram for the dynamical system in (I.5). The steady states of the two equations in (I.5)

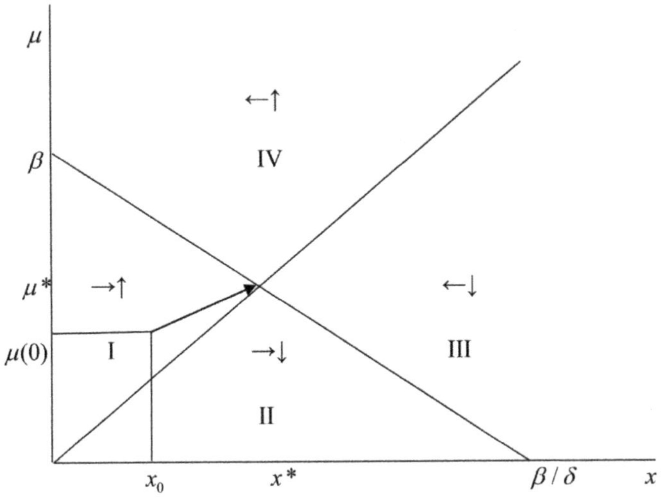

Figure 9.2. System dynamics.

are given by the conditions $\beta - \mu - \delta x = 0$ and $(\rho + \delta)\mu - \gamma x = 0$, respectively, and are depicted as two lines in the (x, μ)-plane in Figure 9.2. The two lines divide the plane into four areas, i.e. I, II, III, and IV. Area I is below the line representing the steady states of x, so the right-hand side of the first equation of (I.5) is positive and the stock of pollution x is increasing. Area I is also above the line representing the steady states of μ, so the right-hand side of the second equation of (I.5) is positive and the total marginal damage (which is equal to the tax rate) μ is increasing. Similarly, in area II, the pollution stock still increases but the tax rate decreases. In area III, the pollution stock and the tax rate decrease both, and in area IV, the pollution stock still decreases but the tax rate now increases. This already gives much information on the optimal path of $(x(t), \mu(t))$. If the initial level of the pollution stock x_0 is lower than the steady-state level x^*, the initial level of tax rate $\mu(0)$ must be sufficiently high but still below the steady-state level μ^* so that the optimal path of $(x(t), \mu(t))$ starts in area I and moves upward and to the right toward the steady state (x^*, μ^*): see Figure 9.2. Finding the precise path usually requires a computer package. Many computer packages for optimal control problems are available and work according to the idea presented above. These packages solve what is called a two-point boundary value problem, with initial conditions and conditions in the long run.

9.2.5 *Connecting resources and pollution*

Section 7.2.2 formulates welfare maximization subject to the extraction of a non-renewable resource, where welfare is direct utility of the extracted quantity. Section 9.2.2 formulates welfare maximization subject to the accumulation of stock pollution, where welfare is the benefit of the production minus the damage of the stock pollution. These are building blocks for a more general welfare analysis. The non-renewable resource is an input into the production. Welfare is the utility of the consumption minus the damage of the stock pollution. Production splits into consumption and investment in capital. The capital accumulates by the investment, net of depreciation, and is another input into the production (Ramsey growth model, see also Section 8.3.2). Welfare analysis requires determining the paths of the resource extraction $q(t)$ and the consumption $c(t)$, with the aim to maximize the present value of the total net welfare

$$\int_0^{\infty} e^{-\rho t}[U(c(t)) - D(x(t))]dt, \tag{9.6}$$

where U denotes utility, D damage, and ρ the discount rate, subject to

$$\begin{aligned}
\dot{s}(t) &= -q(t), s(0) = s_0, \\
\dot{x}(t) &= e(t) - \delta x(t), x(0) = x_0, \\
\dot{k}(t) &= f(k(t), q(t)) - c(t), k(0) = k_0,
\end{aligned} \tag{9.7}$$

where s denotes the stock of the resource, q the resource extraction, x the stock of pollution, e the emissions, δ the natural assimilation rate, k the stock of capital, and f the production net of depreciation, with s_0, x_0, and k_0 as the initial stocks. By connecting emissions with production, the problem is well defined. This is a standard Ramsey growth model from macroeconomics with a non-renewable resource as an additional input into the production, and emissions causing stock pollution as an additional output. A good example is the output of CO_2 emissions, causing climate change, from using fossil fuels as an input into the production. It is possible to solve the problem with a dynamical optimization technique, but this is beyond the scope of these lecture notes. The results of the analyses in this lecture and Lecture 7, however, carry over. The Hotelling rule gives the price path and the optimal extraction path for the resource. This price is the shadow value for reducing the stock of the resource in the first equation in (9.7). The shadow value for the second equation in (9.7) yields the tax rate on emissions as the discounted sum of all the future marginal damages of the stock of pollution. Finally, the shadow value for the third equation in (9.7) leads to the standard result in macroeconomics on balancing consumption and investment. Lecture 10 returns to the issue of growth and the environment.

9.2.6 *Summary*

The previous sections focus on the pollution that arises from using resources in production, such as greenhouse gas emissions that arise from using fossil fuels and cause climate change. The emissions accumulate into a stock of pollution. The analysis abstracts from the relation between the inputs and outputs in the production function and focuses on the trade-off between the benefits of production and the damage of the stock pollution. The main difference with the flow pollution in Lectures 1 and 2 is that the stock pollution requires that marginal benefits are equal to the present value of all future marginal damages, and not to the instantaneous marginal damage. This yields again a tax rate that the government levies for correcting the pollution externality. Since it is a dynamical optimization problem, the optimal tax rate changes over time, but the optimal steady-state tax rate is a good option to use in practice.

A precise analysis of stock pollution requires the use of a dynamical optimization technique (see Appendix I). This leads to a two-dimensional dynamical system in the stock of pollution and the shadow value (or the tax) of a change in the stock of pollution. The dynamics of this system can be represented in a phase diagram to give a picture of the development over time of the stock of pollution and the shadow value or the tax.

Connecting the use of a non-renewable resource and the resulting emissions by introducing a production function and adding the extraction of a non-renewable resource (from Lecture 7) and the accumulation of the emissions (considered in this lecture) to an economic growth model with production, provides a model for the maximization of the utility of consumption minus the damage of the stock pollution. This issue returns in Lecture 10.

9.3 Global Stock Pollution

The previous sections assume that the policymaker can levy a tax on emissions to correct for the pollution externality. However, in the case of a global stock-pollution problem like climate change, there is not a world government with an immediate mandate to levy a worldwide tax. The countries can decide to enter an agreement and to levy a tax together, but if they fail to reach an agreement, each country levies a tax on their own. Such a tax corrects for the pollution externality within the country but not for the pollution externalities to the other countries. This section shows the difference between the full cooperative tax and the non-cooperative tax and is the extension to stock pollution of the basic issues in Lectures 4 and 5.

Suppose that n identical countries are involved. Each country i, $i = 1, 2, \ldots, n$, produces or emits y_i, and the global stock of pollution x accumulates according to

$$x(t+1) - x(t) = \sum_{i=1}^{n} y_i(t) - \delta x(t), \quad x(0) = x_0. \tag{9.8}$$

The benefits in country i, $i = 1, 2, \ldots, n$, are given by $B(y_i) = \beta y_i - 0.5 y_i^2$, and the global damages to each country (a public bad) are given by $D(x) = 0.5\gamma x^2$. In case the countries do not reach an agreement, each country ignores the damage that the emissions of that country cause in the other countries. In the steady state $(y_1^*, y_2^*, \ldots, y_n^*, x^*)$, the optimality condition that marginal benefits $\beta - y_i^*$ are equal to the sum of a series of marginal damages γx^* yields for each country i

$$\beta - y_i^* = \frac{1}{r+\delta}\gamma x^*, \quad i = 1, 2, \ldots, n. \tag{9.9}$$

Using the steady-state condition $ny_i^* = \delta x^*$, the optimal steady state becomes

$$\begin{aligned} y_i^* &= \frac{\beta\delta(\rho+\delta)}{n\gamma + \delta(\rho+\delta)}, \quad i = 1, 2, \ldots, n, \\ x^* &= \frac{\beta n(\rho+\delta)}{n\gamma + \delta(\rho+\delta)}, \end{aligned} \tag{9.10}$$

and the tax rate in country i becomes

$$\tau_i^* = \frac{1}{\rho+\delta}\gamma x^* = \frac{\beta n\gamma}{n\gamma + \delta(\rho+\delta)}, \quad i = 1, 2, \ldots, n. \tag{9.11}$$

If the government in country i levies the tax rate τ_i^*, the optimality condition is $\beta - y_i = \tau_i^*$, which realizes $y_i^* = \beta - \tau_i^*$ in (9.10) as the optimal level of production or emissions. Note that the total level of production or emissions ny_i^* equals the natural assimilation δx^*. The tax rates $\tau_i^*, i = 1, 2, \ldots, n$, form the Nash equilibrium of the game between the n countries (see Lecture 4). Optimization in each country i is the best reply to whatever the other countries do. Consistency of the best replies yields the Nash equilibrium.

For example, if $n = 2$, $\beta = 0.2$, $\gamma = 0.005$, $\delta = 0.05$, and $\rho = 0.03$, the optimal steady state becomes $(y_i^*, x^*) = (0.057, 2.286)$, with the optimal steady-state tax rate $\tau_i^* = 0.143$.

In case the countries reach an agreement, each country takes the damage into account that the emissions of that country cause in the other countries. The optimality condition is that marginal benefits $\beta - y_i^*$ in the steady state are now equal to the sum of a series of *global* marginal damages $n\gamma x^*$. This yields for each country i the optimality condition

$$\beta - y_i^* = \frac{1}{\rho+\delta}n\gamma x^*, \quad i = 1, 2, \ldots, n. \tag{9.12}$$

Using the steady-state condition $ny_i^* = \delta x^*$, the optimal steady state becomes

$$\begin{aligned} y_i^* &= \frac{\beta\delta(\rho+\delta)}{n^2\gamma + \delta(\rho+\delta)}, \quad i = 1, 2, \ldots, n, \\ x^* &= \frac{\beta n(\rho+\delta)}{n^2\gamma + \delta(\rho+\delta)}. \end{aligned} \tag{9.13}$$

The worldwide tax rate is equal to the sum of the series of global marginal damages on the right-hand side of equation (9.12) and becomes

$$\tau^* = \frac{1}{\rho + \delta} n\gamma x^* = \frac{\beta n^2 \gamma}{n^2\gamma + \delta(\rho + \delta)}. \tag{9.14}$$

If all governments levy the tax rate τ^*, the optimality conditions are $\beta - y_i = \tau^*$, which realize $y_i^* = \beta - \tau^*$ in (9.13) as the optimal levels of production or emissions. For $n > 1$, the worldwide tax rate τ^* in (9.14) is larger than the tax rate τ_i^* in (9.11). In the example, the worldwide tax rate is $\tau^* = 0.167$, with the optimal steady state $(y_i^*, x^*) = (0.033, 1.33)$. In case of cooperation, the countries take account of the pollution externalities between them. The production or emission levels y_i^* are smaller (in the example, $0.033 < 0.057$), but the stock of pollution x^* is so much smaller (in the example, $1.33 < 2.286$) that the net benefits become higher. In the example, the net benefits increase from -0.0033 to $+0.0016$. Cooperation turns negative net benefits here into positive net benefits. The analysis in this section focuses on the steady state, but it is possible to solve this game with the accumulation of the stock of pollution x given by equation (9.1), using a dynamical optimization technique (van der Ploeg and de Zeeuw, 1992).

It is interesting to compare the non-cooperative tax rate τ_i^*, given in equation (9.11), and the cooperative tax rate τ^*, given in equation (9.14), with the tax rate for local stock pollution in Section 9.2.3, given in equation (9.5). For $n = 1$, all these tax rates are the same because there is only one country, so stock pollution is only local, and cooperation is not an issue. If $n > 1$, the non-cooperative tax rate τ_i^* is larger than the tax rate for local stock pollution (in the example, $0.143 > 0.111$). The reason is that the countries must share the room for natural assimilation, so each country has to levy a higher tax rate in order to lower its production or emissions. The cooperative tax rate τ^* is the highest (in the example, $0.167 > 0.143$) because the countries take account of the reciprocal pollution externalities.

This section clearly shows an important problem for the control of global stock pollution, as is seen in the discussions regarding climate change. It is best for each country that all countries levy the worldwide tax rate τ^* on CO_2 emissions. However, if the countries plan to do this, each country has an incentive to lower its tax rate to τ_i^* that corrects for the pollution externality within the country but does not correct for the pollution externalities to the other countries. In this way, cooperation breaks down, and the countries end up in a Nash equilibrium. This is another example of a (symmetric) prisoner's dilemma as introduced in Lecture 4.

9.4 Conclusion

In the late 80s of the last century, the societal concern shifted from the threat of depletion of non-renewable resources to the threat of pollution resulting from the use of these resources. The obvious example is climate change resulting from the emissions of CO_2 by burning oil and other fossil fuels. This is an issue of stock pollution, as introduced in Lecture 1, because climate change results from the accumulation of CO_2 emissions in the atmosphere. This lecture analyzes stock pollution and shows that the tax rate, with the purpose of correcting for the pollution externalities, is equal to the present value of all future marginal damages.

In the case of a global stock-pollution problem, such as climate change, this optimal tax rate requires cooperation between the countries. However, each country has an incentive to lower the tax rate by only considering the pollution externalities within the country and not the pollution externalities to the other countries. Giving in to these incentives leads to the Nash equilibrium, in which the countries are worse off. This is another example of a (symmetric) prisoner's dilemma as introduced and discussed in Lectures 4 and 5.

References

Keeler, E., Spence, M., and Zeckhauser, R. 1972. The optimal control of pollution. *Journal of Economic Theory* 4, 1: 19–34.

Nordhaus, W.D. 1992. The DICE model: Background and structure of a dynamic integrated climate-economy model of the economics of global warming. *Cowles Foundation Discussion Papers* 1009, Yale University.

van der Ploeg, F. and de Zeeuw, A.J. 1992. International aspects of pollution control. *Environmental & Resource Economics* 2, 2: 117–139.

Lecture 10

Economic Growth and the Environment

10.1 Introduction

Economic growth is a core concept in economics, and it is *the* core concept in the debate on economics and the environment. Economic growth in the sense of saving, investing in capital, and increasing the capacity to produce goods and services is the basic mechanism for improving welfare over time. On the other hand, environmentalists argue that economic growth is the main driver of environmental deterioration, and it should therefore not be continued: the earth is finite, and pollution threatens the availability of resources and, more importantly, the living conditions for humanity. However, it is not clear that these two positions are contradictory. Economic growth may be possible without deterioration of the environment. Furthermore, while a growing quantity and quality of valuable goods and services contributes to improving welfare, welfare encompasses more than only the consumption of goods and services: good living conditions are a prerequisite for welfare and the deterioration of the environment has a direct and an indirect effect on welfare. It is essential to bring the extreme positions together. Lectures 6 and 7 on resources and Lecture 9 on stock pollution are building blocks for the analysis of economic growth and the connection with the natural environment. This lecture incorporates the essence of those lectures in an analysis of economic growth and the environment.

The concern for the natural environment has gradually increased over time. Initially, after the Second World War, the full focus was on increasing the production and consumption of goods and services. Lecture 7 refers to the report *The Limits to Growth* (Meadows *et al.*, 1972), which contained serious warnings for the deterioration of the environment, but it lasted another 20 years before the societal concern raised to a point where ignoring this was not an option anymore. The main issues now are pollution, climate change, and the reduction of biodiversity. It can be argued that this sequence of events has been necessary. The idea is that people need food, shelter, and a reasonable level of welfare before they start worrying about the environment. In the developed part of the world, people had the time for these different stages because initially, the condition of the environment was not very pressing. However, developing countries are in a different position now. They need economic growth in goods and services to alleviate poverty, but they need to take account of the natural environment at the same time to provide a safe environment in the long run. This tension between alleviating poverty and protecting the natural environment has become the most important challenge for economics.

The main part of this lecture focuses on extending the basic neo-classical economic growth model of Solow (1956) and Swan (1956) with resources and pollution. In this model, the saving or investment rate is fixed and exogenous. The question is how the main message from the analysis of economic growth in macroeconomics changes when resources and pollution are also considered. Since it may be possible to compensate the scale effect of economic growth by decreasing the intensity of resource use and pollution per unit of economic activity, it is important to separate the scale and the intensity. Technology is the main driver of economic growth, but technology also reduces the intensity of resource use and pollution. Previous lectures have shown the complexity of dynamical models. The economic growth model is also a dynamical model. To focus on the main questions, this lecture starts with an analysis in terms of growth rates, rather than levels. In the second part of the lecture, a welfare analysis turns the basic model into the Ramsey economic growth model, where the saving rate or investment rate is endogenous (Ramsey, 1928). At this point, also a connection can be made to stock pollution in Lecture 9.

This lecture has two goals. The first is to show how to reconcile economic growth and the reduction of resource use and pollution. The second is to extend the economic growth model with the connections to the natural environment.

Section 10.2 discusses the concepts of scale and intensity. Section 10.3 extends the Solow–Swan economic growth model, in which saving is exogenous. Section 10.4 extends the Ramsey economic growth model, maximizing a welfare indicator. Section 10.5 concludes.

10.2 Growth Rates, Scale, and Intensity

Lecture 6 started with the simple growth model, $g = \dot{s}(t)/s(t)$, with constant growth rate g, so the stock s develops according to $\dot{s}(t) = gs(t)$ or $s(t) = s(0)e^{gt}$. Lecture 7 introduced the Hotelling rule, which says that the price p grows at the rate of interest r, so $r = \dot{p}(t)/p(t)$ or $\dot{p}(t) = rp(t)$ or $p(t) = p(0)e^{rt}$. In short, the growth rates for the stock s and the price p are denoted as $\hat{s}$ and $\hat{p}$, so the growth model simplifies to $g = \hat{s}$ and the Hotelling rule simplifies to $r = \hat{p}$. The analysis in this lecture builds on growth rates.

The relationship between economic growth and emission of pollutants is not one-to-one. Grossman and Krueger (1995) observed that the pattern of emissions for several pollutants had the form of an inverted U. The emissions first increased with economic growth but at some turning point, the emissions started decreasing. Such a curve is called the Environmental Kuznets Curve because Kuznets (1955) observed the same pattern for economic growth and income inequality. More research has shown that these observations do not hold forever. Usually, at some point, the emissions start increasing again, as income inequality did as well. However, it made clear that the analysis of pollution requires more precision than just the scale effect (see also Lecture 3 on trade). Explanations for an inverted U-curve are that economic growth and a decrease in emissions can go together because of changes in the technology and the structure of the economy, or changes in preferences and policy. In general, the idea is that a decrease in the intensity of pollution per unit of economic activity can compensate and even overtake the scale effect.

In a macroeconomic context, the concept of scale is the total production in the economy, whereas intensity refers to the pollution per unit of production. If y denotes the total production and e the total level of emissions of pollutants, intensity is given by e/y. It follows that the total level of emissions decomposes into scale and intensity by the identity $e = y(e/y)$. The emissions increase if the scale increases or if the intensity increases. This also allows for a representation in terms of growth rates. It is not difficult to show that the growth rate of the product of two variables is equal to the sum of the two growth rates, so

$$\hat{e} = \hat{y} + \widehat{e/y}. \tag{10.1}$$

The reason is that by using the product rule of differentiation (Appendix A), the time derivative of, for example, $u(t)v(t)$ is equal to $\dot{u}(t)v(t)+u(t)\dot{v}(t)$. Dividing by $u(t)v(t)$ yields $\dot{u}(t)/u(t)+\dot{v}(t)/v(t) = \hat{u}+\hat{v}$, which is the growth rate of uv.

Equation (10.1) decomposes the growth in emissions into the growth in production and the growth in emission intensity. For example, if the growth rate of production is 2% and if the growth rate of emission intensity is 1%, the growth rate of emissions is 3%. Note that if the emission intensity decreases by 2% (a negative growth rate), the production can grow by 2% without growth in total emissions. The question is if technological progress with the purpose of reducing emission intensity is sufficiently large to offset the scale effect of economic growth.

The IPAT identity (Ehrlich and Holdren, 1971) shows how **I**mpact on the environment results from **P**opulation, **A**ffluence, and **T**echnology. This identity $e = \pi(y/\pi)(e/y)$ decomposes total emissions e into population π, affluence or income per capita y/π, and technology or the emission intensity of production e/y. In terms of growth rates,

$$\hat{e} = \hat{\pi} + \widehat{y/\pi} + \widehat{e/y}. \tag{10.2}$$

The first two terms on the right-hand side of equation (10.2) represent the scale effect and split the growth of the total production into population growth and the growth of income per capita. The third term represents the intensity effect of total emissions per unit of production. The question is again if technological progress with the purpose of reducing emission intensity is sufficiently large to offset the combined effect of population growth and the growth in affluence.

10.3 Economic Growth, Resources, and Pollution

Economic growth arises from the investments expanding the future productive capacity. Natural resources are an essential input into production and pollution is a by-product of production. Resource scarcity and environmental policy affect the process of growth and the first question is whether economic growth is possible under restrictions of resource use and pollution. The analysis uses the Solow–Swan economic growth model, with a fixed exogenous saving or investment rate. In a later section, the saving or investment rate becomes endogenous by using a welfare indicator and by switching to the Ramsey economic growth model. Finally, damage costs of stock pollution are added to the Ramsey economic growth model.

10.3.1 *Production, growth, and resources*

The total production in an economy is determined by the inputs (capital, labor, and resource use) and the productivity of these inputs, i.e. total factor productivity (TFP) α. Abstracting from the labor input, production y is a function f of capital k and resource use q. The sequel uses the Cobb–Douglas production function

$$y = f(k, q) = \alpha k^{\beta_k} q^{\beta_q}, \tag{10.3}$$

where $\beta_k > 0$, $\beta_q > 0$ and $\beta_k + \beta_q < 1$. The time derivative of $k^{\beta_k}(t)$ is equal to $\beta_k k^{\beta_k - 1}(t)\dot{k}(t)$, so the growth rate of k^{β_k} is $\beta_k \dot{k}(t)/k(t) = \beta_k \hat{k}$. It follows that the growth rate of total production is a simple function of the growth rates of TFP, capital, and resource use:

$$\hat{y} = \hat{\alpha} + \beta_k \hat{k} + \beta_q \hat{q}. \tag{10.4}$$

The emissions of pollutants follow physically from the use of resources. For example, burning fossil fuels transforms the carbon in coal, oil, and gas into the emission of CO_2 that ends up in the atmosphere and in the oceans. The transformation means that emissions of pollutants are a one-to-one by-product of the use of resources, i.e. $e = q$ (with the proper choice of dimensions), and in terms of growth rates $\hat{e} = \hat{q}$. It is possible to reduce the emission of CO_2 by switching from coal to gas because the carbon content of gas is lower, but the transformation remains the same. It is also possible to reduce emissions, for example, by capturing and storing CO_2. However, these measures are limited and at some point, reduction of emissions requires reduction of resource use. In the sequel, it is assumed that $e = q$, and thus $\hat{e} = \hat{q}$. This means that resource conservation and emission reduction have the same effect on the economy. According to equation (10.3), both imply a loss of production, ceteris paribus. Using equation (10.4) in growth rates, a reduction of 2% in the growth rate $\hat{e} = \hat{q}$ of emissions or resource use implies a loss of $2\beta_q$% in the growth rate $\hat{y}$ of production (but not necessarily a loss in welfare, of course).

Equation (10.4) also reveals that the reduction of emissions does not necessarily imply that the economy stops growing. For example, if TFP α and capital k both grow at a rate of 1% or $\hat{\alpha} = \hat{k} = 1\%$ and the production elasticities of capital and resource use are $\beta_k = 0.5$ and $\beta_q = 0.3$, the growth rate of production $\hat{y}$ can still be positive while emissions are reduced. Equation (10.4) shows that $\hat{y} > 0$, if $\hat{e} > -(1 + 0.5)/0.3 = -5\%$, which means that the growth rate of emissions $\hat{e}$ can be reduced without decreasing the production. The reason is that the Cobb–Douglas production function allows for substitution: technological progress and investments in capital can compensate for a decrease in resource use. The economy allows for changes in the emission intensity e/y, as introduced in equation (10.1), to counter the scale effect of economic growth. Substitution is key in the process. A set of papers in an issue of *The Review of Economic Studies* in 1974 formed the start for this way of modeling economic growth and resources (Dasgupta and Heal, 1974; Solow, 1974; Stiglitz, 1974a, 1974b).

10.3.2 *Investments in capital*

An important driver of economic growth is the investment in the capital stock, to increase the capacity to produce goods and services. In this section, the growth rates of TFP $\hat{\alpha}$ and resource use $\hat{q}$ are exogenous, but the change in the capital stock k results from the investment decisions. It is also assumed that the saving or investment rate is exogenous and equal to a fraction σ of total output y, so $\dot{k}(t) = \sigma y(t)$ (abstracting from depreciation). The growth rate of capital becomes $\hat{k} = \dot{k}(t)/k(t) = \sigma y(t)/k(t)$. This lecture assumes that the growth rates are constant and that the economy is in a situation of so-called *balanced growth*. In that case, total output y and capital k must grow at the same rate, i.e. $\hat{y} = \hat{k}$, because otherwise the numerator $\sigma y(t)$ in the expression for $\hat{k}$ increases faster or slower than the denominator $k(t)$, so $\hat{k}$ is not constant. The growth rates of TFP, capital, and resource use may differ and may be negative, particularly resource use. Note that this situation differs from the economic growth model in Section 8.3.2 of Lecture 8 where in steady state, the stock of capital is fixed and given by the golden rule. In this lecture, the steady state is one where the variables have constant growth rates.

Substitution of $\hat{k} = \hat{y}$ in equation (10.4) yields the growth rate of production

$$\hat{y} = \frac{\hat{\alpha} + \beta_q \hat{q}}{1 - \beta_k}. \tag{10.5}$$

Equation (10.5) shows a direct link between the growth rate of production and the growth rate of resource use $\hat{q}$. Lowering the growth rate of resource use $\hat{q}$ lowers the growth rate of production. The production elasticity becomes $\beta_q/(1-\beta_k)$, which is larger than the elasticity β_q in equation (10.4). The reason is that reducing resource use not only affects the production directly but also indirectly by affecting investment and capital formation. The total effect represents the cost of reducing resource use or emission of pollutants. It is reasonable to assume that $\beta_k + \beta_q < 1$, so the elasticity $(\beta_q/(1-\beta_k)) < 1$. In the example above with the elasticities $\beta_q = 0.3$ and $\beta_k = 0.5$, the production elasticity $\beta_q/(1-\beta_k)$ in equation (10.5) becomes 0.6. In practice, this number is usually smaller because the direct output elasticity of resource use β_q and the output elasticity of capital β_k are smaller. This elasticity measures the costs, in terms of the production growth rate, of reducing resource use or emission of pollutants by combining the direct effect on the production and the indirect effect via slower capital accumulation.

Equation (10.5) also provides an important conclusion on the role of technological change. It shows that the growth rate of production $\hat{y}$ is positive if the growth rate of TFP $\hat{\alpha}$ is sufficiently large, i.e. $\hat{y} > 0$ if $\hat{\alpha} > -\beta_q\hat{q}$. Even if the growth rate of resource use $\hat{q}$ is negative, which means that resource use decreases, growth in TFP α can compensate for that, especially if the production elasticity of resource use β_q is small. Figure 10.1

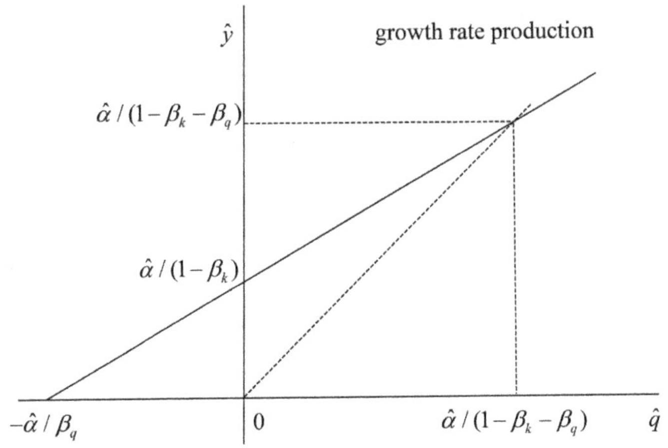

Figure 10.1. Growth, technology, and resource use.

depicts this situation. The solid line depicts the growth rate of production $\hat{y}$ as a function of the growth rate of resource use $\hat{q}$. The points on the line to the left of the vertical axis, where $-\hat{\alpha}/\beta_q < \hat{q}$ so that $\hat{y} > 0$, are combinations of decreasing resource use and increasing production (for a numerical example, see above Figure 10.2). The most important conclusion is that it is possible to have growth in production and to reduce resource use or emission of pollutants simultaneously if the technological progress is sufficiently fast. In the analysis of the IPAT identity in Section 10.2, it was concluded that technological progress with the aim to reduce emission intensity can compensate for the combined impact on the environment of population growth and the growth in affluence. In the analysis here, technological progress can compensate for the reduced contribution of resources to production.

10.3.3 *Supply and demand of resources*

Resources used in production are extracted from a renewable or non-renewable resource stock. The Hotelling model in Lecture 7 forms the supply side of a non-renewable resource. The fishery model in Lecture 6 can be seen as the supply side of a renewable resource.

Lecture 7 concludes that the net price for a unit of a non-renewable resource is equal to the shadow cost of extracting a unit from the stock of the resource. It grows at the rate of interest r (Hotelling rule). In case of a constant marginal extraction cost, the path of the gross price differs from the path of the shadow cost but in the long run, the price p grows at the rate of interest r. In case of a renewable resource, with a growth function G as introduced in Lecture 6, the net price grows at the rate $r - G'$ because the value of the growth of a unit left in the stock of the renewable resource is taken into account. Furthermore, Lecture 6 concludes that in case of open access, i.e. in the absence of property rights, the profits converge to 0, by entry and exit of the suppliers of the resource. This implies that the net price converges to 0, and the argument of Hotelling does not apply. It is thus reasonable to assume that the growth rate of the price $\hat{p}$ lies somewhere between the interest rate r (the Hotelling rule) and 0 (open access). The analysis in this section focuses on these two extreme cases, $\hat{p} = 0$ and $\hat{p} = r$.

For the case $\hat{p} = r$, the model requires a solution for the interest rate r, which is also the price of the capital. The production function (10.3) shows that one more unit of capital increases the production by the marginal product $\partial y/\partial k$, which is equal to $\beta_k y/k$. This is the price the producers are maximally willing to pay for the capital. The inverse demand function for the capital becomes $r = \beta_k y/k$. Using $\hat{k} = \sigma y/k$ from Section 10.3.2, this yields $r = \beta_k \hat{k}/\sigma$, or $r = \beta_k \hat{y}/\sigma$ because the growth rate of capital is equal to the growth rate of production.

The demand for resources is represented by the willingness-to-pay for the resources. The production function (10.3) shows that one more unit of a resource increases the production by the marginal product $\partial y/\partial q$, which is equal to $\beta_q y/q$. This is the price the producers are maximally willing to pay for the resource. The inverse demand function for resources becomes $p = \beta_q y/q$, which in terms of growth rates becomes $\hat{p} = \hat{y} - \hat{q}$ (see Section 10.2; $\hat{\beta}_q = 0$ since β_q is constant). Eliminating the growth rate of production $\hat{y}$ by using equation (10.5) yields

$$\hat{p} = \hat{y} - \hat{q} = \frac{\hat{\alpha} + \beta_q \hat{q}}{1 - \beta_k} - \hat{q} = \frac{\hat{\alpha} - (1 - \beta_k - \beta_q)\hat{q}}{1 - \beta_k}. \tag{10.6}$$

Figure 10.2 depicts the demand and supply of resources as functions of the growth rate of resource use $\hat{q}$. The demand line (10.6) is downward sloping and passes through the point $\hat{\alpha}/(1 - \beta_k)$ on the $\hat{p}$-axis where $\hat{q} = 0$ and the point $\hat{\alpha}/(1 - \beta_k - \beta_q)$ on the $\hat{q}$-axis where $\hat{p} = 0$.

For example, if $\hat{\alpha} = 0.02$, $\beta_q = 0.3$, and $\beta_k = 0.5$, the solid line in Figure 10.1 represents equation (10.5) and becomes $\hat{y} = 0.04 + 0.6\hat{q}$. It shows that combinations of decreasing resource use and increasing production are possible, such as $\hat{q} = -0.05$ and $\hat{y} = 0.01$. The demand line in Figure 10.2 becomes $\hat{p} = 0.04 - 0.4\hat{q}$.

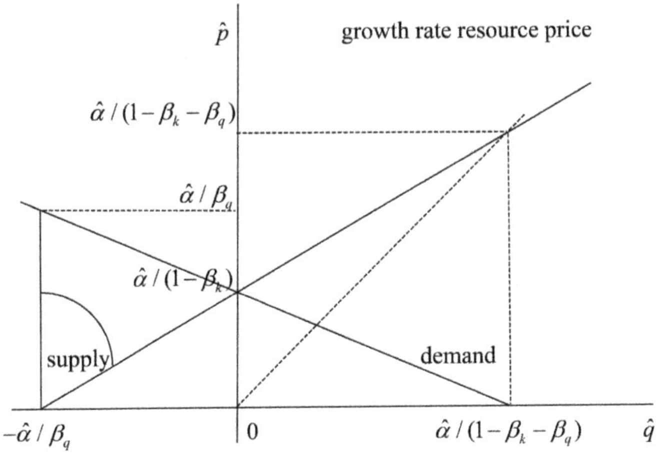

Figure 10.2. Demand and supply of resources.

On the supply side of resources, the two extreme cases for the growth rate of the resource price are $\hat{p} = 0$ and $\hat{p} = r$. In case 1, the resource is exploited under open access, which implies that in the long run $\hat{p} = 0$. In Figure 10.2, the supply line $\hat{p} = 0$ is the $\hat{q}$-axis. Intersection with the demand line yields $\hat{q} = \hat{\alpha}/(1 - \beta_k - \beta_q)$, so according to Figure 10.1, $\hat{y} = \hat{\alpha}/(1 - \beta_k - \beta_q)$ as well. In the example, $\hat{q} = \hat{y} = 0.1$. If there is open access to the resource and the resource is not regulated, the growth rates of production $\hat{y}$ and resource use $\hat{q}$ only depend on the growth rate of TFP $\hat{\alpha}$. This shows that without policy, only growth drives resource use: technological progress allows the economy to grow but also results in unregulated resource use or pollution. Note that when resource management or pollution policy stabilizes the use of resources, so $\hat{q} = 0$, Figure 10.2 and Figure 10.1 show that the price p and the production y grow at the same rate, which is $\hat{p} = \hat{y} = \hat{\alpha}/(1 - \beta_k)$. In the example, $\hat{p} = \hat{y} = 0.04$.

In case 2, the resource is non-renewable and extracted under full property rights, without extraction costs or tax. The Hotelling rule implies that the price grows at the rate of interest, i.e. $\hat{p} = r$. It was shown above that the interest rate, or the price of capital, is given by $r = \beta_k \hat{y}/\sigma$. Using equation (10.5) again, the supply equation becomes

$$\hat{p} = \frac{\beta_k \hat{y}}{\sigma} = \frac{\beta_k}{\sigma} \frac{\hat{\alpha} + \beta_q \hat{q}}{1 - \beta_k}. \tag{10.7}$$

Figure 10.2 depicts two possible supply lines, which are both upward-sloping, for different values of the saving rate σ. If $\sigma = \beta_k$, $\hat{p} = \hat{y}$, and the supply line (10.7) is the same as the solid line in Figure 10.1. In the example, this supply line becomes $\hat{p} = 0.04 + 0.6\hat{q}$. This line intersects the demand line in $\hat{p} = \hat{\alpha}/(1 - \beta_k)$. It follows that the resource use does not grow, i.e. $\hat{q} = 0$, and that the production y grows at the same rate as the price p, so $\hat{y} = \hat{\alpha}/(1 - \beta_k)$. In the example, $\hat{p} = \hat{y} = 0.04$. Note that all the lines representing the supply equation (10.7) intersect the $\hat{q}$-axis in $\hat{q} = -\hat{\alpha}/\beta_q$ where $\hat{p} = 0$. If $\sigma < \beta_k$, the supply line rotates upward from the line for $\sigma = \beta_k$ and if $\sigma > \beta_k$, the supply line rotates downward. The other supply line depicted in Figure 10.2 is the vertical supply line in the limit for $\sigma \to 0$. This supply line intersects the demand line (10.6) in $\hat{p} = \hat{\alpha}/\beta_q$, where growth in resource use is negative, i.e. $\hat{q} = -\hat{a}/\beta_q$, and growth in production stops, i.e. $\hat{y} = 0$. In the example, $\hat{p} = 0.067$ and $\hat{q} = -0.067$. The two depicted supply lines in Figure 10.2 determine the area where the resource use is declining, i.e. $\hat{q} < 0$, and the production is growing, i.e. $\hat{y} > 0$. By decreasing the saving rate σ down from $\sigma = \beta_k$, the growth rate of resource use becomes more negative and according to Figure 10.1, the growth rate of production decreases. This implies that a trade-off occurs between the decline in resource use and the growth in production. A relatively high saving rate σ is good for the growth of production but bad for the reduction of resource use, whereas the opposite holds for a relatively low saving rate σ. The choice depends on the implications for welfare.

10.3.4 *Summary*

These sections focus on the question of whether economic growth can be compatible with a reduction in resource use. This reduction may be needed because the resource is non-renewable and substitutes are not available, or the use of a renewable resource exceeds the natural growth of the resource, or the use of the resource leads to environmental pollution that is damaging. It is assumed that substitution is possible between the inputs into production by using a Cobb–Douglas production function, that depends on technology, capital, and resource use. Considering a situation of balanced growth, where the growth rates of the variables are constant, the dynamical analysis of investment and resource extraction simplifies to an analysis in terms of growth rates. The basic model is the Solow–Swan economic growth model that has an exogenous saving rate.

The need to reduce resource use lowers the growth rate of production. However, it remains possible to have growth in production together with declining resource use, for a sufficiently large growth in total factor productivity. Lectures 6 and 7 analyze resource supply. The extreme cases are open access, where the growth of the price is zero, and the Hotelling rule for a non-renewable resource, where the price grows at the rate of interest, i.e. the price of capital. Resource demand follows from the production function. In the case of open access, the growth rates of production and resource use are the same and only depend on the growth rate of TFP, so this case cannot be sustainable. In the case of the Hotelling rule, a range of equilibria between the resource demand and supply exist in which the growth rate of production is positive while resource use is declining. The saving rate must be sufficiently low, and a decreasing saving rate increases the reduction of resource use but decreases the growth rate of production.

10.4 Optimal Growth, Resources, and Pollution

The previous sections use the Solow–Swan economic growth model in which the saving or investment rate is exogenous. This section considers the Ramsey economic growth model where the decision to consume or to invest follows from the maximization of welfare as a function of consumption (Ramsey, 1928). Investment means giving up some consumption now and increasing capital to enjoy more future production and consumption. This intertemporal trade-off yields an optimal consumption rate, and thus an optimal saving rate or investment rate. Resource use leads to pollution that either affects productivity (see Section 8.3.2) or directly affects welfare.

10.4.1 *The Keynes–Ramsey rule*

As in Section 7.2 in Lecture 7, the argument of no-arbitrage gives an immediate insight in the intertemporal trade-off between consumption and investment. The value or the price of giving up one unit of consumption now must be the same as investing this unit and enjoying the utility of consuming the extra production later. Denote the consumption by c, and the utility by U. The value or the price of one unit of c is given by the marginal utility $U'(c)$. Following the idea behind the Hotelling rule in Lecture 7, a unit of production that is invested grows at the rate of interest r, and becomes e^{rt} at time t. The price of consumption at time t is equal to $U'(c(t))$. Denote the rate of time preference, or the utility discount rate, by ρ. Note that this discount rate ρ and the interest rate r are different now. The discounted value at time 0 of the extra consumption at time t, that results from one unit of investment, becomes $e^{-\rho t}U'(c(t))e^{rt}$. The argument of no-arbitrage requires that the price of one unit of consumption at time 0 must be equal to the discounted value of the resulting consumption at time t, or

$$U'(c(0)) = e^{-\rho t}U'(c(t))e^{rt}. \tag{10.8}$$

The left-hand side of equation (10.8) is a constant, so the growth rate is 0. The growth rates of $e^{-\rho t}$ and e^{rt} at the right-hand side of equation (10.8) are equal to $-\rho$ and r, respectively. The time derivative of $U'(c(t))$ is equal to $U''(c(t))\dot{c}(t)$, and dividing this by $U'(c(t))$ yields the growth rate of this term. The elasticity of the marginal utility $U'(c)$ with respect to consumption c is a measure how fast the marginal utility or the price decreases with the increase in consumption. This elasticity is given by $\eta = -cU''(c)/U'(c) > 0$. For a constant elasticity η, the growth rate of the marginal utility $U'(c(t))$ becomes $-\eta\dot{c}(t)/c(t)$ or $-\eta\hat{c}$. Using the rule in Section 10.2, equation (10.8) in terms of growth rates becomes

$$0 = -\rho - \eta\hat{c} + r \Rightarrow r = \rho + \eta\hat{c}. \tag{10.9}$$

Equation (10.9) is the Keynes–Ramsey rule. Note that the utility function $U(c) = c^{1-\eta}/(1-\eta)$ has a constant elasticity of marginal utility

η because $U'(c) = c^{-\eta}$ and $U''(c) = -\eta c^{-\eta-1}$, implying that $-cU''(c)/U'(c) = \eta$. Also note that for $\hat{c} = 0$, equation (10.9) yields the condition for the steady state with zero growth. If the production is a function f of capital k, the condition for the steady-state stock of capital k^* becomes $f'(k^*) = \rho$ because the interest rate r is equal to the marginal productivity of capital $f'(k)$. This is the golden rule used in Section 8.3.2 in Lecture 8. Appendix J derives the Keynes–Ramsey rule as a result from general welfare maximization, with a dynamical optimization technique.

10.4.2 *The Ramsey–Hotelling model*

On the supply side, when the resource is non-renewable and extracted under full property rights, without extraction costs or tax, the Hotelling rule implies that the price grows at the rate of interest, i.e. $\hat{p} = r$. In the Ramsey economic growth model, equation (10.9) yields $\hat{p} = \rho + \eta\hat{c}$. On a balanced growth path, consumption c and production y grow at the same rate, i.e. $\hat{c} = \hat{y}$. Using equation (10.5), it follows that the supply equation becomes

$$\hat{p} = \rho + \eta\hat{y} = \rho + \eta\frac{\hat{\alpha} + \beta_q\hat{q}}{1 - \beta_k}. \tag{10.10}$$

The supply equation (10.10) has two parameters, i.e. η for the utility function and ρ for the utility discount rate, whereas the supply equation (10.7) only has one parameter σ for the saving rate. In Figure 10.2, the supply lines (10.10) shift up with ρ (assume $\rho < \hat{\alpha}/\beta_q$) from $\hat{q} = -\hat{\alpha}/\beta_q$ on the $\hat{q}$-axis and then rotate with changes in the parameter η, as the supply lines (10.7) rotate with changes in the parameter σ. The intersection points with the demand line (10.6) yield the optimal rate for resource use $\hat{q}$ and the optimal growth rate for production $\hat{y}$:

$$\hat{q} = -\frac{(\eta - 1)\hat{\alpha} + \rho(1 - \beta_k)}{(\eta - 1)\beta_q + 1 - \beta_k}, \quad \hat{y} = \frac{\hat{\alpha} + \beta_q\hat{q}}{1 - \beta_k}. \tag{10.11}$$

For $\eta > 1 - (\rho(1 - \beta_k)/\hat{\alpha})$, it follows that $-\hat{\alpha}/\beta_q < \hat{q} < 0$ and $\hat{y} > 0$, so resource use declines and production increases. For the example in Section 10.3.3, the condition becomes $\eta > 0.75$ for $\rho = 0.01$. This solution provides the optimal long-run growth rate in the case that non-renewable resources are used in production. It maximizes intertemporal welfare for given preferences (the parameters η and ρ) and given technology (the parameters $\hat{a}$, β_k, and β_q). The Hotelling rule ensures the optimal path of resource extraction, and the Ramsey economic growth model ensures the optimal path of consumption. The values of the parameters determine whether it is possible to have economic growth with declining resource use. As the appendices for Lectures 6, 7, and 9, Appendix J presents a formal analysis by using a dynamical optimization technique.

10.4.3 *Stock pollution*

Pollution has an indirect and a direct effect on welfare. For example, climate change affects welfare indirectly by lowering total factor productivity (Section 8.3.2 in Lecture 8) but also directly by a change in weather conditions. To take another example, because of air pollution, health issues arise which not only affect the productivity of workers but also have a direct negative effect on welfare. Moreover, pollution destroys nature which implies an indirect welfare loss in terms of the loss of resources and a direct welfare loss in terms of the loss of amenities that nature provides. In these situations, especially stock pollution causes this type of damage.

Section 9.2.1 in Lecture 9 shows the way to model stock pollution. The accumulation of emissions means that at each time t, the increase in the stock of pollution x is equal to the flow of emissions e minus the natural assimilation of pollution:

$$\dot{x}(t) = e(t) - \delta x(t), \quad x(0) = x_0, \tag{10.12}$$

where δ denotes the assimilative capacity of the environment, and x_0 the initial stock. Note that in this lecture (Section 10.3.1), it is assumed that emissions e are equal to resource use q but in Lecture 9, it is assumed that emissions e are equal to production y. The main result in Lecture 9 is that optimality requires that the marginal benefits of production are equal to the present value of all future marginal damages of stock pollution. This can be implemented by a tax on production that is equal to the present value of all marginal damages. Similarly, it is possible to add equation (10.12) to the Ramsey economic growth model in this lecture and to find such a tax on emissions e or on resource use q. Appendix K provides the analysis, but it is not possible to give the precise expression for the tax in these lecture notes. The net price of the resource $p-\tau$, where τ denotes the tax, grows at the rate of interest r. This tax affects the price and thus the use of resources, and it is the optimal policy with the aim to regulate the pollution and to balance the marginal damage of stock pollution and the marginal benefits of consumption. A full analysis combines the previous building blocks but is beyond the scope of these lecture notes.

10.4.4 *Summary*

These sections move from the exogenous saving rate or investment rate in the Solow–Swan model for economic growth to welfare maximization in the Ramsey model for economic growth. The optimal consumption rate or investment rate now follows from the rate of time preference (or the utility discount rate) and the elasticity of the marginal utility of consumption. This yields the Keynes–Ramsey rule, which connects the interest rate (or the consumption discount rate) to the rate of time preference, this elasticity, and the growth rate of consumption. In case the Hotelling rule holds, the Keynes–Ramsey rule also connects the price of the resource to the growth rate of consumption or production, which provides the supply equation for the resource. In Section 10.3.3, the Solow–Swan economic growth model determines the saving rates for which the growth rate of production is positive while the resource use is declining. In Section 10.4.2, the Ramsey economic growth model derives the optimal combination of the production growth and the declining resource use, for a given intertemporal welfare indicator.

The connection of the economic system and the natural environment raises two concerns. The limited availability of non-renewable resources is one, and damage of pollution is the other. Pollution can damage the total factor productivity, like in the DICE model on climate change, but pollution can also reduce welfare directly by damaging amenities that nature provides. Lecture 9 develops a tax on emissions to balance the marginal benefits with all future marginal damages of stock pollution. Incorporating this tax in the Ramsey economic growth model controls the price and the extraction of the resources that produce the emissions.

10.5 Conclusion

The main question in this lecture is whether economic growth and the reduction of resource use and pollution can go together. First, note that reduction of the scale of economic activities is not the only way to reduce resource use and pollution. It is also possible to reduce the intensity of resource use and pollution. Second, note that substitution within production is a crucial concept. If these options are available, technological progress and a tax on pollution can put the economy on a path with growth of production and a reduction of resource use and pollution. Growth rates will be lower than when ignoring the natural environment, but welfare will be higher by lowering pollution and preserving the goods and services of nature.

References

Dasgupta, P. and Heal, G. 1974. The optimal depletion of exhaustible resources. *The Review of Economic Studies* 41, 5: 3–28.

Ehrlich, P.R. and Holdren, J.P. 1971. Impact of population growth. *Science* 171, 3977: 1212–1217.

Grossman, G.M. and Krueger, A.B. 1995. Economic growth and the environment. *The Quarterly Journal of Economics* 110, 2: 353–377.

Kuznets, S. 1955. Economic growth and income inequality. *The American Economic Review* 45, 1: 1–28.

Meadows, D.H., Meadows, D.L., Randers, J., and Behrens III, W.W. 1972. *The Limits to Growth: A Report for the Club of Rome's Project on the Predicament of Mankind.* New York: Universe Books.

Ramsey, F.P. 1928. A mathematical theory of saving. *The Economic Journal* 38, 152: 543–559.

Solow, R.M. 1956. A contribution to the theory of economic growth. *The Quarterly Journal of Economics* 70, 1: 65–94.

Solow, R.M. 1974. Intergenerational equity and exhaustible resources. *The Review of Economic Studies* 41, 5: 29–45.

Stiglitz, J.E. 1974a. Growth with exhaustible natural resources: Efficient and optimal growth paths. *The Review of Economic Studies* 41, 5: 123–137.

Stiglitz, J.E. 1974b. Growth with exhaustible natural resources: The competitive economy. *The Review of Economic Studies* 41, 5: 139–152.

Swan, T.W. 1956. Economic growth and capital accumulation. *Economic Record* 32, 2: 334–361.

Appendices to the Lecture Notes

Appendix A: Static Optimization

Optimization is a standard technique in economic theory. For example, the maximization of utility or profit is basic to theoretical economic analysis. Suppose that F denotes the objective function and x the variable of choice. If the function F is twice differentiable, the conditions for optimality are that the first derivative $F'(x)$ is 0 and the second derivative $F''(x)$ is either positive, which yields a minimum, or negative, which yields a maximum. For example, if $F(x) = x^2$, so that $F'(x) = 2x$ and $F''(x) = 2$, the objective F has a minimum at $2x = 0$ or $x = 0$. The reason is that a positive second derivative means that the first derivative is increasing. It follows that the first derivative is negative for $x < 0$ and positive for $x > 0$, so the objective F is decreasing for $x < 0$ and increasing for $x > 0$ and has a minimum at $x = 0$. This objective function F is called a convex function. If $F(x) = -x^2$, the objective F has a maximum at $x = 0$ because the second derivative is negative and the opposite holds. This objective function F is called a concave function. If $F(x) = x^3$, so that $F'(x) = 3x^2$ and $F''(x) = 6x$, the second derivative changes sign at $x = 0$, and the first derivative is positive for $x < 0$ and for $x > 0$, so the objective F always increases and does not have a minimum or a maximum. Finally, consider the objective function $F(x) = x^3 - 3x$, with $F'(x) = 3x^2 - 3$

and $F''(x) = 6x$. The condition $F'(x) = 0$ yields $x_1 = -1$ and $x_2 = 1$. In the neighborhood of $x_1 = -1$, the second derivative is negative, so the objective F has a maximum at $x_1 = -1$. This is a local maximum because F is larger for large x. In the neighborhood of $x_2 = 1$, the second derivative is positive, so the objective F has a minimum at $x_2 = 1$. This is now a local minimum because F is smaller for small x. At $x = 0$, the second derivative changes sign, and the first derivative is negative. The objective F decreases, and the first derivative F' has a minimum at $x = 0$. This objective function F is called a concave-convex function. Optimization first solves the *first-order condition* $F'(x) = 0$ and then checks the *second-order condition* on $F''(x)$. Usually, the objective functions in economic theory are concave, so the maximization only requires solving the first-order condition, i.e. differentiate the objective function F and set the derivative equal to 0. The basic rules of differentiation are as follows:

$$F(x) = ax^b \Rightarrow F'(x) = abx^{b-1}, \quad F(x) = e^x \Rightarrow F'(x) = e^x,$$

$$F(x) = \ln x \Rightarrow F'(x) = 1/x,$$

$$F(x) = f(x)g(x) \Rightarrow F'(x) = f'(x)g(x) + f(x)g'(x) \text{ (product rule)},$$

$$F(x) = \frac{f(x)}{g(x)} \Rightarrow F'(x) = \frac{f'(x)g(x) - f(x)g'(x)}{(g(x))^2} \text{ (quotient rule)},$$

$$F(x) = f(g(x)) \Rightarrow F'(x) = f'(g(x))g'(x) \text{ (chain rule)}.$$

If the objective function F is a function of two variables x and y, the first-order conditions are that the partial derivatives with respect to x and y, $F_x(x, y)$ and $F_y(x, y)$, are 0. For example, if $F(x, y) = x^2 + y^2$, so $F_x(x, y) = 2x$ and $F_y(x, y) = 2y$, the first-order conditions yield $x = 0$ and $y = 0$. The second-order conditions in general are complicated but it is clear that this F has a minimum 0 for $x = y = 0$ because F is larger for any other combination of x and y.

Many optimization problems have constraints. For example, utility maximization has a budget constraint or profit maximization has a constraint on the inputs into the production. If the constraint is easy to solve, so x is a function of y or y is a function of x, substitution of this function in $F(x, y)$ turns the problem into a problem with only one choice variable. For example, if $F(x, y) = xy$ and the constraint is $x + y = a$, it follows that $y = a - x$, and the objective becomes $F(x) = ax - x^2$, with $F'(x) = a - 2x$

and $F''(x) = -2$. This implies that the objective F has its maximum at $x = 0.5a$, with $y = 0.5a$. If the constraint is not easy to solve, it is convenient to introduce a so-called Lagrange multiplier λ and to solve the first-order conditions of the Lagrange function. Formally, the optimization problem with an equality constraint is given by

$$\max_{x,y} F(x,y), \text{ subject to } f(x,y) = 0. \tag{A.1}$$

The Lagrange function becomes

$$L(x,y,\lambda) = F(x,y) + \lambda f(x,y), \tag{A.2}$$

with the first-order conditions

$$\begin{aligned} &F_x(x,y) + \lambda f_x(x,y) = 0, \\ &F_y(x,y) + \lambda f_y(x,y) = 0, \\ &f(x,y) = 0. \end{aligned} \tag{A.3}$$

For the example with $F(x,y) = xy$ and $f(x,y) = a - x - y$, this yields the first-order conditions $y - \lambda = 0$, $x - \lambda = 0$, and $x + y = a$. It follows that $x = y$, so $x = y = 0.5a$ and $\lambda = 0.5a$. The Lagrange multiplier is a shadow value that measures the marginal increase in the objective F for an increase in the constraint a, where a denotes income, for example.

Appendix B: Logistic Growth

The solution to the Verhulst model (6.1) is the time path

$$s(t) = \frac{s_{\max}}{1 + ke^{-gt}}, \quad k = \frac{s_{\max} - s(0)}{s(0)}. \tag{B.1}$$

The proof is simply that differentiating $s(t)$ in (B.1) with respect to time t yields

$$\dot{s}(t) = \frac{g s_{\max} k e^{-gt}}{(1 + ke^{-gt})^2} = gs(t)\frac{ke^{-gt}}{1 + ke^{-gt}} = gs(t)\left(1 - \frac{s(t)}{s_{\max}}\right), \tag{B.2}$$

which is equation (6.1). The value for the parameter k follows from $s(0) = s_{\max}/(1 + k)$.

The time path (B.1) is called the logistic growth curve.

Figure B.1 sketches this curve.

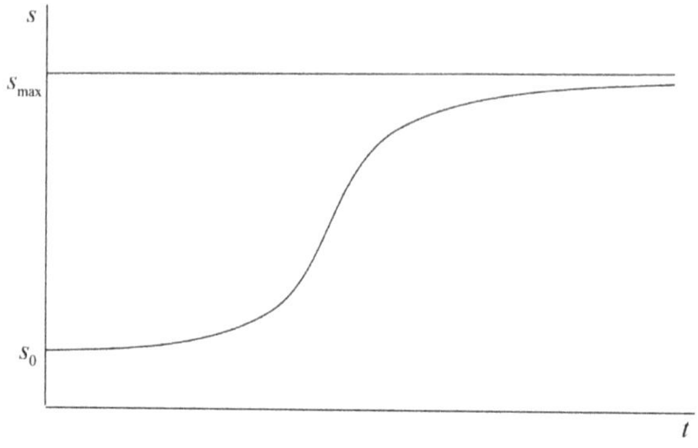

Figure B.1. Logistic growth curve.

Appendix C: Dynamical Optimization

Dynamical optimization is quite standard in economic theory. For example, maximization of welfare subject to the accumulation of capital is basic economic theory. The technique that is widely used is the so-called *maximum principle*, developed by Pontryagin and his students in 1962. This appendix presents this dynamical optimization technique. Considering a two-period problem first, the idea of the maximum principle becomes clear. Many books are available on dynamical optimization or *optimal control*, as it is usually called. A very good textbook on optimal control with economic applications is Seierstad and Sydsaeter (1987).

Consider a simple general two-period problem (time $t = 0, 1, 2$) where a path of *controls* (u_0, u_1) is chosen in order to maximize the sum of *objectives*

$$F(x_0, u_0) + F(x_1, u_1) + F_2(x_2), \tag{C.1}$$

where F is a function of the *state* x and the *control* u, and F_2 attaches a value to the final state x_2. The state x develops from a given state x_0 according to

$$x_1 = f(x_0, u_0), x_2 = f(x_1, u_1). \tag{C.2}$$

By viewing the dynamical equation (C.2) as equality constraints, the optimization problem can be solved (see Appendix A). With the Lagrange multipliers (λ_0, λ_1) and the Lagrange function

$$L = F(x_0, u_0) + F(x_1, u_1) + F_2(x_2) + \lambda_0(f(x_0, u_0) - x_1) + \lambda_1(f(x_1, u_1) - x_2), \tag{C.3}$$

the first-order conditions become (C.2) (i.e. the derivatives with respect to λ_0 and λ_1) and

$$F_u(x_t, u_t) + \lambda_t f_u(x_t, u_t) = 0, \quad t = 0, 1, \tag{C.4}$$

$$\lambda_1 = F_2'(x_2), \quad \lambda_0 = F_x(x_1, u_1) + \lambda_1 f_x(x_1, u_1), \tag{C.5}$$

where the subscripts u and x denote the partial derivatives with respect to u and x, respectively. Conditions (C.5) are written in this way because it shows that this produces a dynamical equation in λ, but backward in time, starting with λ_1. Conditions (C.4) are the first-order conditions for the optimal controls u_0 at time $t = 0$ and u_1 at time $t = 1$. This is the basic idea of the maximum principle. The optimization of the path of controls (u_0, u_1) is simplified by translating it into static optimizations at each point in time, at the expense of an additional dynamical equation in λ. The idea is to solve the static optimizations (C.4), substitute the results in (C.2) and (C.5), and solve the resulting dynamical system consisting of (C.2) and (C.5).

An elegant way of formulating the maximum principle uses the so-called Hamilton function

$$H(x, u, \lambda) = F(x, u) + \lambda f(x, u). \tag{C.6}$$

The dynamical optimization of (C.1), subject to (C.2), is translated into static optimizations of the Hamilton function (C.6), with first-order conditions (C.4) and the Hamiltonian system

$$\begin{aligned} x_{t+1} &= H_\lambda(x_t, u_t) = f(x_t, u_t), t = 0, 1, \\ \lambda_{t-1} &= H_x(x_t, u_t, \lambda_t) = F_x(x_t, u_t) + \lambda_t f_x(x_t, u_t), t = 1, \lambda_1 = F_2'(x_2), \end{aligned} \tag{C.7}$$

which is the same as (C.2) and (C.5). The subscript λ denotes the partial derivative with respect to λ. For this simple problem, the solution looks clumsy, but the power of the maximum principle becomes evident when extending this technique to general optimal-control problems.

A general optimal-control problem in continuous time requires to determine the path $u(t)$ in order to maximize the objective function

$$\int_0^T e^{-\rho t} F(x(t), u(t)) dt + e^{-\rho T} F_T(x(T)), \tag{C.8}$$

where ρ denotes the discount rate, subject to the state equation

$$\dot{x}(t) = f(x(t), u(t)), x(0) = x_0. \tag{C.9}$$

If discounting is ignored, i.e. $\rho = 0$, the Hamilton function is given by (C.6) and according to the maximum principle, the optimality conditions are (no proof here)

$$\begin{aligned} &H_u(x(t), u(t), \lambda(t)) = 0, \\ &\dot{x}(t) = H_\lambda(x(t), u(t)) = f(x(t), u(t)), x(0) = x_0, \\ &\dot{\lambda}(t) = -H_x(x(t), u(t), \lambda(t)), \lambda(T) = F_T'(x(T)). \end{aligned} \tag{C.10}$$

The minus sign on the right-hand side of the third condition in (C.10) reflects that the dynamical equation in λ runs backward in time.

If $\rho > 0$, it is common to include the role of the discounting term $e^{-\rho t}$ in the following way. The Hamilton function for this problem is $e^{-\rho t}F(x, u) + \mu f(x, u)$. By writing $\mu = e^{-\rho t}\lambda$, the Hamilton function becomes (C.6) times $e^{-\rho t}$. Therefore, the first optimality condition in (C.10) is the same. The second optimality condition in (C.10) is the state equation and remains the same as well. The left-hand side of the dynamical equation in μ becomes $\dot{\mu}(t) = e^{-\rho t}\dot{\lambda}(t) - re^{-\rho t}\lambda(t)$. The term $e^{-\rho t}$ cancels out with $e^{-\rho t}$ in $-e^{-\rho t}F_x(x(t), u(t))$ and $-e^{-\rho t}\lambda(t)f_x(x(t), u(t))$ in the right-hand side of the dynamical equation in μ. It follows that the optimality conditions become

$$\begin{aligned} &H_u(x(t), u(t), \lambda(t)) = 0, \\ &\dot{x}(t) = H_\lambda(x(t), u(t)) = f(x(t), u(t)), x(0) = x_0, \\ &\dot{\lambda}(t) - \rho\lambda(t) = -H_x(x(t), u(t), \lambda(t)), \lambda(T) = F_T'(x(T)). \end{aligned} \tag{C.11}$$

The dynamical optimization problem (C.8) and (C.9) has been translated into static optimization problems at each time t (the first condition of (C.11)) and a dynamical system in the state x and the so-called co-state λ (the second and third condition of (C.11)).

The last step is extending the objective function (C.8) to the infinite horizon, i.e.

$$\int_0^\infty e^{-\rho t}F(x(t), u(t))dt, \tag{C.12}$$

which implies that the co-state λ does not get a value at a finite time T. Otherwise, the solution is the same as (C.11). This means that the maximum principle requires maximizing the Hamilton function H in (C.6) with respect to u, which yields the optimal control $u^*(x, \lambda)$, and then solving the dynamical system

$$\begin{aligned}\dot{x}(t) &= f[x(t), u^*(x(t), \lambda(t))], x(0) = x_0, \\ \dot{\lambda}(t) &= \rho\lambda(t) - H_x[x(t), u^*(x(t), \lambda(t)), \lambda(t)].\end{aligned} \tag{C.13}$$

This dynamical system has an initial condition on the state x but not a final condition on the co-state λ. However, from optimality considerations, it can usually be argued that the optimal path has to converge to the steady state of the system (C.13). As in Section 6.3.1, a phase diagram can provide a general picture for the solution path of the dynamical system (C.13) (see Lecture 9) but generally, a computer package is needed to provide the precise solution. After this long analysis, it may be a bit disappointing that so many issues remain to be solved. Dynamical optimization is simply rather complicated!

Appendix D: The Optimal Dynamics of a Fishery

Returning to Section 6.3.4, optimal management of a simple fishery requires determining the path of the harvest $h(t)$ with the aim of maximizing the total discounted revenues

$$\int_0^\infty e^{-rt} p h(t) dt, \tag{D.1}$$

where p denotes the price and r denotes the interest or discount rate, subject to

$$\dot{s}(t) = g s(t)\left(1 - \frac{s(t)}{s_{\max}}\right) - h(t) := G(s(t)) - h(t), \quad s(0) = s_0, \tag{D.2}$$

where s denotes the stock of fish, g the growth parameter, $s_{\max}$ the carrying capacity, and G the growth function.

According to the maximum principle in Appendix C, the first-order conditions can be expressed in terms of the Hamilton function. This function becomes

$$H(s, h, \lambda) = ph + \lambda(G(s) - h) = (p - \lambda)h + \lambda G(s). \tag{D.3}$$

The parameter λ in the Hamilton function is often referred to as the *shadow value*. It attaches a benefit or a cost to a change in the stock of fish

s, given by the right-hand side of equation (D.2). By harvesting below the growth, the stock of fish increases and more fish is available in the future. Harvesting above the growth has the opposite effect. Maximization of the Hamilton function H with respect to the harvest h poses a new problem. The function H in (D.3) is linear in the harvest h. If the coefficient $p - \lambda$ of h is negative, the optimal harvest h^* is 0, and if $p - \lambda$ is positive, h^* is as large as possible. This coefficient denotes the marginal revenue of an extra unit of harvest h net of the shadow cost λ. In the steady state of the fish stock, the price p is equal to the shadow cost λ, and the optimal harvest h^* is equal to the growth.

According to (C.13), the maximum principle yields the dynamical system

$$\begin{aligned} \dot{s}(t) &= G(s(t)) - h^*(t), \quad s(0) = s_0, \\ \dot{\lambda}(t) &= (r - G'(s(t)))\lambda(t). \end{aligned} \tag{D.4}$$

In the steady state (s^*, λ^*) of the dynamical system (D.4), the optimal harvest level $h^* = G(s^*)$, $G'(s^*) = r$, and $\lambda^* = p$, which was concluded above. The condition $G'(s^*) = r$ is called the *golden rule* of the fishery: this yields the optimal steady-state fish stock s^*. The structure of the solution for the optimal management of the fishery is clear now. When the fish stock $s(t)$ is below s^*, $G'(s(t)) > G'(s^*)$, so $r - G'(s(t)) < r - G'(s^*) = 0$, and λ is decreasing according to the second equation of (D.4). During this process, the shadow cost $\lambda(t)$ is larger than the price p. It follows that if the initial fish stock $s_0 < s^*$, a moratorium ($h^* = 0$) on fishing is required, so the fish stock can grow until the steady-state level s^* is reached. Harvesting can then continue forever at the steady-state level ($h^* = G(s^*)$). When the fish stock $s(t)$ is above s^*, the opposite holds, and λ is increasing. During this process, the shadow cost $\lambda(t)$ is smaller than the price p. It follows that if the initial fish stock $s_0 > s^*$, the fish has to be harvested down to the steady-state fish stock s^* as quickly as possible. In optimal-control theory, this type of solution is called a *most rapid approach path* to the steady state.

Appendix E: From Multi-Period to Continuous Time

If the frequency of interest payments in each period is increased from 1 to n, the price at time t in the multi-period Hotelling rule (7.3) becomes

$$p(t) = \left(1 + \frac{r}{n}\right)^{nt} p(0) \tag{E.1}$$

with compound interest at an average interest rate r/n. When taking the frequency n of interest payments in each period to infinity, the interest payments are provided in smaller and smaller time steps, so that in the limit the continuous version results. By using the definition of the number e (see Wikipedia), the price at time t becomes

$$p(t) = \lim_{n\to\infty} \left(1 + \frac{r}{n}\right)^{nt} p_0 = \left(\lim_{n\to\infty} \left(1 + \frac{r}{n}\right)^{\frac{n}{r}}\right)^{rt} p(0) = e^{rt} p(0), \quad \text{(E.2)}$$

where $p(t) = p(0)e^{rt}$ is the solution to the no-arbitrage condition $\dot{p}(t) = rp(t)$ in Section 7.2. This is the Hotelling rule in continuous time.

It is also possible to derive this result by formulating the problem in continuous time from the start, and by applying a dynamical optimization technique: see Appendix G.

Appendix F: The Hotelling Rule in Discrete Time

Section 7.2.2 uses the argument that if $q(0), q(1), \ldots$ is the optimal path of extraction, it is not beneficial to swap one unit of extraction from period 0 to period t, or vice versa, which leads to (7.6) and the Hotelling rule (7.3). Formally, the maximization of welfare requires to determine the extraction path $q(0), q(1), \ldots$ that maximizes the discounted sum of utilities

$$\sum_{t=0}^{T} \left(\frac{1}{(1+r)^t} U(q(t))\right), \quad \text{(F.1)}$$

where T denotes the time of depletion, subject to the constraint that the total sum of extractions is equal to the initial stock of the resource s_0, i.e. $\sum_{t=0}^{T} q(t) = s_0$. Using the Lagrange function

$$\sum_{t=0}^{T} \left(\frac{1}{(1+r)^t} U(q(t))\right) + \lambda \left(s_0 - \sum_{t=0}^{T} q(t)\right), \quad \text{(F.2)}$$

with Lagrange parameter λ, the optimality conditions become

$$U'(q(0)) = \lambda, \frac{1}{(1+r)^t} U'(q(t)) = \lambda, \quad t = 1, 2, \ldots, \quad \text{(F.3)}$$

which implies equation (7.6) and thus equation (7.3). All discounted marginal utilities are equal to the shadow value λ of extracting one unit of the resource.

Section 7.2.1 uses Hotelling's argument to derive the Hotelling rule in (7.3) under perfect competition. Formally, the owner of the resource determines the extraction path $q(0), q(1), \ldots$ to maximize the discounted sum of revenues, which yields the Lagrange function

$$\sum_{t=0}^{T}\left(\frac{1}{(1+r)^t}p(t)q(t)\right)+\lambda\left(s_0-\sum_{t=0}^{T}q(t)\right). \tag{F.4}$$

The maximization is different from (F.2) because the objectives are linear in $q(t), t = 0, 1, \ldots,$ with the coefficients $p(t)/(1+r)^t - \lambda$. If these coefficients are not equal to 0, the owner of the resource extracts either everything or nothing, which cannot be in equilibrium. It follows that $p(0) = \lambda$ and $p(t)/(1+r)^t = \lambda$, which yields the Hotelling rule in discrete time (7.3).

Appendix G: The Hotelling Rule in Continuous Time

The optimal extraction of a non-renewable resource is a dynamical optimization problem. Sections 7.2.1–7.2.3 derive the basic Hotelling rule for a two-period problem, without using a dynamical optimization technique, but the use of such a technique generalizes this analysis and makes it easier. The technique is easy to apply but hard to prove. Appendix C above introduces Pontryagin's *maximum principle*. By applying this technique, Appendix G generalizes the analysis for a two-period problem in Sections 7.2.1–7.2.3 to the general dynamical problem. The appendix starts with welfare analysis and then compares perfect competition and monopoly.

Extraction of a non-renewable resource simply means that at each time t, the decrease in the stock of the resource is equal to the extraction:

$$\dot{s}(t) = -q(t), \quad s(0) = s_0, \tag{G.1}$$

where s denotes the stock of the resource, q the extracted quantity, and s_0 the initial stock of the resource. The optimal extraction of a non-renewable resource requires to determine the path of extraction $q(t)$ with the aim to maximize the total discounted utility

$$\int_0^{\infty} e^{-rt}U(q(t))dt, \tag{G.2}$$

where r denotes the interest or discount rate, subject to (G.1). The Hamilton function is

$$H(s, q, \lambda) = U(q) + \lambda(-q), \tag{G.3}$$

so the first-order conditions become (note that $H_s = 0$)

$$\begin{aligned} &U'(q(t)) = \lambda(t), \\ &\dot{s}(t) = -q(t), s(0) = s_0, \\ &\dot{\lambda}(t) = r\lambda(t). \end{aligned} \tag{G.4}$$

The main result is immediately available. Since the marginal utility $U'(q)$ is equal to the price p, the first equation in (G.4) implies that the price p is equal to the shadow cost λ of a decrease in the stock of the resource s. The Hotelling rule, $\dot{p}(t) = rp(t)$, results from the third equation in (G.4). Both the shadow cost λ and the price p grow at the rate of interest r.

Following the same steps as in Sections 7.2.1–7.2.3, it is possible to compare the case of perfect competition with the case of monopoly. If an owner of the non-renewable resource reacts to the market price $p(t)$, the optimal extraction of a non-renewable resource requires to determine the path of extraction $q(t)$ with the aim to maximize the total discounted profits

$$\int_0^{\infty} e^{-rt} p(t) q(t) dt, \tag{G.5}$$

subject to (G.1).

The Hamilton function depends on time t via $p(t)$ and becomes

$$H(s, q, \lambda, p(t)) = p(t)q + \lambda(-q) = (p(t) - \lambda)q. \tag{G.6}$$

The Hamilton function is linear in the extraction q. If $p(t) > \lambda$, the owner of the resource will extract the whole remaining stock at time t and if $p(t) < \lambda$, the owner of the resource will extract nothing. This cannot be part of an equilibrium, so $p(t) = \lambda(t)$ for all t. The third equation in (G.4) holds again and implies the Hotelling rule, i.e. $\dot{p}(t) = rp(t)$.

As a monopolist, the owner of the renewable resource takes the inverse demand function $p(q)$ into account. The optimal extraction requires to determine the path of extraction $q(t)$ with the aim to maximize the total discounted profits

$$\int_0^{\infty} e^{-rt} p(q(t)) q(t) dt, \tag{G.7}$$

subject to (G.1).

The Hamilton function becomes

$$H(s, q, \lambda) = p(q)q + \lambda(-q), \tag{G.8}$$

so the first-order conditions become

$$\begin{aligned} &p'(q(t))q(t) + p(q(t)) = \lambda(t),\\ &\dot{s}(t) = -q(t), s(0) = s_0,\\ &\dot{\lambda}(t) = r\lambda(t). \end{aligned} \tag{G.9}$$

The first equation in (G.9) expresses that the marginal revenue of the monopolist is equal to the shadow cost λ. The other equations in (G.9) are the same as in (G.4). It follows that the marginal revenue grows at the rate of interest r, which is the same for perfect competition and monopoly. In case of perfect competition, the marginal revenue is equal to the price p, and the Hotelling rule results. In case of monopoly, the marginal revenue is equal to $p'(q)q + p(q)$.

Finally, it is straightforward to perform the analysis for a renewable resource, by adding a growth function to the dynamical constraint (G.1), which yields

$$\dot{s}(t) = G(s(t)) - q(t), s(0) = s_0. \tag{G.10}$$

The Hamilton function (G.3) becomes

$$H(s, q, \lambda) = U(q) + \lambda(G(s) - q), \tag{G.11}$$

so the first-order conditions (G.4) become (note that $H_s = \lambda G'(s)$)

$$\begin{aligned} &U'(q(t)) = \lambda(t),\\ &\dot{s}(t) = G(s(t)) - q(t), s(0) = s_0,\\ &\dot{\lambda}(t) = (r - G'(s(t))\lambda(t). \end{aligned} \tag{G.12}$$

It follows that the price equation for a renewable resource becomes $\dot{p}(t) = (r - G'(s(t))p(t)$. The growth rate $(r - G'(s(t))$ of the price p is lower than for a non-renewable resource because the no-arbitrage condition includes the value of the resource growth $G'(s(t))p(t)$.

Appendix H: Geometric Series

A geometric series is defined as

$$a, ab, ab^2, \ldots, \tag{H.1}$$

where the first term is a, and each term results from the previous one by multiplication with b. The sum of a geometric series is equal to $a/(1-b)$ because

$$(1-b)(a+ab+ab^2+\cdots) = a+ab+ab^2+\cdots-ab-ab^2-\cdots = a. \quad \text{(H.2)}$$

With $a = 1/(1+r)$ and $b = (1-\delta)/(1+r)$, the sum between brackets in equation (22) becomes

$$\frac{1}{1+r}\bigg/\left(1-\frac{1-\delta}{1+r}\right) = \frac{1}{1+r}\bigg/\frac{r+\delta}{1+r} = \frac{1}{r+\delta}. \quad \text{(H.3)}$$

Appendix I: Stock Pollution

The social optimum requires to determine the path of production or emissions $y(t)$ with the aim to maximize the total discounted net benefits, given by

$$\int_0^\infty e^{-\rho t}[B(y(t)) - D(x(t))]dt, \quad \text{(I.1)}$$

subject to (9.1), where B denotes the benefits of production y, D the damage of stock pollution x, and ρ the discount rate. This is a dynamical optimization problem, which can be solved by applying the maximum principle as presented in Appendix C.

By taking the quadratic forms $B(y) = \beta y - 0.5y^2$ for the benefits and $D(x) = 0.5\gamma x^2$ for the damage, the analysis becomes tractable. The Hamilton function H becomes

$$H(x, y, \mu) = \beta y - 0.5y^2 - 0.5\gamma x^2 - \mu(y - \delta x), \quad \text{(I.2)}$$

where μ denotes the shadow cost of adding one unit to the stock of pollution. The minus sign in front of μ is not essential but it supports the intuition that this term is a cost. According to the maximum principle, the first-order conditions become

$$\begin{aligned} &H_y = 0 \Rightarrow \beta - y(t) = \mu(t), \\ &\dot{x} = H_\mu \Rightarrow \dot{x}(t) = y(t) - \delta x(t), x(0) = x_0, \\ &-\dot{\mu} + \rho\mu = -H_x \Rightarrow \dot{\mu}(t) = (\rho + \delta)\mu(t) - \gamma x(t). \end{aligned} \quad \text{(I.3)}$$

The first equation of (I.3) means that the marginal benefits $\beta - y$ of production are equal to the shadow costs μ of adding emissions to the stock of pollution. The second equation of (I.3) is the accumulation of the stock of pollution. The third equation of (I.3) is the dynamical equation that gives the development for the shadow costs of the increases in the stock of pollution.

In steady state, the first and third equation of (I.3) yield

$$\beta - y^* = \mu^* = \frac{\gamma x^*}{\rho + \delta}. \tag{I.4}$$

Equation (I.4) has a clear interpretation. The instantaneous marginal benefits $\beta - y^*$ are equal to the present value of all future marginal damages γx^*, discounted by the discount rate ρ plus the assimilation rate δ. Using the steady-state condition $y^* = \delta x^*$ from the second equation of (I.3) yields the solutions for y^*, x^* and $\tau^* = \mu^*$ in equations (9.4) and (9.5).

After substituting the first equation of (I.3) into the second equation, the optimal path toward the steady state results from the solution of the two-dimensional dynamical system

$$\begin{aligned} \dot{x}(t) &= \beta - \mu(t) - \delta x(t), x(0) = x_0, \\ \dot{\mu}(t) &= (\rho + \delta)\mu(t) - \gamma x(t). \end{aligned} \tag{I.5}$$

The variable x has the initial condition x_0, but the variable μ does not have an initial condition. However, optimality requires the optimal path to converge to the steady state of the system (I.5), which allows finding the optimal path: see Section 9.2.4.

Appendix J: The Ramsey–Hotelling Model

The Ramsey economic growth model in Section 10.4 is a dynamical optimization problem. It maximizes the intertemporal welfare by choosing the optimal consumption path or saving path. Appendix C presents the maximum principle, which is a technique for dynamical optimization that provides an alternative here for the analysis in Section 10.4.

Welfare maximization requires to determine the path of consumption $c(t)$ and the path of resource extraction $q(t)$ with the aim to maximize the total discounted utility

$$\int_0^\infty e^{-\rho t} U(c(t))dt, \tag{J.1}$$

subject to

$$\begin{aligned} \dot{k}(t) &= y(t) - c(t), \quad k(0) = k_0, \quad y = \alpha k^{\beta_k} q^{\beta_q}, \\ \dot{s}(t) &= -q(t), \quad s(0) = s_0, \end{aligned} \tag{J.2}$$

where U denotes utility, ρ the rate of time preference, y the production, α the total factor productivity, k the capital stock, k_0 the initial stock, s the resource stock, s_0 the initial stock, and β_k and β_q the production elasticities. The Hamilton function becomes

$$H(k, s, c, q, \lambda, \mu) = U(c) + \lambda(y - c) + \mu(-q), \tag{J.3}$$

where λ denotes the shadow value of investing one unit of production in the capital stock, and μ the shadow value of leaving one unit of the resource in the resource stock.

Consider first the subset of necessary conditions representing the Ramsey part of the model:

$$\begin{aligned} &U'(c) = \lambda, \\ &\dot{k}(t) = y(t) - c(t), \quad k(0) = k_0, \\ &\dot{\lambda}(t) = (\rho - y_k(t))\lambda(t). \end{aligned} \tag{J.4}$$

Differentiation of the first equation of (J.4) with respect to time t yields $U''(c(t))\dot{c}(t) = \dot{\lambda}(t)$, so the third equation of (J.4) becomes

$$U''(c(t))\dot{c}(t) = (\rho - y_k(t))U'(c(t)). \tag{J.5}$$

The elasticity of the marginal utility of consumption $U'(c)$ is $\eta = -cU''(c)/U'(c)$, so

$$\dot{c}(t) = \eta^{-1}(y_k(t) - \rho)c(t). \tag{J.6}$$

Equation (J.6) is the Keynes–Ramsey rule. Note that $y_k = \beta_k y/k$, and this is equal to the interest rate r. On the balanced growth path, the growth rate $\hat{c}$ is constant, so the interest rate r is constant. It follows from equation (J.6) that $r = \rho + \eta\hat{c}$, which is equation (10.11) in the main text. Section 10.3.2 shows that $\hat{y} = \hat{k}$ on the balanced growth path, and thus $\hat{c} = \hat{y} = \hat{k}$. Consumption c, capital stock k, and production y all grow at the same rate.

Consider now the additional necessary conditions representing the Hotelling part of the model:

$$\begin{aligned} \lambda y_q &= \mu, \\ \dot{s}(t) &= -q(t), \quad s(0) = s_0, \\ \dot{\mu}(t) &= \rho\mu(t). \end{aligned} \tag{J.7}$$

Note that $y_q = \beta_q y/q$, and this is equal to the price of the resource p. The third equation of (J.7) yields $\hat{\mu} = \dot{\mu}(t)/\mu(t) = \rho$, and the third equation of (J.4) yields $\hat{\lambda} = \dot{\lambda}(t)/\lambda(t) = \rho - r$. Using the rules in Section 10.2, the first equation of (J.7) in terms of growth rates becomes $\rho - r + \hat{p} = \rho$. It follows that $\hat{p} = r$, which is the Hotelling rule.

Appendix K: Stock Pollution in the Ramsey–Hotelling Model

This Appendix extends Appendix J with the damage of stock pollution.

Welfare maximization requires to determine the path of consumption $c(t)$ and the path of resource extraction $q(t)$ with the aim to maximize the total discounted welfare

$$\int_0^\infty e^{-\rho t} \left(U(c(t)) - D(x(t))\right) dt, \tag{K.1}$$

subject to

$$\begin{aligned} \dot{k}(t) &= y(t) - c(t), k(0) = k_0, y = \alpha k^{\beta_k} q^{\beta_q} \\ \dot{s}(t) &= -q(t), s(0) = s_0, \\ \dot{x}(t) &= q(t) - \delta x(t), x(0) = x_0, \end{aligned} \tag{K.2}$$

where U denotes utility, D the damage, ρ the rate of time preference, y the production, α the total factor productivity, k the capital stock, k_0 the initial stock, s the resource stock, s_0 the initial stock, x the pollution stock, x_0 the initial stock, and β_k and β_q the production elasticities. The Hamilton function becomes

$$H(k, s, x, c, q, \lambda, \mu, \nu) = U(c) - D(x) + \lambda(y - c) + \mu(-q) - \nu(q - \delta x), \tag{K.3}$$

where λ denotes the shadow value of investing one unit of production in the capital stock, μ the shadow value of leaving one unit of the resource in the resource stock, and ν the shadow cost of adding one unit to the pollution stock. The minus sign in front of ν is not essential but it supports the intuition that this term is a cost.

The Ramsey part of the model does not change and yields the Keynes–Ramsey rule (J.6).

The additional necessary conditions representing the Hotelling part as well as the stock pollution part of the model become

$$\begin{aligned} &\lambda y_q = \mu + \nu, \\ &\dot{s}(t) = -q(t), s(0) = s_0, \\ &\dot{x}(t) = q(t) - \delta x(t), x(0) = x_0, \\ &\dot{\mu}(t) = \rho\mu(t), \\ &\dot{\nu}(t) = (\rho + \delta)\nu(t) - D'(x(t)). \end{aligned} \tag{K.4}$$

The set of dynamical equations (K.4) is difficult to solve. However, the last equation of (K.4) is basically the same as the third equation of (I.3) in Appendix I. In this growth model, the tax on emissions or resource extraction is also based on the present value of marginal damages $D'(x(t))$, discounted by the utility discount rate ρ and the assimilation rate δ. Note that as in Appendix J, the fourth equation of (K.4) yields $\hat{\mu} = \dot{\mu}(t)/\mu(t) = \rho$ or $\mu(t) = \mu(0)e^{\rho t}$, and the third equation of (J.4) yields $\hat{\lambda} = \dot{\lambda}(t)/\lambda(t) = \rho - r$ or $\lambda(t) = \lambda(0)e^{(\rho - r)t}$. Dividing the first equation of (K.4) by λ, it follows that the price of the resource $p(t)$ or $y_q(t)$ has a first term $\mu(t)/\lambda(t) = (\mu(0)/\lambda(0))e^{rt}$ that grows at the rate of interest r and a second term that gives the tax $\tau(t)$ on the resource use. The difference with the result in Appendix J is that the price of the resource now depends on both the shadow value of leaving one unit of the resource in the resource stock and the tax that regulates adding one unit of emissions to the pollution stock. The net price of the resource $p(t) - \tau(t)$ still grows at the rate of interest r.

References

Pontryagin, L.S., Boltyanskii, V.G., Gamkrelidze, R.V., and Mishchenko, E.F. 1962. *The Mathematical Theory of Optimal Processes*. New York: Interscience.

Seierstad, A. and Sydsaeter, K. 1987. *Optimal Control Theory with Economic Applications*. Amsterdam: North Holland.

Index

D

E

F

www.ingramcontent.com/pod-product-compliance
Lightning Source LLC
Chambersburg PA
CBHW071219060126
37764CB00004B/238

9789819808014